Carpentry Forms

Level Three

Trainee Guide
Fourth Edition

Upper Saddle River, New Jersey
Columbus, Ohio

National Center for Construction Education and Research
President: Don Whyte
Director of Product Development: Daniele Stacey
Carpentry Project Manager: Daniele Stacey
Production Manager: Jessica Martin
Curriculum Maintenance Supervisor: Debie Ness
Editor: Brendan Coote
Desktop Publisher: Jessica Martin

Writing and development services provided by Topaz Publications, Liverpool, New York.

Pearson Education, Inc.
Product Manager: Lori Cowen
Project Manager: Stephen C. Robb
Design Coordinator: Diane Y. Ernsberger
Text Designer: Kristina D. Holmes
Cover Designer: Kristina D. Holmes
Copy Editor: Sheryl Rose
Scanning Technician: Janet Portisch
Operations Supervisor: Pat Tonneman
Marketing Manager: Derril Trakalo

This book was set in Palatino and Helvetica by Carlisle Communications, Ltd. It was printed and bound by Courier Kendallville, Inc. The cover was printed by Phoenix Color Corp.

This information is general in nature and intended for training purposes only. Actual performance of activities described in this manual requires compliance with all applicable operating, service, maintenance, and safety procedures under the direction of qualified personnel. References in this manual to patented or proprietary devices do not constitute a recommendation of their use.

Pearson Prentice Hall™ is a trademark of Pearson Education, Inc.
Pearson® is a registered trademark of Pearson plc
Prentice Hall® is a registered trademark of Pearson Education, Inc.

Pearson Education Ltd.
Pearson Education Singapore Pte. Ltd.
Pearson Education Canada, Ltd.
Pearson Education—Japan

Pearson Education Australia Pty. Limited
Pearson Education North Asia Ltd.
Pearson Educación de Mexico, S.A. de C.V.
Pearson Education Malaysia Pte. Ltd.

10 9 8 7 6 5 4 3 2
ISBN-13: 978-0-13-228600-8
ISBN-10:   0-13-228600-9

Preface

TO THE TRAINEE

Congratulations! If you're ready to start training with *Carpentry Forms: Level Three*, you've already mastered the fundamental skills necessary for a career in the carpentry trade. In *Carpentry Forms: Level Three*, you'll be building upon these foundation skills—in many cases—multiple stories high. In fact, it's the form carpenter who gets to work on some of the largest structures in the world.

Form carpenters build skyscrapers, stadiums, bridges, tunnels, cathedrals, and monuments. They build places where people live, work, and play, and, as many form carpenters will tell you, no two jobs are ever alike. Form carpentry is also a leader in use of new technologies, from stronger, lighter form materials to computer equipment and software for locating the forms.

Structures are being built taller and larger thanks to advanced building technology. As the structures grow, so do the challenges to build them—and so do the opportunities for those entering this unique and evolving field.

We wish you success on your journey through this training program. Should you have any comments on how NCCER might improve upon this text, please complete the user feedback form located at the back of each module and send it to us. We will always consider and respond to input from our customers.

NEW WITH *CARPENTRY FORMS: LEVEL THREE*

NCCER and Prentice Hall are pleased to present the fourth edition of *Carpentry Forms: Level Three*. This edition has been greatly enhanced to address the training needs of carpenters employed in heavy construction work. Improvements include the addition of modules on rigging equipment, rigging practices, trenching and excavation, and tilt-up concrete construction. Coverage of foundation work and form construction has been significantly expanded, and modules dealing with concrete and concrete reinforcing have been updated.

For a glimpse into the world of form carpentry and heavy construction work, check out the opening pages to each of the ten modules in this textbook. These images depict projects managed by Birmingham, Alabama-based Brasfield & Gorrie General Contractors. Brasfield & Gorrie is a full-service general contracting, construction management, and design/build service provider. The firm's expertise spans healthcare, industrial, office, institutional, retail, educational, and water treatment facilities—perfect examples of the diverse opportunities open to people entering this trade. You can learn more about Brasfield & Gorrie by visiting their website at www.brasfieldgorrie.com.

We also invite you to visit the NCCER website at **www.nccer.org** for the latest releases, training information, newsletter, Contren® product catalog, and much more. Your feedback is welcome. You may email your comments to **curriculum@nccer.org** or send general comments and inquiries to **info@nccer.org**.

NEW FORM CARPENTRY CREDENTIALING AVAILABLE THROUGH THE NATIONAL REGISTRY

A completion credential in Form Carpentry is now available through NCCER's National Registry after trainees have successfully completed both the written and performance tests from *Carpentry Fundamentals: Level One* and *Carpentry Forms: Level Three*.

If you're training through a traditional registered apprenticeship program, NCCER still meets the time-based requirements set forth by the Department of Labor's Office of Apprenticeship. As such, NCCER's traditional credential for a pure "Carpentry Level Three" completion is still available as well.

Submit Form 200 to report course completions to the National Registry. Contact the Registry Department at 1-888-NCCER20 for more information.

Now there's even more reason to train under an NCCER-accredited training sponsor—multitiered credentialing! And nothing gives the job-seeker more of an edge than an industry-recognized credential. If you're not training through an NCCER-accredited training sponsor, find out where one exists near you. Call NCCER at 1-888-NCCER20 or visit **www.nccer.org**.

CONTREN® LEARNING SERIES

The National Center for Construction Education and Research (NCCER) is a not-for-profit 501(c)(3) education foundation established in 1995 by the world's largest and most progressive construction companies and national construction associations. It was founded to address the severe workforce shortage facing the industry and to develop a standardized training process and curricula. Today, NCCER is supported by hundreds of leading construction and maintenance companies, manufacturers, and national associations. The Contren® Learning Series was developed by NCCER in partnership with Prentice Hall, the world's largest educational publisher.

Some features of NCCER's Contren® Learning Series are as follows:

- An industry-proven record of success
- Curricula developed by the industry for the industry
- National standardization providing portability of learned job skills and educational credits
- Compliance with Office of Apprenticeship requirements for related classroom training (*CFR 29:29*)
- Well-illustrated, up-to-date, and practical information

NCCER also maintains a National Registry that provides transcripts, certificates, and wallet cards to individuals who have successfully completed modules of NCCER's Contren® Learning Series. *Training programs must be delivered by an NCCER Accredited Training Sponsor in order to receive these credentials.*

Contren® Curricula

NCCER's training programs comprise more than 40 construction, maintenance, and pipeline areas and include skills assessments, safety training, and management education.

Boilermaking
Cabinetmaking
Careers in Construction
Carpentry
Concrete Finishing
Construction Craft Laborer
Construction Technology
Core Curriculum: Introductory Craft Skills
Currículo Básico
Electrical
Electronic Systems Technician
Heating, Ventilating, and Air Conditioning
Heavy Equipment Operations
Highway/Heavy Construction
Hydroblasting
Instrumentation
Insulating
Ironworking
Maintenance, Industrial
Masonry
Millwright
Mobile Crane Operations
Painting
Painting, Industrial
Pipefitting
Pipelayer
Plumbing
Reinforcing Ironwork
Rigging
Scaffolding
Sheet Metal
Site Layout
Sprinkler Fitting
Welding

Pipeline

Control Center Operations, Liquid
Corrosion Control
Electrical and Instrumentation
Field Operations, Liquid
Field Operations, Gas
Maintenance
Mechanical

Safety

Field Safety
Orientación de Seguridad
Safety Orientation
Safety Technology

Management

Introductory Skills for the Crew Leader
Project Management
Project Supervision

Special Features of This Book

In an effort to provide a comprehensive user-friendly training resource, we have incorporated many different features for your use. Whether you are a visual or hands-on learner, this book will provide you with the proper tools to get started in the construction industry.

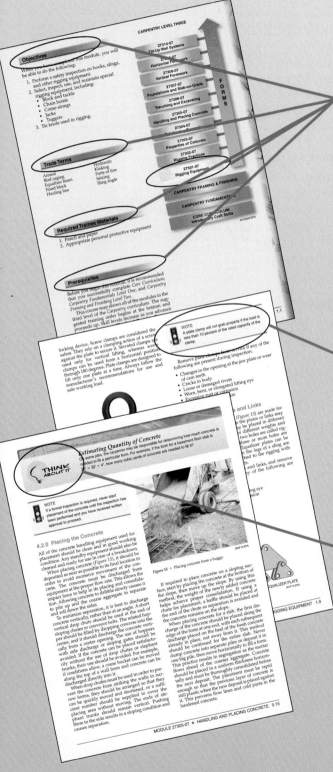

Introduction Page

This page is found at the beginning of each module and lists the Objectives, Trade Terms, Required Trainee Materials, Prerequisites, and Course Map for that module. The Objectives list the skills and knowledge you will need in order to complete the module successfully. The list of Trade Terms identifies important terms you will need to know by the end of the module. Required Trainee Materials list the materials and supplies needed for the module. The Prerequisites for the module are listed and illustrated in the Course Map. The Course Map also gives a visual overview of the entire course and a suggested learning sequence for you to follow.

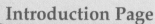

Notes, Cautions, and Warnings

Safety features are set off from the main text in highlighted boxes and organized into three categories based on the potential danger of the issue being addressed. Notes simply provide additional information on the topic area. Cautions alert you of a danger that does not present potential injury but may cause damage to equipment. Warnings stress a potentially dangerous situation that may cause injury to you or a co-worker.

Think About It

Think About It features use "What if?" questions to help you apply theory to real-world experiences and put your ideas into action.

Step-by-Step Instructions

Step-by-step instructions are used throughout to guide you through technical procedures and tasks from start to finish. These steps show you not only how to perform a task but how to do it safely and efficiently.

Color Illustrations and Photographs

Full-color illustrations and photographs are used throughout each module to provide vivid detail. These figures highlight important concepts from the text and provide clarity for complex instructions. Each figure is denoted in the text in *italic type* for easy reference.

Inside Track

Inside Track features provide a head start for those entering the carpentry field by presenting technical tips and professional practices from master carpenters in a variety of disciplines. Inside Tracks often include real-life scenarios similar to those you might encounter on the job site.

Trade Terms

Each module presents a list of Trade Terms that are discussed within the text, defined in the Glossary at the end of the module. These terms are denoted in the text with blue bold type upon their first occurrence. To make searches for key information easier, a comprehensive Glossary of Trade Terms from all modules is found at the back of this book.

Review Questions

Review Questions are provided to reinforce the knowledge you have gained. This makes them a useful tool for measuring what you have learned.

Contents

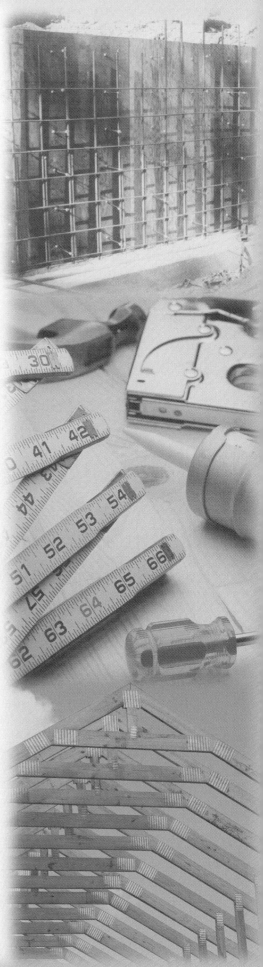

Acknowledgments

This curriculum was revised as a result of the farsightedness and leadership of the following sponsors:

Alfred State College
Bowden Contracting Company
Brasfield & Gorrie, LLC
Cianbro Corporation

Fransen Pittman General Contractors
Onslow-Sheffield, Inc.
The Shaw Group

This curriculum would not exist were it not for the dedication and unselfish energy of those volunteers who served on the Authoring Team. A sincere thanks is extended to the following:

Steve Anderson
Howard Davis
Curt Haskins
Dan McNally

Thomas G. Murphy
Mike Noble
Mark Onslow

A final note: This book is the result of a collaborative effort involving the production, editorial, and development staff at Prentice Hall and the National Center for Construction Education and Research. Thanks to all of the dedicated people involved in the many stages of this project.

NCCER PARTNERING ASSOCIATIONS

American Fire Sprinkler Association
API
Associated Builders & Contractors, Inc.
Associated General Contractors of America
Association for Career and Technical Education
Association for Skilled & Technical Sciences
Carolinas AGC, Inc.
Carolinas Electrical Contractors Association
Center for Improvement of Construction
   Management & Processes
Construction Industry Institute
Construction Users Roundtable
Design Build Institute of America
Electronic Systems Industry Consortium
Merit Contractors Association of Canada
Metal Building Manufacturers Association
NACE International
National Association of Minority Contractors

National Association of Women in Construction
National Insulation Association
National Ready Mixed Concrete Association
National Systems Contractors Association
National Technical Honor Society
National Utility Contractors Association
NAWIC Education Foundation
North American Crane Bureau
North American Technician Excellence
Painting & Decorating Contractors of America
Portland Cement Association
SkillsUSA
Steel Erectors Association of America
Texas Gulf Coast Chapter ABC
U.S. Army Corps of Engineers
University of Florida
Women Construction Owners & Executives, USA

Rigging Equipment
27301-07

27301-07
Rigging Equipment

Topics to be presented in this module include:

Overview

Everyone who works in a construction craft participates in rigging activity because most of the materials used in construction must be lifted and moved by cranes or other lifting devices. Roof trusses are usually placed with a crane. In high-rise construction, curtain walls are lifted into place using cranes. Concrete form sections and prestressed beams are also moved into place with cranes. A lot of the rigging process involves simply moving materials such as lumber, metal studs, rebar, and structural steel from where they are stored to where they are needed.

Rigging is all about safety. Anyone involved in rigging must know how to inspect rigging equipment to make sure it is safe to use and must be able to select the right rigging equipment for a given load and a given type of lift.

Objectives

When you have completed this module, you will be able to do the following:

1. Perform a safety inspection on hooks, slings, and other rigging equipment.
2. Select, inspect, use, and maintain special rigging equipment, including:
   - Block and tackle
   - Chain hoists
   - Come-alongs
   - Jacks
   - Tuggers
3. Tie knots used in rigging.

Trade Terms

Anneal	Hydraulic
Bird caging	Kinking
Equalizer beam	Parts of line
Fixed block	Seizing
Hauling line	Sling angle

Required Trainee Materials

1. Pencil and paper
2. Appropriate personal protective equipment

Prerequisites

Before you begin this module, it is recommended that you successfully complete *Core Curriculum*; *Carpentry Fundamentals Level One*; and *Carpentry Framing and Finishing Level Two*.

This course map shows all of the modules in the third level of the *Carpentry* curriculum. The suggested training order begins at the bottom and proceeds up. Skill levels increase as you advance on the course map. The local Training Program Sponsor may adjust the training order.

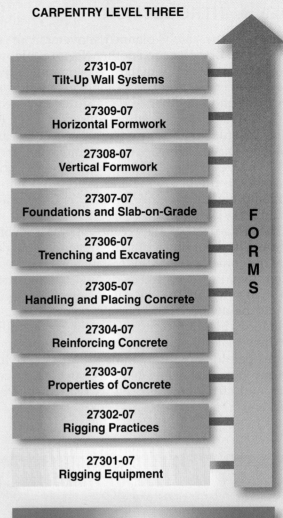

CARPENTRY LEVEL THREE

FORMS

- 27310-07 Tilt-Up Wall Systems
- 27309-07 Horizontal Formwork
- 27308-07 Vertical Formwork
- 27307-07 Foundations and Slab-on-Grade
- 27306-07 Trenching and Excavating
- 27305-07 Handling and Placing Concrete
- 27304-07 Reinforcing Concrete
- 27303-07 Properties of Concrete
- 27302-07 Rigging Practices
- 27301-07 Rigging Equipment

CARPENTRY FRAMING & FINISHING

CARPENTRY FUNDAMENTALS

CORE CURRICULUM: Introductory Craft Skills

301CMAP.EPS

1.0.0 ◆ INTRODUCTION

Rigging is the safely planned movement of an object from one place to another (*Figure 1*). However, it does not apply to the actual operation of a crane. It may also include moving an object from one position to another or tying down an object. For example, tools and equipment must often be lifted several floors to get them where they are needed. This moving operation must be done safely and effectively. This module reviews and expands on the hardware and procedural information previously learned in the *Core Curriculum* module, *Basic Rigging*.

The rigger and the crane operator work together in preparing a lift. The rigger must make sure the crane operator understands what is to be lifted, what it weighs, and any complexities involving the lift. At the same time, the rigger should be aware of the crane's capabilities and limitations in order to ensure that the crane is able to safely make the lift. As a team, the rigger and crane operator should examine the area of the lift for any potential safety hazards, such as power lines and structures, as well as risks to nearby workers.

Figure 1 ◆ A rigging application.

2.0.0 ◆ RIGGING HARDWARE

Hardware used in rigging includes hooks, shackles, eyebolts, spreader and equalizer beams, and blocks. These hardware items must be carefully matched to the lifting capability of the crane or hoist and the slings used in each application. Mixing items with different safe working loads makes it impossible to determine if the lift will be safe. Careful inspection and maintenance of all lifting hardware is essential for continuous operation. Hardware should always be inspected before each use.

NOTE

Rigging hooks must be properly marked or tagged with the manufacturer's ratings and application information. If a hook is not properly marked, don't use it. Also, rigging hardware must never be modified because modifications could affect its capacity.

2.1.0 Hooks

Rigging hooks are used to attach to slings or loads. There are six basic types of rigging hooks, with the eye-type hook being the most commonly used. Rigging hooks are equipped with safety latches to prevent a sling attachment from coming off the hook when a sling is slackened. The capacity of a rigging hook, in tons, is determined by its size and physical dimensions. Information about a specific hook's capacity is readily available from the hook manufacturer.

The safe working load of the hook is accurate only when the load is suspended from the saddle of the hook. If the working load is applied anywhere between the saddle and the hook tip, the safe working load is considerably reduced, as shown in *Figure 2*. Some manufacturers do not permit their hooks to be used in any other position.

NOTE

There are hooks specifically made for tip loading.

Always inspect hooks before each use. Look for wear in the saddle of the hook. Also, look for cracks, severe corrosion, and twisting of the hook body. The safety latch should be in good working order. Measure the hook throat opening; if a hook has been overloaded or if it is beginning to weaken, the throat will open. OSHA regulations require that the hook be replaced if the throat has opened 15 percent from its original size or if the body has been twisted 10 degrees from its original plane. *Figure 3* shows the location of inspection points for a hook.

Never use a sling eye over a hook with a body diameter larger than the natural width of the eye. Never force the eye onto the hook. Always use an eye with at least the nominal diameter of the hook.

2.2.0 Shackles

A shackle is used to attach an item to a load or to attach slings together. It can be used to attach the end of a wire rope to an eye fitting, hook, or other type of connector. Shackles are made in several configurations (*Figure 4*).

Shackles used for overhead lifting are made of forged alloy steel. They are sized by the diameter of the steel in the bow section rather than the pin size.

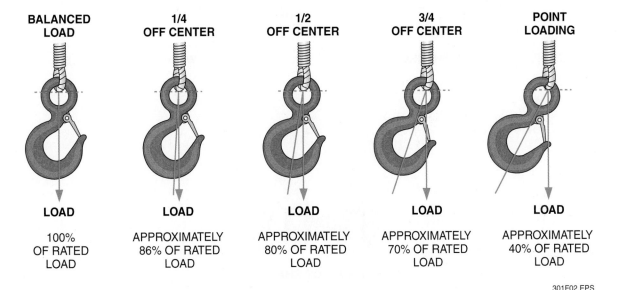

| BALANCED LOAD | 1/4 OFF CENTER | 1/2 OFF CENTER | 3/4 OFF CENTER | POINT LOADING |

LOAD — 100% OF RATED LOAD

LOAD — APPROXIMATELY 86% OF RATED LOAD

LOAD — APPROXIMATELY 80% OF RATED LOAD

LOAD — APPROXIMATELY 70% OF RATED LOAD

LOAD — APPROXIMATELY 40% OF RATED LOAD

301F02.EPS

Figure 2 ◆ Rigging hook rated load versus load location.

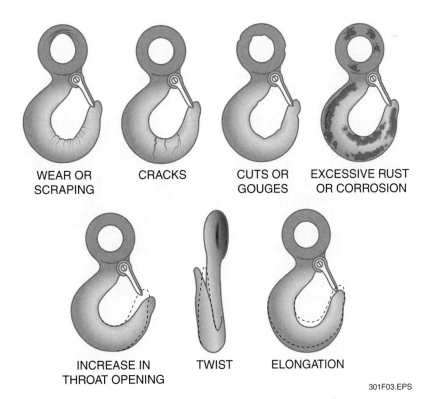

WEAR OR SCRAPING   CRACKS   CUTS OR GOUGES   EXCESSIVE RUST OR CORROSION

INCREASE IN THROAT OPENING   TWIST   ELONGATION

301F03.EPS

Figure 3 ◆ Rigging hook inspection points.

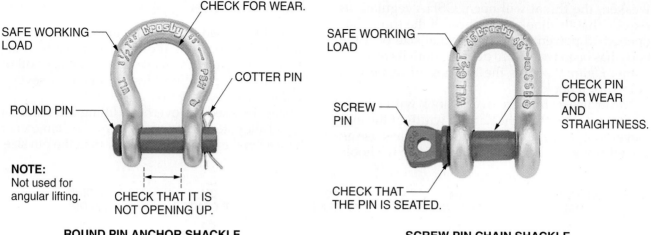

CHECK FOR WEAR.

SAFE WORKING LOAD

COTTER PIN

ROUND PIN

NOTE:
Not used for angular lifting.

CHECK THAT IT IS NOT OPENING UP.

ROUND PIN ANCHOR SHACKLE

SAFE WORKING LOAD

CHECK PIN FOR WEAR AND STRAIGHTNESS.

SCREW PIN

CHECK THAT THE PIN IS SEATED.

SCREW PIN CHAIN SHACKLE

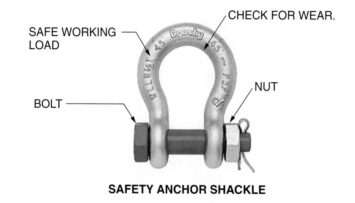

CHECK FOR WEAR.

SAFE WORKING LOAD

NUT

BOLT

THE CROSBY GROUP, INC.

SAFETY ANCHOR SHACKLE

301F04.EPS

Figure 4 ◆ Shackles.

When using shackles, be sure that all pins are straight, all screw pins are completely seated, and cotter pins are used with all round pin shackles. A shackle must not be used in excess of its rated load.

Shackle pins should never be replaced with a bolt or a shackle pin from another shackle. Bolts cannot take the bending force normally applied to a pin. Shackles that are stretched or that have crowns or pins worn more than 10 percent should be destroyed and replaced. If a shackle is pulled out at an angle, the capacity is reduced. Use spacers to center the load being hoisted on the pin. Only shackles of suitable load ratings can be used for lifting. When using a shackle on a hook, the pin of the shackle should be hung on the hook. Spacers can be used on the pin to keep the shackle hanging evenly on the hook (*Figure 5*). Never use a screw-pin shackle in a situation where the pin can roll under load, as shown in *Figure 6*.

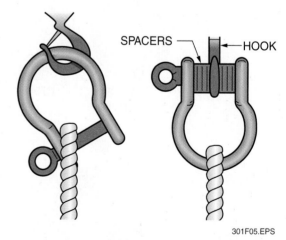

SPACERS

HOOK

301F05.EPS

Figure 5 ◆ Spacers used with a shackle to keep it hanging evenly.

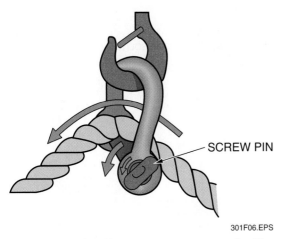

SCREW PIN

301F06.EPS

Figure 6 ◆ Example of how a rope can cause a shackle screw-pin to roll under load.

 WARNING!

Shackles may not be loaded at an angle unless approved by the manufacturer. Check the manufacturer's literature for derating instructions.

2.3.0 Eyebolts

Eyebolts (*Figure 7*) are often attached to heavy loads by a manufacturer in order to aid in hoisting the load. One type of eyebolt, called a ringbolt, is equipped with an additional movable lifting ring. Eyebolts and ringbolts can be of either the shoulder or shoulderless type. The shoulder type is recommended for use in hoisting applications because it can be used with slightly angled lifting pulls, whereas the shoulderless type is designed only for lifting a load vertically. Loads should always be applied to the plane of the eye to reduce bending. This procedure is particularly important when bridle slings are used.

When installed, the shoulder of the eyebolt must be at right angles to the axis of the hole and must be in full contact with the working surface when the nuts are properly fastened. Washers or other suitable spacers may be used to ensure that the shoulders are in firm contact with the working surface. Tapped holes used with screwed-in eyebolts should have a minimum depth of 1½ times the bolt diameter. Swivel eyebolts may be installed instead of fixed eyebolts. These devices swivel to the desired lift position and do not require any load rating reduction.

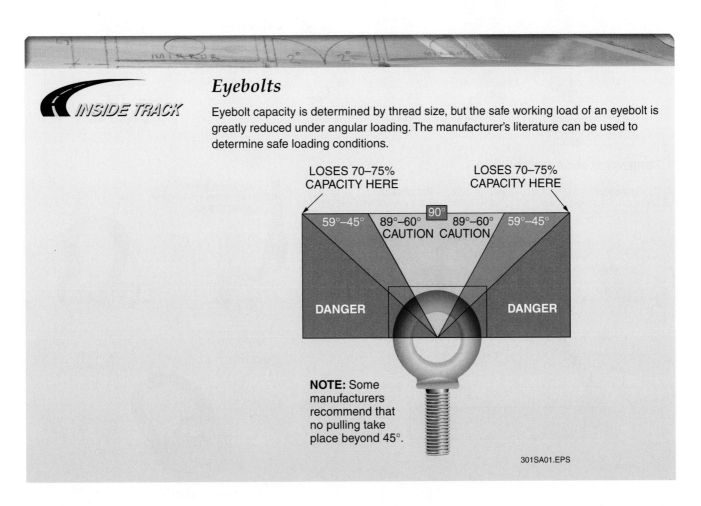

Eyebolts

Eyebolt capacity is determined by thread size, but the safe working load of an eyebolt is greatly reduced under angular loading. The manufacturer's literature can be used to determine safe loading conditions.

LOSES 70–75% CAPACITY HERE

LOSES 70–75% CAPACITY HERE

90°

59°–45° 89°–60° CAUTION CAUTION 89°–60° 59°–45°

DANGER

DANGER

NOTE: Some manufacturers recommend that no pulling take place beyond 45°.

301SA01.EPS

USE OF EYEBOLTS

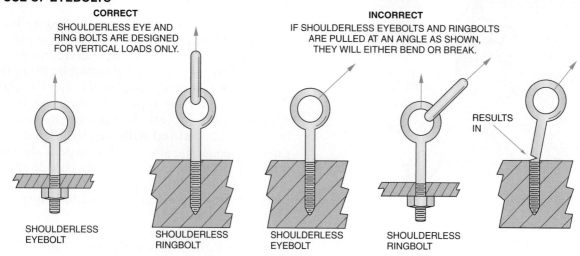

CORRECT
SHOULDERLESS EYE AND RING BOLTS ARE DESIGNED FOR VERTICAL LOADS ONLY.

INCORRECT
IF SHOULDERLESS EYEBOLTS AND RINGBOLTS ARE PULLED AT AN ANGLE AS SHOWN, THEY WILL EITHER BEND OR BREAK.

RESULTS IN

SHOULDERLESS EYEBOLT

SHOULDERLESS RINGBOLT

SHOULDERLESS EYEBOLT

SHOULDERLESS RINGBOLT

USE OF SHOULDER TYPE EYEBOLTS AND RINGBOLTS

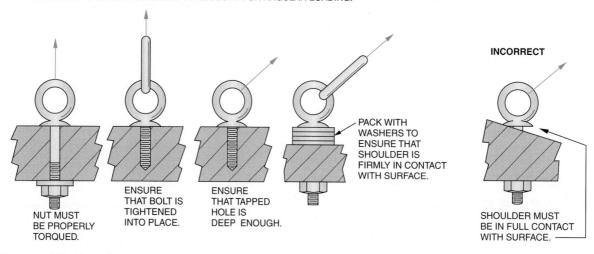

CORRECT
FOR SHOULDER TYPE EYEBOLTS AND RINGBOLTS PROVIDING LOADS ARE REDUCED TO ACCOUNT FOR ANGULAR LOADING.

PACK WITH WASHERS TO ENSURE THAT SHOULDER IS FIRMLY IN CONTACT WITH SURFACE.

INCORRECT

NUT MUST BE PROPERLY TORQUED.

ENSURE THAT BOLT IS TIGHTENED INTO PLACE.

ENSURE THAT TAPPED HOLE IS DEEP ENOUGH.

SHOULDER MUST BE IN FULL CONTACT WITH SURFACE.

ORIENTATION OF EYEBOLTS

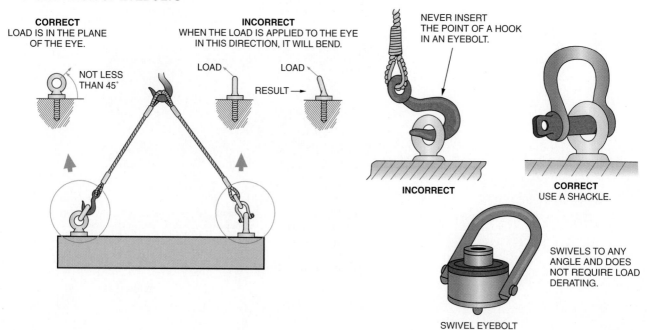

CORRECT
LOAD IS IN THE PLANE OF THE EYE.

NOT LESS THAN 45°

INCORRECT
WHEN THE LOAD IS APPLIED TO THE EYE IN THIS DIRECTION, IT WILL BEND.

LOAD

LOAD

RESULT

NEVER INSERT THE POINT OF A HOOK IN AN EYEBOLT.

INCORRECT

CORRECT
USE A SHACKLE.

SWIVELS TO ANY ANGLE AND DOES NOT REQUIRE LOAD DERATING.

SWIVEL EYEBOLT

301F07.EPS

Figure 7 ◆ Eyebolt and ringbolt installation and lifting criteria.

2.4.0 Lifting Lugs

Lifting lugs (*Figure 8*) are typically welded, bolted, or pinned by a manufacturer to the object to be lifted. They are designed and located to balance the load and support it safely. Lifting lugs should be used for straight, vertical lifting only, unless specifically designed for angular loads. This is because they can bend if loaded at an angle.

Lifting lugs should be inspected before each use for deformation, cracks, corrosion, and defective welds. A lifting lug must be removed from service if such conditions are found.

2.5.0 Turnbuckles

Turnbuckles are available in a variety of sizes. They are used to adjust the length of rigging connections. Three common types of turnbuckles are the eye, jaw, and hook ends (*Figure 9*). They can be used in any combination. The safe working load for turnbuckles can be found in the manufacturer's catalog and is based on the diameter of the threaded rods. The safe working load of turnbuckles with hook ends is less than that of the same size turnbuckles with other types of ends.

Consider the following when selecting turnbuckles for rigging:

- Turnbuckles should be made of alloy steel and should not be welded.
- When using turnbuckles with multi-leg slings, do not use more than one turnbuckle per leg.
- Do not use jamb nuts on turnbuckles that do not come equipped with them.
- Turnbuckles should not be overtightened. Do not use a cheater to tighten them. Perform tightening with a wrench of the proper size, using as much force as a person can achieve by hand.
- Turnbuckles must not be used for angular loading unless permitted by the manufacturer. If angular loading is permitted, the capacity must be derated accordingly.

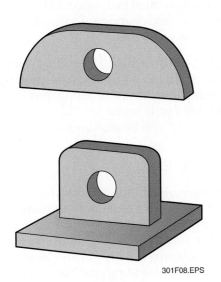

Figure 8 ◆ Two types of lifting lugs.

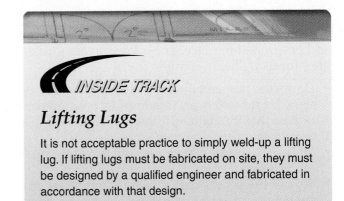

INSIDE TRACK

Lifting Lugs

It is not acceptable practice to simply weld-up a lifting lug. If lifting lugs must be fabricated on site, they must be designed by a qualified engineer and fabricated in accordance with that design.

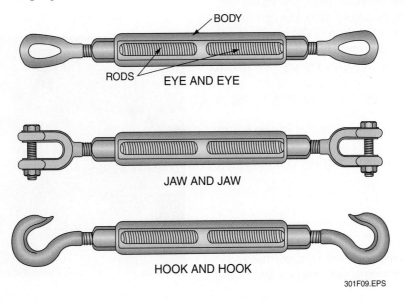

Figure 9 ◆ Turnbuckles.

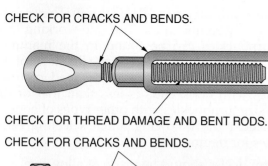

CHECK FOR CRACKS AND BENDS.

CHECK FOR THREAD DAMAGE AND BENT RODS.

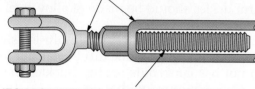

CHECK FOR CRACKS AND BENDS.

CHECK FOR THREAD DAMAGE AND BENT RODS.

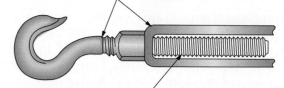

CHECK FOR CRACKS AND BENDS.

CHECK FOR THREAD DAMAGE AND BENT RODS.

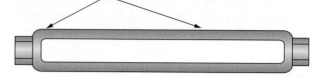

CHECK FOR CRACKS AND DEFORMATIONS.

301F10.EPS

Figure 10 ◆ Turnbuckle inspection points.

Turnbuckles should be inspected as shown in *Figure 10*. If a turnbuckle is damaged, remove it from service.

2.6.0 Beam Clamps

Beam clamps (*Figure 11*) are used to connect hoisting devices to beams, so the beams can be lifted and positioned in place. The following are guidelines for using beam clamps:

- Do not use homemade clamps unless they are designed, load tested, and stamped by an engineer.
- Ensure that the clamp fits the beam and is of the correct capacity.
- Make sure beam clamps are securely fastened to the beam.
- Be careful when using beam clamps where angle lifts are to be made. Most are designed for essentially straight vertical lifts only. However, some manufacturers allow two clamps to be used with a long bridle sling if the angle of lift does not exceed 25 degrees from the vertical.
- Be certain the capacity appears on the beam clamp.
- Attach rigging to the beam clamp using a shackle.
- Do not place a hoist hook directly in the beam clamp lifting eye.
- Never overload a beam clamp beyond its rating capacity.

WARNING!

Check with an engineer when lifting overhead steel to be sure the load can be supported.

Beam clamps must be inspected before each use and removed from service if you observe any of the following problems:

- The jaws of the beam clamp have been opened more than 15 percent of their normal opening.
- The lifting eye is bent or elongated.
- The lifting eye is worn.
- The capacity and beam size are unreadable.

2.7.0 Plate Clamps

Plate clamps attach to structural steel plates to allow for easier rigging attachment and handling of the plate. There are two basic types of plate clamps: the serrated jaw type and the screw type.

Serrated clamps (*Figure 12*) are designed to grip a single plate for hoisting and are available with a

301F11.EPS

Figure 11 ◆ Typical beam clamp application.

locking device. Screw clamps are considered the safest. They rely on a clamping action of a screw against the plate to secure it. Serrated clamps are used only for vertical lifting, whereas screw clamps can be used from a horizontal position through 180 degrees. Plate clamps are designed to lift only one plate at a time. Always follow the manufacturer's recommendations for use and safe working load.

NOTE

A plate clamp will not grab properly if the load is less than 10 percent of the rated capacity of the clamp.

Remove plate clamps from service if any of the following are present during inspection:

- Changes in the opening at the jaw plate or wear of cam teeth
- Cracks in body
- Loose or damaged rivets
- Worn, bent, or elongated lifting eye
- Excessive rust or corrosion
- Unreadable capacity size

2.8.0 Rigging Plates and Links

Rigging plates and links (*Figure 13*) are made for specific uses. The holes in the plates or links may be different sizes and may be placed in different locations in the plates for different weights and types of lifts. Plates with two holes are called rigging links. Plates with three or more holes are called equalizer plates. Equalizer plates can be used to level loads when the legs of a sling are unequal. Plates are attached to the rigging with high-strength pins or bolts.

Inspect rigging plates and links, and remove them from service if any of the following are present:

- Cracks in body
- Worn or elongated lifting eye
- Excessive rust or corrosion

301F12.EPS

Figure 12 ◆ Serrated-jaw lifting clamp.

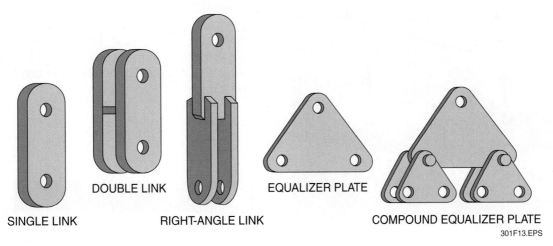

SINGLE LINK   DOUBLE LINK   RIGHT-ANGLE LINK   EQUALIZER PLATE   COMPOUND EQUALIZER PLATE

301F13.EPS

Figure 13 ◆ Rigging links and plates.

2.9.0 Spreader and Equalizer Beams

Spreader beams (*Figure 14*) are used to support long loads during lifting operations. If used properly, they help eliminate the hazard of the load tipping, sliding, or bending. They reduce low **sling angles** and the tendency of the slings to crush loads. Equalizer beams are used to balance the load on sling legs and to maintain equal loads on dual hoist lines when making tandem lifts.

Both types of beams are usually fabricated to suit a specific application. They are often made of heavy pipe, I-beams, or other suitable material. Custom-fabricated spreader or equalizer beams must be designed by an engineer and have their capacity clearly stamped on the side. They should be tested at 125 percent of rated capacity. Information on the beams should be kept on file. The capacity of beams designed for use with multiple attachment points depends on the distance between attachment points.

Before use, a spreader or equalizer beam should be inspected for the following:

* Solid welds
* No cracks, nicks, gouges, or corrosion
* Condition of attachment points
* Capacity rating
* Sling angle tension at the points of attachment

3.0.0 ◆ SLINGS

The common types of slings include wire rope slings, synthetic slings, chain slings, and metal mesh slings. Wire rope and synthetic slings were covered in the *Core Curriculum* module, *Basic Rigging*. Metal mesh slings (*Figure 15*) are typically made of wire or chain mesh. They are similar in appearance to web slings and are suited for situations where the loads are abrasive, hot, or tend to cut other types of slings. Metal mesh slings resist abrasion and cutting, grip the load firmly without stretching, can withstand temperatures up to 550°F, are smooth, conform to irregular shapes, do not **kink** or tangle, and resist corrosion. These slings are available in several mesh sizes and can be coated with a variety of substances, such as rubber or plastic, to help protect the load they are handling.

3.1.0 Sling Capacity

Sling capacities depend on the sling material, construction, size of hitch configuration, quantity, and angle for the specific type of sling being used. The amount of tension on the sling is directly affected by the angle of the sling (*Figure 16*). For this reason, proper sling angles are crucial to safe rigging. This information, along with other pertinent rigging information, is available from rigging equipment manufacturers and rigging trade organizations in the form of easy-to-use pocket guides like the ones shown in *Figure 17*. Sling capacity information is also given in *OSHA Regulation 29 CFR, Section 1926.251*, titled *Rigging Equipment for Material Handling*. *Table 1* shows an example of a typical capacity table used with wire rope slings.

301F14.EPS

Figure 14 ◆ Typical use of a spreader beam.

301F15.EPS

Figure 15 ◆ Metal mesh sling.

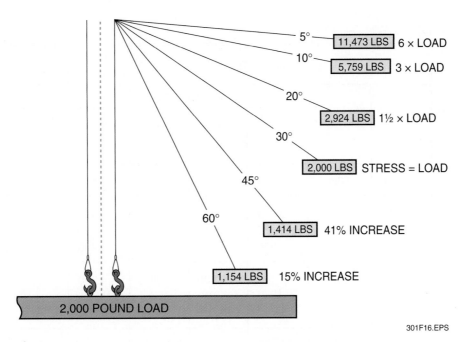

$5°$ 11,473 LBS   6 × LOAD

$10°$ 5,759 LBS   3 × LOAD

$20°$ 2,924 LBS   1½ × LOAD

$30°$ 2,000 LBS   STRESS = LOAD

$45°$ 1,414 LBS   41% INCREASE

$60°$ 1,154 LBS   15% INCREASE

2,000 POUND LOAD

301F16.EPS

Figure 16 ◆ Sling angles.

301F17.EPS

Figure 17 ◆ Rigging pocket guides.

NOTE

Figure 16 shows that the rigging must be upgraded for angles below 30 degrees.

The D/d ratio applies to wire rope slings. It refers to the relationship between the diameter of the surface (D) the sling is around and the diameter of the sling (d). This relationship, specifically the severity of the bends in the sling, has an impact on the capacity of the sling. Efficiency charts have been developed to help determine the actual sling capacity. *Figure 18* shows load and hook diameter examples and a D/d ratio chart.

For example, consider a 1-inch-diameter rope sling in a basket hitch around a 2-inch shackle pin.

The capacity of the sling in the basket hitch is listed as 17 tons. Look across the bottom of the chart for the 2-inch D/d ratio and find the line that meets the ratio curve. It is opposite 65 percent efficiency. Multiply the rated load of 17 tons by 65 percent and you will get an actual capacity of 11 tons. Sling eyes with pin or body sizes that are at least equal to the rope diameter should be used with shackles and hooks. Always refer to the tag when selecting a wire rope sling.

CAUTION

A rule of thumb is 20:1. A sling can be damaged if used on a pin with too small a diameter.

3.2.0 Sling Care and Storage

You learned about inspection criteria for slings in the *Core Curriculum* module, *Basic Rigging*. The following are some important reminders for sling inspection, care, and storage:

• Store slings in a rack to keep them off the ground. The rack should be in an area free of moisture and away from acid or acid fumes and extreme heat.
• Never let slings lie on the ground in areas where heavy machinery may run over them.
• Slings should be inspected at each use for broken wires, kinks, rust, or damaged fittings. Any slings found to be defective should be destroyed.

Table 1 Example of a Wire Rope Sling Capacity Table

CLASS	SIZE (IN.)	RATED CAPACITY - LBS.*						EYE DIMENSIONS (APPROXIMATE)	
		VERTICAL	CHOKER**	BASKET HITCH				WIDTH (IN.)	LENGTH (IN.)
				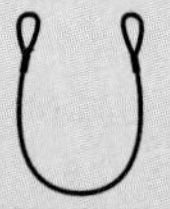 ⋃	30°	60°	90°		
6 × 19 IWRC	¼	1,120	820	2,200	2,200	1,940	1,580	2	4
	⁵⁄₁₆	1,740	1,280	3,400	3,400	3,000	2,400	2½	5
	⅜	2,400	1,840	4,800	4,600	4,200	3,400	3	6
	⁷⁄₁₆	3,400	2,400	6,800	6,600	5,800	4,800	3½	7
	½	4,400	3,200	8,800	8,600	7,600	6,200	4	8
	⁹⁄₁₆	5,600	4,000	11,200	10,800	9,600	8,000	4½	9
	⅝	6,800	5,000	13,600	13,200	11,800	9,600	5	10
	¾	9,800	7,200	19,600	19,000	17,000	13,800	6	12
	⅞	13,200	9,600	26,000	26,000	22,000	18,600	7	14
	1	17,000	12,600	34,000	32,000	30,000	24,000	8	16
	1⅛	20,000	15,800	40,000	38,000	34,000	28,000	9	18
6 × 37 IWRC	1¼	26,000	19,400	52,000	50,000	46,000	36,000	10	20
	1⅜	30,000	24,000	60,000	58,000	52,000	42,000	11	22
	1½	36,000	28,000	72,000	70,000	62,000	50,000	12	24
	1⅝	42,000	32,000	84,000	82,000	72,000	60,000	13	26
	1¾	50,000	38,000	100,000	96,000	86,000	70,000	14	28
	2	64,000	48,000	128,000	124,000	110,000	90,000	16	32
	2¼	78,000	60,000	156,000	150,000	136,000	110,000	18	36
	2½	94,000	74,000	188,000	182,000	162,000	132,000	20	40

*RATED CAPACITIES FOR UNPROTECTED EYES APPLY ONLY WHEN ATTACHMENT IS MADE OVER AN OBJECT NARROWER THAN THE NATURAL WIDTH OF THE EYE AND APPLY FOR BASKET HITCHES ONLY WHEN THE D/d RATIO IS 25 OR GREATER, WHERE D=DIAMETER OF CURVATURE AROUND WHICH THE BODY OF THE SLING IS BENT, AND d=NOMINAL DIAMETER OF THE ROPE.
**SEE CHOKER HITCH RATED CAPACITY ADJUSTMENT CHART.

301T01.EPS

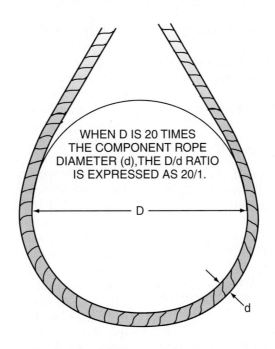

WHEN D IS 20 TIMES
THE COMPONENT ROPE
DIAMETER (d), THE D/d RATIO
IS EXPRESSED AS 20/1.

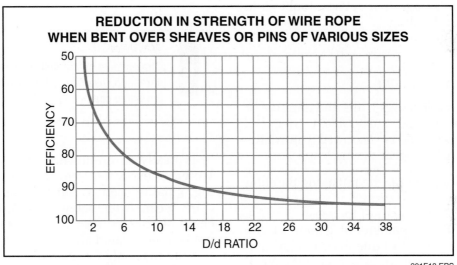

301F18.EPS

Figure 18 ◆ Load and hook diameter and D/d ratio chart for wire rope.

3.2.1 Wire Rope Slings

Wire rope slings should be discarded if you discover any of the following conditions:

- *Broken wires* – Serious breakage is indicated by ten randomly distributed broken wires in one rope lay, five broken wires in one strand in one rope lay, or any broken wire at any fitting.
- *Diameter reduction* – Wear should not exceed one-third of the original rope diameter. This type of wear is often caused by excessive abrasion of the outside wires, loss of core support, internal or external corrosion, inner wire failure, loosening of the rope lay, or stretching due to overloading.

- *Heat damage* – Usually indicated by the discoloration and pitting associated with high-temperature sources.
- *Corrosion* – Any noticeable rusting, pitting, or discoloration in the rope or end fittings. Corrosion around end fittings is typically associated with broken wires near the end fittings. Corrosion can be difficult to detect when it develops internally in areas not visible from outside inspection.
- *Damaged end fittings* – This type of damage is easily detected and includes cracks, gouges, nicks, severe corrosion, and evidence that the end fitting is creasing into the rope.

- *Rope distortion* – Includes kinking, crushing, and **bird caging**.
- *Core protrusion* – Involves the core sticking out from between the strands or the strands separating, exposing the core.
- *Unlaying of a splice* – Unraveling of a splice.

3.2.2 Synthetic Web and Round Slings

When inspecting synthetic and round slings, look for the following conditions. If any of these appear, discard the slings immediately:

- Acid or caustic burns
- Melting or charring of any part of the sling
- Holes, cuts, tears, or snags
- Broken or worn stitching in loadbearing splices
- Excessive abrasive wear (to the point where the colored yarns are showing)
- Knots in any part of the sling
- Excessive pitting or corrosion, or cracked, distorted, or broken fittings
- Other visible damage that causes doubt as to the strength of the sling
- Missing or illegible tag

3.2.3 Metal Mesh Slings

Although metal mesh slings withstand abrasive or hot loads, they are still vulnerable to damage. Metal mesh slings should be discarded if any of the following conditions appear during inspection:

- A broken welded or brazed joint along the sling edge
- A broken wire in any part of the mesh
- A reduction of wire diameter of 25 percent due to abrasion or 15 percent due to corrosion
- Lack of flexibility due to distortion of the mesh
- Distortion of the choker fitting so that the depth of the slot is increased by 10 percent
- Distortion of either end fitting so that the width of the eye opening is decreased by more than 10 percent
- A 15 percent reduction in the original cross-sectional area of metal at any point

3.3.0 Chain Slings

Some jobs are better suited for chain slings than for wire rope or web slings. Use of chain slings is recommended when lifting rough castings that would quickly destroy wire slings by bending the wires over rough edges. They are also used in high-heat applications or where wire chokers are not suitable, and for dredging and other marine work because they withstand abrasion and corrosion better than cable. Information pertaining to sling angles and sling capacities described earlier for rope and web slings also apply to chain slings. *Figure 19* shows some common configurations of chain slings and hooks.

A chain link consists of two sides. The failure of either side would cause the link to open and drop the load. Wire rope is frequently composed of as many as 114 individual wires, all of which must fail before it breaks. Chains have less reserve strength and should be more carefully inspected. They must never be used for routine lifting operations.

Chains will stretch under excessive loading. This causes elongating and narrowing of the links until they bind on each other, giving visible warning. If overloading is severe, the chain will fail with less warning than a wire rope. If a weld should break, there is little, if any, warning.

WARNING!

Chains must be carefully inspected for weak or damaged links. The failure of one link can cause the entire chain to fail.

Typically, iron-hoisting chains should be **annealed** every two years to relieve work hardening. Chains used as slings should be annealed every year. After being annealed six times, the chain should be destroyed. Steel chains should not be heat-treated after leaving the factory.

Note that only Grade 8 or higher chain is permitted for overhead lifting.

3.3.1 Chain Sling Storage

To store chains properly, hang them inside a building or vehicle on racks to reduce deterioration due to rust or corrosion from the weather. Never let chain slings lie on the ground in areas where heavy machinery can run over them. Some manufacturers suggest lubrication of alloy chains while in use; however, slippery chains increase handling hazards. Chains coated with oil or grease accumulate dirt and grit, which may cause abrasive wear. Before storing chains in exposed areas, coat them with a film of oil or grease for rust and corrosion protection.

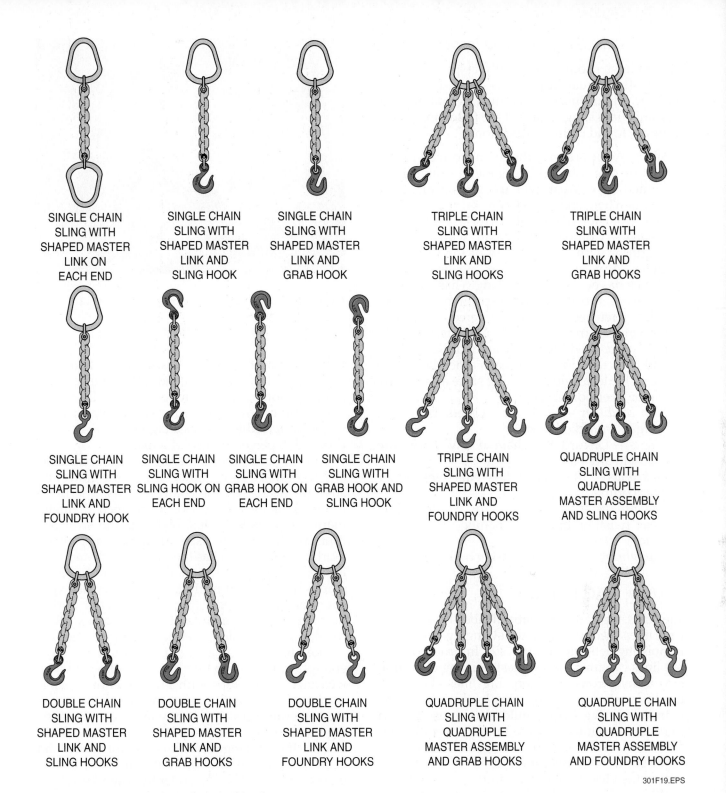

SINGLE CHAIN
SLING WITH
SHAPED MASTER
LINK ON
EACH END

SINGLE CHAIN
SLING WITH
SHAPED MASTER
LINK AND
SLING HOOK

SINGLE CHAIN
SLING WITH
SHAPED MASTER
LINK AND
GRAB HOOK

TRIPLE CHAIN
SLING WITH
SHAPED MASTER
LINK AND
SLING HOOKS

TRIPLE CHAIN
SLING WITH
SHAPED MASTER
LINK AND
GRAB HOOKS

SINGLE CHAIN
SLING WITH
SHAPED MASTER
LINK AND
FOUNDRY HOOK

SINGLE CHAIN
SLING WITH
SLING HOOK ON
EACH END

SINGLE CHAIN
SLING WITH
GRAB HOOK ON
EACH END

SINGLE CHAIN
SLING WITH
GRAB HOOK AND
SLING HOOK

TRIPLE CHAIN
SLING WITH
SHAPED MASTER
LINK AND
FOUNDRY HOOKS

QUADRUPLE CHAIN
SLING WITH
QUADRUPLE
MASTER ASSEMBLY
AND SLING HOOKS

DOUBLE CHAIN
SLING WITH
SHAPED MASTER
LINK AND
SLING HOOKS

DOUBLE CHAIN
SLING WITH
SHAPED MASTER
LINK AND
GRAB HOOKS

DOUBLE CHAIN
SLING WITH
SHAPED MASTER
LINK AND
FOUNDRY HOOKS

QUADRUPLE CHAIN
SLING WITH
QUADRUPLE
MASTER ASSEMBLY
AND GRAB HOOKS

QUADRUPLE CHAIN
SLING WITH
QUADRUPLE
MASTER ASSEMBLY
AND FOUNDRY HOOKS

301F19.EPS

Figure 19 ◆ Common chain slings and hooks.

Chain slings should be visually inspected before every lift. Annual inspections are also required and records of inspections must be maintained. Discard chain slings if any of the following conditions are found during inspection:

- *Wear* – Any portion of the chain worn by 15 percent or more should be removed from service immediately. Wear will usually occur at the points where chain links bear on each other or on the outside of the link barrels.
- *Stretch* – Compare the chain with its rated length or with a new length of the same type chain. Any length increase means wear or stretch has occurred. If the length has increased 3 percent, further careful inspection is needed. If it is stretched more than 5 percent, it should be removed from service immediately. Significantly stretched links have an hourglass shape, and links tend to bind on each other. Be sure to check for localized stretching since a chain link can be overlooked easily.
- *Link condition* – Look for twisted, bent, cut, gouged, or nicked links.
- *Cracks* – Discard the chain if any cracks are found in any part.
- *Link welds* – Lifted fins at the weld edges signify overloading.
- *End fittings* – Check for signs of stretching, wear, twisting, bending, opening up, and corrosion.
- *Capacity tag* – Check for missing or illegible tags.

4.0.0 ◆ TAG LINES

Tag lines typically are natural fiber or synthetic rope lines used to control the swinging of the load in hoisting activities (*Figure 20*). Improper use of tag lines can turn the simplest hoisting operation into a dangerous situation. Tag lines should be used to control swinging of the load when a crane is traveling. Tag lines should also be used when the crane is rotated if rotation of the load is hazardous. A tag line with a tag line insulator is required during operation of a mobile crane within the vicinity of power lines.

When selecting a tag line, take certain factors into consideration. Compared to synthetic rope, natural fiber rope is inexpensive and the most common type used for tag lines. However, it is notably weaker than synthetic fiber (nylon, polyester, polypropylene, or polyethylene) ropes of the same size, and it is subject to ultraviolet deterioration and damage from heat and chemicals. Manila rope can also become a conductor of electricity when wet. Synthetic ropes are light and strong for

301F20.EPS

Figure 20 ◆ Use of a tag line to control swinging of a suspended load.

their size, and most are resistant to chemicals. When dry, they are poor conductors of electricity, although some synthetic ropes will readily absorb water and conduct electricity. Dry polypropylene line is preferred for use as a tag line. However, no rope is 100 percent nonconductive.

Number one natural manila is strong, durable, and recognized by its light color. As the grade and strength decreases, the color darkens. The minimum breaking strength of a one-inch diameter manila rope is 9,000 lbs. Nylon is the strongest rope available. It is used in marine and water work because nylon has the most stretch and flexibility, is highly abrasion resistant, and can be stored wet without rotting. Polyester is also very common. It has less stretch than nylon and is twice as strong as manila. It also has an excellent resistance to abrasion, chemicals, and weathering.

The diameter of a tag line should be large enough so that it can be gripped well even when wearing gloves. Rope with a diameter of ½ inch is common, but ¾-inch- and 1-inch-diameter ropes are sometimes used on heavy loads or where the tag line must be extremely long. Tag lines should be of sufficient length to allow control of the load from its original lift location until it is safely placed or control is taken over by coworkers. Special consideration should be given to situations where a long tag line would interfere with safe handling of loads, such as steel erection or catalyst pours.

Tag lines should be attached to loads at a location that gives the best mechanical advantage in controlling the load. Long loads should have tag lines attached as close to the ends as possible. The tag line should be located in a place that allows personnel to remove it easily after the load is

Tag Line Insulator

Any tag line, including polypropylene line, can conduct enough high-voltage electricity to kill a person. Such electrical energy can come from a lightning strike or from contact with a high-voltage power line. For that reason, the use of a tag line insulator is strongly recommended.

301SA02.EPS

placed. Knots used to attach tag lines should be tied properly to prevent slipping or accidental loosening, but they need to be easily untied after the load is placed. Some recommended knots are the clove hitch with overhand safety and bowline. Riggers use different knots for different purposes. *Figure 21* shows several knots commonly used in rigging. As much as possible, tag lines should be of one continuous length, free of knots and splices, and seized on both ends. If joining two tag lines together is necessary, it should be done by splicing the lines. Knots tied in the middle or with free ends of tag lines can create difficulties.

To properly handle a tag line, determine the mechanical advantage intended by the tag line and stand away from the load in order to have a clear area. When possible, stand where you can see the crane being used for lifting. Keep yourself and the tag line in view of the crane operator. Stay alert. Do not become complacent during the lift. Be aware of the location of any excess rope, and do not allow it to become fouled or entangled on anything.

Large loads often require the use of more than one tag line. In such cases, tag line personnel must work as a team and coordinate their actions.

BOWLINE

ROUND TURN AND
TWO HALF-HITCHES

CLOVE HITCH

SQUARE KNOT

TIMBER HITCH

RUNNING BOWLINE

HALF-HITCH SAFETY

OVERHAND SAFETY

301F21.EPS

Figure 21 ◆ Common rigging knots.

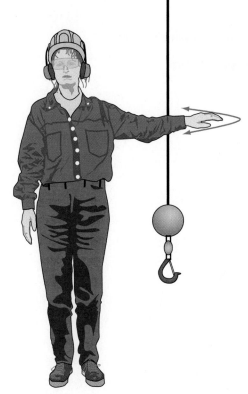

STOP: Arm extended, palm down, move arm back and forth horizontally.

EXPECTED MACHINE MOVEMENT: None. All movement of the machine ceases.

302F12.EPS

Figure 12 ◆ Stop.

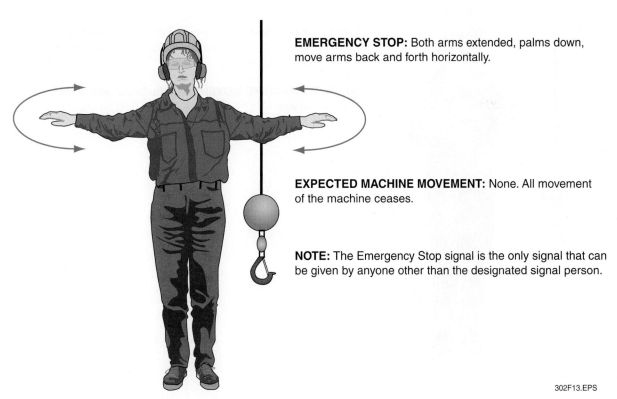

EMERGENCY STOP: Both arms extended, palms down, move arms back and forth horizontally.

EXPECTED MACHINE MOVEMENT: None. All movement of the machine ceases.

NOTE: The Emergency Stop signal is the only signal that can be given by anyone other than the designated signal person.

302F13.EPS

Figure 13 ◆ Emergency stop.

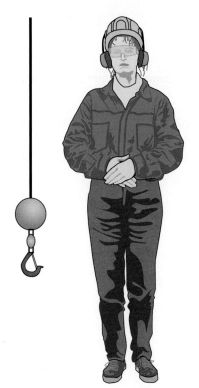

DOG EVERYTHING: Clasp hands in front of body.

EXPECTED MACHINE MOVEMENT: None.

302F14.EPS

Figure 14 ◆ Dog everything.

TRAVEL (BOTH TRACKS): Position both fists in front of body and move them in a circular motion, indicating the direction of travel (forward or backward).

EXPECTED MACHINE MOVEMENT: Machine travels in the direction chosen.

302F15.EPS

Figure 15 ◆ Travel (both tracks).

TRAVEL (ONE TRACK): Lock track on side of raised fist. Travel opposite track in direction indicated by circular motion of other fist, rotated vertically in front of body.

EXPECTED MACHINE MOVEMENT: Machine turns in the direction chosen.

302F16.EPS

Figure 16 ◆ Travel (one track).

There are certain requirements that mandate the presence of a signal person. When the operator of the crane can't see the load, the landing area, or the path of motion, or can't judge distance, a signal person is required. A signal person is also required if the crane is operating near power lines or another crane is working in close proximity.

Not just anyone can be a signal person. Signal persons must be qualified by experience, be knowledgeable in all established communication methods, be stationed in full view of the operator, have a full view of the load path, and understand the load's intended path of travel in order to position themselves accordingly. In addition, they must wear high-visibility gloves and/or clothing, be responsible for keeping everyone out of the operating radius of the crane, and never direct the load over anyone.

NOTE

Do not give signals to the crane operator unless you have been designated as the signal person. However, if a dangerous situation is observed, anyone can signal the crane operator to stop.

Although personnel involved in lifting operations are expected to understand these signals when they are given, it is acceptable for a signal person to give a verbal or nonverbal signal to an operator that is not part of the *ASME B30.5* standard. In cases where such nonstandardized signals are given, it is important that both the operator and the signal person have a complete understanding of the message that is being sent.

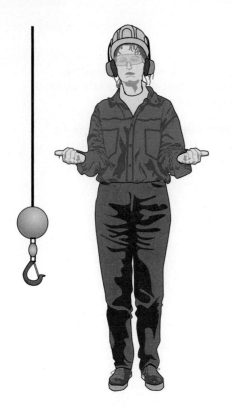

EXTENDING BOOM (TELESCOPING BOOM): Both fists in front of body with thumbs pointing outward.

EXPECTED MACHINE MOVEMENT: Boom sections telescope out. The load radius is increased, possibly decreasing machine capacity and stability. The load (block or ball) rises.

A. TWO-HANDED

EXTENDING BOOM (TELESCOPING BOOM): One fist in front of body with thumb pointing toward body.

EXPECTED MACHINE MOVEMENT: Boom sections telescope out. The load radius is increased, possibly decreasing machine capacity and stability. The load (block or ball) rises.

B. ONE-HANDED

302F17.EPS

Figure 17 ◆ Extend boom.

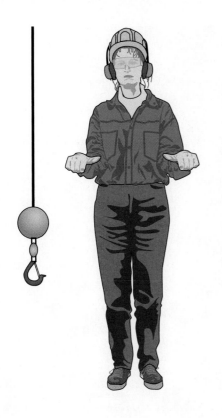

RETRACT BOOM (TELESCOPING BOOM): Both fists in front of body with thumbs pointing toward each other.

EXPECTED MACHINE MOVEMENT: Boom sections retract. The load radius is decreased, possibly increasing machine capacity and stability. The load (block or ball) lowers.

A. TWO-HANDED

RETRACT BOOM (TELESCOPING BOOM): One fist in front of body with thumb pointing outward.

EXPECTED MACHINE MOVEMENT: Boom sections retract. The load radius is decreased, possibly increasing machine capacity and stability. The load (block or ball) lowers vertically.

B. ONE-HANDED

302F18.EPS

Figure 18 ◆ Retract boom.

3.0.0 ◆ GENERAL RIGGING SAFETY

You must be aware of the unavoidable hazards associated with rigging. You will be directing the movement of loads above and around other workers, where falling equipment and material can present a grave safety hazard (*Figure 19*). You may also work during extreme weather conditions where winds, slippery surfaces, and unguarded work areas exist. When working near cranes, always look up and be mindful of the hazards above and around you.

As a result of tighter regulations established by the Occupational Safety and Health Administration (OSHA), and more lost work days experienced by construction employees, individual construction trade contractors have put more stringent safety policies into place.

Safety consciousness is extremely important for the employee. The earning ability of injured employees may be reduced or eliminated for the rest of their lives. The number of employees injured can be lowered if each employee is committed to safety awareness. Full participation in the employer's safety program is your personal responsibility.

Safety consciousness is the key to reducing accidents, injuries, and deaths on the job site. Accidents can be avoided because most result from human error. Mistakes can be reduced by developing safe work habits derived from the principles of on-the-job safety.

3.1.0 Personal Protection

Workers on the job have responsibilities for their own safety and the safety of their fellow workers. Management has a responsibility to each worker to ensure that the workers who prepare and use the equipment, and who work with or around it, are well trained in operating procedures and safety practices.

Always be aware of your environment when working with cranes. Stay alert and know the location of equipment at all times when moving about and working within the job area.

Standard personal protective equipment, including hard hats, safety shoes, gloves, and barricaded work areas (*Figure 20*) are among the important safety requirements at any job site.

3.2.0 Equipment and Supervision

Your employer is responsible for ensuring that all hoisting equipment is operated by experienced,

302F19.EPS

Figure 19 ◆ Overhead hazards.

302F20.EPS

Figure 20 ◆ Barricaded work area.

trained operators. Rigging workers must also be capable of selecting suitable rigging and lifting equipment, and directing the movement of the crane and the load to ensure the safety of all personnel. Rigging operations must be planned and supervised by competent personnel who ensure the following:

- Proper rigging equipment is available.
- Correct load ratings are available for the material and rigging equipment.
- Rigging material and equipment are well maintained and in good working condition.

A rigging supervisor is responsible for the following functions:

- Proper load rigging
- Crew supervision
- Ensuring that the rigged material and equipment meet the required capacity and are in safe condition
- Ensuring that the lifting bolts and other rigging materials and equipment are installed correctly
- Guaranteeing the safety of the rigging crew and other personnel

3.3.0 Basic Rigging Precautions

The most important rigging precaution is determining the weight of all loads before attempting to lift them. When the assessment of the weight load is difficult, safe-load indicators or weighing devices should be attached to the rigging equipment. It is equally important to rig the load so that it is stable and the **center of gravity** is below the hook.

The personal safety of riggers and hoisting operators depends on common sense. Always observe the following safety practices:

- Always read the manufacturer's literature for all equipment with which you work. This literature provides information on required startup checks and periodic inspections, as well as inspection guidelines. Also, this literature provides information on configurations and capacities in addition to many safety precautions and restrictions of use.
- Determine the weight of loads, including rigging and hardware, before rigging. Site management must provide this information if it is not known.
- Know the safe working load of the equipment and rigging, and never exceed the limit.
- Examine all equipment and rigging before use. Discard all defective components.
- Immediately report defective equipment or hazardous conditions to the supervisor. Someone in authority must issue orders to proceed after safe conditions have been ensured.

- Stop hoisting or rigging operations when weather conditions present hazards to property, workers, or bystanders, such as when winds exceed manufacturer's specifications; when the visibility of the rigger or hoist crew is impaired by darkness, dust, fog, rain, or snow.
- Recognize factors that can reduce equipment capacity. Safe working loads of all hoisting and rigging equipment are based on ideal conditions. These conditions are seldom achieved under working conditions.
- Remember that safe working loads of hoisting equipment are applicable only to freely suspended loads and plumb hoist lines. Side loads and hoist lines that are not plumb can stress equipment beyond design limits, and structural failure can occur without warning.
- Ensure that the safe working load of equipment is not exceeded if it is exposed to wind. Avoid sudden snatching, swinging, and stopping of suspended loads. Rapid acceleration and deceleration greatly increase the stress on equipment and rigging.
- Follow all manufacturer's guidelines, and consult applicable standards to stabilize mobile cranes properly (*Figure 21*).

3.4.0 Load Path, Load Control, and Tag Lines

Any load that is hoisted into the air must have a tag line (*Figure 22*). If a load is small and the air conditions will not affect it, a short tag line can be

302F21.EPS

Figure 21 ◆ Mobile crane with outriggers.

used. If it is a large object, multiple tag lines must be used. The length of the tag line will be determined by the height of the object. Tag lines must be long enough so that workers can be off to the side of the load, not directly beneath the load. When workers are using tag lines to control the load, they must talk to each other and fellow workers involved before they start lifting the load. The workers must ensure that the load is balanced before attaching tag lines. They need to talk about the positioning of the load during lifting and installation so they are working with each other and not against each other during the rigging activity. They also need to take landing zone precautions ahead of time such as barricading areas and **blocking** placement. At least two tag lines need to be held onto at all times. Do not wrap the tag lines around your hand or body. Do not tie a knot on the ends of a tag line unless it is a crown knot. A piece of tape on the end is sufficient to keep the rope from unraveling.

 WARNING!
Make sure that the tag line is not wrapped around any part of your body.

3.5.0 Barricades

Barricades should always be used to isolate the area of an overhead lift to prevent the possibility of injuring personnel who may walk into the area. Always follow the individual site requirements for proper barricade erection. If in doubt as to the proper procedure, ask your supervisor for guidance before proceeding with any overhead lifting operation. It is important to remember that accessible areas within the swing radius of the rear of the crane's rotating structure must be barricaded in such a manner as to prevent an employee or others from being struck or crushed by the crane (*Figure 23*).

3.6.0 Load-Handling Safety

The safe and effective control of the load involves the rigger's strict observance of load-handling safety requirements. This includes making sure that the swing path or load path is clear of personnel and obstructions (*Figure 24*). Keep the front and rear swing paths (*Figure 25*) of the crane clear for the duration of the lift. Most people watch the load when it is in motion, which prevents them from seeing the back end of the crane coming around.

Make sure the landing zone is clear of personnel, with the exception of the tag line tenders. Also make sure that the necessary blocking and **cribbing** for the load are in place before you position the load for landing. The practice of lowering the load just above the landing zone and then placing the cribbing and blocking can be dangerous. No one should work under the load. The layout of the cribbing can be completed in the landing zone before you set the load. Blocking of the load may have to be done after the load is set. In this case, do not take the load stress off the sling until the blocking is set and secured. Do not attempt to position the load onto the cribbing by manhandling it.

302F22.EPS

Figure 22 ◆ Using a tag line.

SAFETY BARRIER

302F23.EPS

Figure 23 ◆ Use of a barrier to isolate the swing circle area of a crane.

Figure 24 ◆ Front swing path.

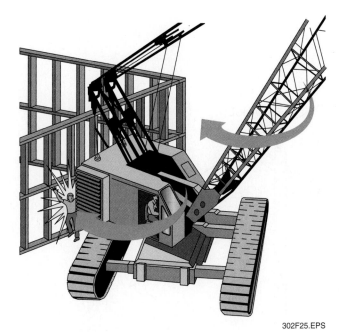

Figure 25 ◆ Rear swing path.

After the rigging has been set and whenever loads are to be handled, follow these procedures:

- Before lifting, make sure that all loads are securely slung and properly balanced to prevent shifting of any part.
- Use one or more tag lines to keep the load under control.
- Safely land and properly block all loads before removing the slings.
- Only use lifting beams for the purpose for which they were designed. Their weight and working load abilities must be visible on the beams.
- Never wrap hoist ropes around the load. Use only slings or other adequate lifting devices.
- Do not twist multiple-part lines around each other.
- Bring the load line over the center of gravity of the load before starting the lift.
- Make sure the rope is properly seated on the drum and in the sheaves if there has been a slack rope condition.
- Load and secure any materials and equipment being hoisted to prevent movement, which, in turn, could create a hazard.
- Keep hands and feet away from pinch points as the slack is taken up.
- Wear gloves.
- See that all personnel are standing clear while loads are being lifted and lowered or when slings are being drawn from beneath the load. The hooks may catch under the load and suddenly fly free. It is prohibited to pull a choker out from under a load that has been set on the choker.
- Never ride on a load that is being lifted.
- Never allow the load to be lifted above other personnel.
- Never work under a suspended load.
- Never leave a load suspended in the air when the hoisting equipment is unattended.
- Never make temporary repairs to a sling.
- Never lift loads with one or two legs of a multi-leg sling until the unused slings are secured.
- Ensure that all slings are made from the same material when using two or more slings on a load.
- Remove or secure all loose pieces from a load before it is moved.
- Lower loads onto adequate blocking to prevent damage to the slings.
- Never allow the load to touch the crane.

4.0.0 ◆ WORKING AROUND POWER LINES

A competent signal person must be stationed at all times to warn the operator when any part of the machine or load is approaching the minimum safe distance from the power line. The signal person must be in full view at all times. *Table 1* and *Figure 26* show the minimum safe distance from power lines.

WARNING!

The most frequent cause of death of riggers and material handlers is electrocution caused by contact of the crane's boom, load lines, or load with electric power lines. To prevent personal injury or death, stay clear of electric power lines. Even though the boom guards, insulating links, or proximity warning devices may be used or required, these devices do not alter the precautions given in this section.

Table 1   High-Voltage Power Line Clearances

CRANE IN OPERATION (1)	
POWER LINE (kV)	BOOM OR MAST MINIMUM CLEARANCES (feet)
0 to 50	10
50 to 200	15
200 to 350	20
350 to 500	25
500 to 750	35
750 to 1000	45
CRANE IN TRANSIT (with no load and the boom or mast lowered) (2)	
POWER LINE (kV)	BOOM OR MAST MINIMUM CLEARANCES (feet)
0 to 0.75	4
0.75 to 50	6
50 to 345	10
345 to 7500	16
750 to 1000	20

Note 1: For voltages over 50kV, clearance increases 5 feet for every 150 kV.

Note 2: Environmental conditions such as fog, smoke, or precipitation may require increased clearances.

302T01.EPS

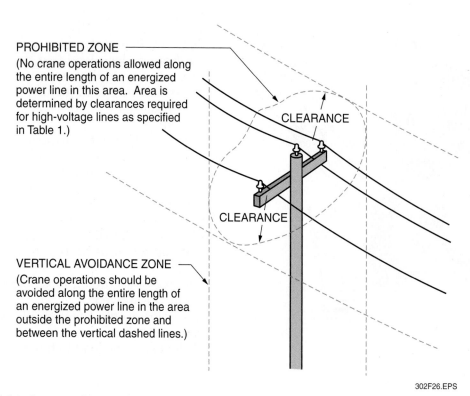

PROHIBITED ZONE
(No crane operations allowed along the entire length of an energized power line in this area. Area is determined by clearances required for high-voltage lines as specified in Table 1.)

CLEARANCE

CLEARANCE

VERTICAL AVOIDANCE ZONE
(Crane operations should be avoided along the entire length of an energized power line in the area outside the prohibited zone and between the vertical dashed lines.)

302F26.EPS

Figure 26 ◆ Prohibited zone and avoidance zone.

The preferred working condition is to have the owner of the power lines de-energize and provide grounding of the lines that are visible to the crane operator. When that is not possible, observe the following procedures and precautions if any part of your boom can reach the power line:

- Make sure a power line awareness permit (see *Appendix*) or equivalent has been prepared.
- Erect nonconductive barricades to restrict access to the work area.
- Use a tag line for load control.
- The qualified signal person(s), whose sole responsibility is to verify that the proper clearances are established and maintained, shall be in constant contact with the crane operator.
- The person(s) responsible for the operation shall alert and warn the crane operator and all persons working around or near the crane about the hazards of electrocution or serious injury, and instruct them on how to avoid these hazards.
- All nonessential personnel shall be removed from the crane work area.
- No one shall be permitted to touch the crane or load unless the signal person indicates it is safe to do so.

If a crane or load comes in contact with or becomes entangled in power lines, assume that the power lines are energized unless the lines are visibly grounded. Any other assumption could be fatal.

The following guidelines should be followed if the crane comes in contact with an electrical power source:

- The operator should stay in the cab of the crane unless a fire occurs.
- Do not allow anyone to touch the crane or the load.
- If possible, the operator should reverse the movement of the crane to break contact with the energized power line.
- If the operator cannot stay in the cab due to fire or arcing, the operator should jump clear of the crane, landing with both feet together on the ground. Once out of the crane, the operator must take very short steps or hops with feet together until well clear of the crane.
- Call the local power authority or owner of the power line.
- Have the lines verified as secure and properly grounded within the operator's view before allowing anyone to approach the crane or the load.

Power Lines

Working around cranes can be very dangerous. Nearly 40 percent of the injuries and deaths recorded over a 10-year period resulted from electrocution, which often occurs when the boom of a crane comes into contact with power lines. As a rigger, it is vitally important to keep an eye out for the proximity of power lines.

302SA01.EPS

5.0.0 ◆ SITE SAFETY

It takes a combined effort by everyone involved in crane operations to make sure no one is injured or killed. Site hazards and restrictions as well as the crane manufacturer's requirements must be observed for safe crane operation.

WARNING!

Transmitters such as radio towers can also represent a hazard. These transmitters generate high-power radio frequency (RF) energy that can induce a hazardous voltage into the boom of a nearby crane. OSHA requires that the transmitter be de-energized in such situations, or that appropriate grounding methods be used to protect workers. Always consult your supervisor or site safety officer in such situations.

While induced RF voltages from transmitters are not an electrocution hazard like power line voltages, they can result in sparks to any object or person. The sparks can cause fires or explosions of combustible or flammable materials. They can also result in painful burns and shocks to personnel that come in close contact with the crane or the load being lifted by the crane.

5.1.0 Site Hazards and Restrictions

There are many site hazards and restrictions related to crane operations. These hazards include the following:

- Underground utilities such as gas, oil, electrical, and telephone lines; sewage and drainage piping; and underground tanks
- Electrical lines or high-frequency transmitters
- Structures such as buildings, excavations, bridges, and abutments

WARNING!

Power lines and environmental issues such as weather are common causes of injury and death during crane operations.

The operator and riggers should inspect the work area and identify hazards or restrictions that may affect the safe operation of the crane. This includes the following actions:

- Ensuring the ground can support the crane and the load
- Checking that there is a safe path to move the crane around on site
- Making sure that the crane can rotate in the required quadrants for the planned lift

The operator must follow the manufacturer's recommendations and any locally established restrictions placed on crane operations, such as traffic considerations or time restrictions for noise abatement.

6.0.0 ◆ EMERGENCY RESPONSE

Operators and riggers must react quickly and correctly to any crane malfunction or emergency situation that might arise. They must learn the proper responses to emergency situations. The first priority is to prevent injury and loss of life. The second priority is to prevent damage to equipment or surrounding structures.

6.1.0 Fire

Judgment is crucial in determining the correct response to fire. The first response is to cease crane operation and, if time permits, lower the load and secure the crane. In all cases of fire, evacuate the area even if the load cannot be lowered or the crane secured. After emergency services have been notified, a qualified individual may judge if the fire can be combated with a fire extinguisher. A fire extinguisher can be successful at fighting a small fire in its beginning stage, but a fire can get out of control very quickly. Do not be overconfident, and keep in mind that priority number one is preventing loss of life or injury to anyone. Even trained firefighters using the best equipment can be overwhelmed and injured by fires.

6.2.0 Malfunctions During Lifting Operations

Mechanical malfunctions during a lift can be very serious. If a failure causes the radius to increase unexpectedly, the crane can tip or the boom could collapse. Loads can also be dropped during a mechanical malfunction. A sudden loss of load on the crane can cause a whiplash effect that can tip the crane or cause the boom to fail.

The chance of these types of failures occurring in modern cranes is greatly reduced because of system redundancies and safety backups. However, failures do happen, so stay alert at all times.

If a mechanical problem occurs, the operator should lower the load immediately. Next, the operator should secure the crane, tag the controls out of service, and report the problem to a supervisor. The crane should not be operated until it is repaired by a qualified technician.

6.3.0 Hazardous Weather

Mobile crane operations generally take place outdoors. Under certain environmental conditions, such as extreme hot or cold weather or in high winds, work can become uncomfortable and possibly dangerous. For example, snow and rain can have a dramatic effect on the weight of the load and on ground compaction. During the winter, the tires, outriggers, and crawlers can freeze to the ground. This may lead the operator or rigger to the false conclusion that the crane is on stable ground. In fact, as weight is added during the lifting operation, it may cause an outrigger float, tire, or crawler to sink into the ground below the frozen surface. Severe rain can cause the ground under the crane to become unstable, resulting in instability of the crane due to erosion or loss of compaction of the soil. There are other specific things to be aware of when working under these adverse conditions.

6.3.1 High Winds and Lightning

High winds and lightning may cause severe problems on the job site (*Figure 27*). They are major weather hazards and must be taken seriously. Crane operators and riggers must be prepared to handle extreme weather in order to avoid accidents, injuries, and damages. It is very rare for high winds or lightning to arrive without some warning. This gives operators and riggers time to react appropriately.

High winds typically start out as less dramatic gusts. Operators and riggers must be aware of changing weather conditions, such as worsening winds, to determine when the weather may become hazardous. With high winds, the operator must secure crane operations as soon as it is practical. This involves placing the boom in the lowest possible position and securing the crane. Once this is done, all personnel should seek indoor shelter away from the crane.

Lightning can usually be detected when it is several miles away. As a general rule of thumb, thunder follows lightning by five seconds per mile. Be aware, however, that successive lightning strikes can touch down up to 8 miles apart. That means once you hear thunder or see lightning, it is close enough to present a hazard.

In some high-risk areas, proximity sensors provide warnings when lightning strikes within a 20-mile radius. Once a warning is given or lightning is spotted, crane operations must be secured as soon as practical, following the crane manufacturer's recommendations for doing so.

Once crane operations have been shut down, all personnel should seek indoor shelter away from the crane. Always wait a minimum of 30 minutes from the last observed instance of lightning or thunder before resuming work.

WARNING!
Even in its lowest position, the boom may be taller than surrounding structures and could still be a target for lightning strikes.

6.3.2 Cold Weather

The amount of injury caused by exposure to abnormally cold temperatures depends on wind speed, length of exposure, temperature, and humidity. Freezing is increased by wind and humidity or a combination of the two factors.

Weather

Weather conditions can affect crane operations. Because they extend so high and are made of metal, crane booms are easy targets for lightning. High winds have the potential to topple a crane with a raised boom. The person on the ground working with the crane operator must be alert for weather problems that could affect the crane.

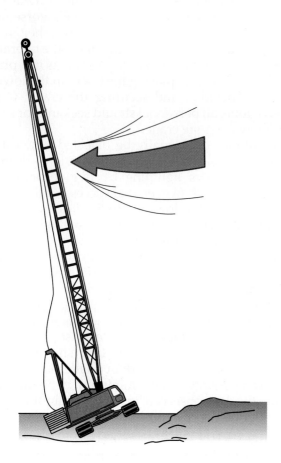
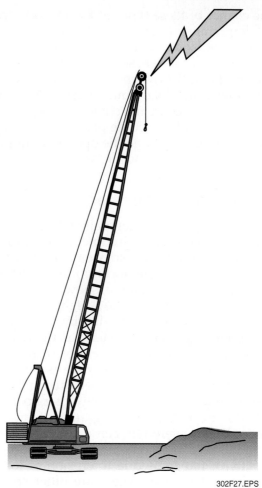

302F27.EPS

Figure 27 ◆ Wind and lightning hazards.

Follow these guidelines to prevent injuries such as frostbite during extremely cold weather:

- Always wear the proper clothing.
- Limit your exposure as much as possible.
- Take frequent, short rest periods.
- Keep moving. Exercise fingers and toes if necessary, but do not overexert yourself.
- Do not drink alcohol before exposure to cold. Alcohol can dull your sensitivity to cold and make you less aware of overexposure.
- Do not expose yourself to extremely cold weather if any part of your clothing or body is wet.
- Do not smoke before exposure to cold. Smoking reduces blood flow to the extremities, which increases the risk of frostbite.
- Learn how to recognize the symptoms of overexposure and frostbite.
- Place cold hands under dry clothing against the body, such as in the armpits.

6.3.3 Cold Exposure Symptoms and Treatment

If you live in a place with cold weather, you will most likely be exposed to it when working. Spending long periods of time in the cold can be dangerous. It is important to know the following symptoms of cold weather exposure and how to treat them:

- Shivering
- Numbness
- Low body temperature
- Drowsiness
- Weak muscles

Follow these steps to treat cold exposure:

Step 1 Get to a warm inside area as quickly as possible.

Step 2 Remove wet or frozen clothing and anything that is binding, such as necklaces, watches, rings, and belts.

Step 3 Rewarm by adding clothing or wrapping in a blanket.

Step 4 Drink hot liquids, but do not drink alcohol.

Step 5 Check for frostbite. If frostbite is found, seek medical help immediately.

6.3.4 Symptoms and Treatment of Frostbite

Frostbite is an injury resulting from exposure to cold elements. It happens when ice crystals form in the fluids and underlying soft tissues of the skin. The nose, cheeks, ears, fingers, and toes are usually affected. Affected skin may be slightly flushed just before frostbite sets in. Symptoms of frostbite include the following:

- Skin becomes white, gray, or waxy yellow. The color indicates deep tissue damage. Victims are often not aware of frostbite until someone else recognizes the pale, glossy skin.
- Skin tingles and then becomes numb.
- Pain in the affected area starts and stops.
- Blisters show up on the area.
- The area of frostbite swells and feels hard.

Use the following steps to treat frostbite:

Step 1 Protect the frozen area from refreezing.

Step 2 Warm the frostbitten part as soon as possible.

Step 3 Get medical attention immediately.

6.3.5 Hot Weather

Hot weather can be as dangerous as cold weather. When someone is exposed to excessive amounts of heat, he or she runs the risk of overheating. The following conditions are associated with overheating:

- *Heat exhaustion* – Heat exhaustion is characterized by pale, clammy skin; heavy sweating with nausea and possible vomiting; a fast, weak pulse; and possible fainting.
- *Heat cramps* – Heat cramps can occur after an attack of heat exhaustion. Cramps are characterized by abdominal pain, nausea, and dizziness. The skin becomes pale with heavy sweating, muscular twitching, and severe muscle cramps.
- *Heat stroke* – Heat stroke is an immediate, life-threatening emergency that requires urgent medical attention. It is characterized by headache, nausea, and visual problems. Body temperature can reach as high as 106°F. This will be accompanied by hot, flushed, dry skin; slow, deep breathing; possible convulsions; and loss of consciousness.

Follow these guidelines when working in hot weather in order to prevent heat exhaustion, cramps, or heat stroke:
- Drink plenty of water.
- Do not overexert yourself.
- Wear lightweight clothing.
- Keep your head covered and face shaded.
- Take frequent, short work breaks.
- Rest in the shade whenever possible.

First aid for heat exhaustion involves these steps:

Step 1 Remove the victim from heat.

Step 2 Have the victim lie down and raise his or her legs six to eight inches.

Step 3 If the victim is nauseous, lay the victim on his or her side.

Step 4 Loosen clothing, and remove any heavy clothing.

Step 5 Apply cool, wet cloths.

Step 6 Fan the victim, but stop if the victim develops goosebumps or shivers.

Step 7 Give the victim one-half glassful of water to drink every 15 minutes if he or she is fully conscious and can tolerate it.

Step 8 If the victim's condition does not improve within a few minutes, call emergency medical services (911).

If you or anyone else experiences heat cramps, follow these guidelines:

- Sit or lie down in a cool area.
- Drink one-half glassful of water every 15 minutes.
- Gently stretch and massage cramped muscles.

First aid for heat stroke involves these steps:

Step 1 Call emergency medical services (911) immediately.

Step 2 Remove the victim from heat.

Step 3 Have the victim lie down on his or her back.

Step 4 If the victim is nauseous, lay the victim on his or her side.

Step 5 Move all nearby objects, as heat stroke may cause convulsions or seizures.

Step 6 Cool the victim by fanning, spraying with cool water mist, covering with a wet sheet, or wiping with a wet cloth.

Step 7 If the victim is alert enough to do so, and not nauseous, give small amounts of cool water (a cup every 15 minutes).

Step 8 Place ice packs under the armpits and groin area.

7.0.0 ◆ USING CRANES TO LIFT PERSONNEL

Although using cranes to lift people was common in the past, OSHA regulations, as spelled out in *29 CFR 1926.550*, now discourage the practice. Using a crane to lift personnel is not specifically prohibited by OSHA, but the restrictions are such that it is only permitted in special situations where no other method is suitable. When it is allowed, certain controls must be in place, including the following:

- The rope design factor is doubled.
- No more than 50 percent of the crane's capacity, including rigging, may be used.
- Free-falling is prohibited.
- **Anti-two-blocking devices** are required on the crane boom.
- The platform must be specifically designed for lifting personnel.
- Before the personnel basket is used, it must be tested with appropriate weight, and then inspected.
- Every intended use must undergo a trial run with weights rather than people.

Figures 28 and *29* illustrate the requirements for personnel lifts.

7.1.0 Personnel Platform Loading

The personnel platform must not be loaded in excess of its rated load capacity or maximum intended load. The number of employees, along with material, occupying the personnel platform must not exceed the limit established for the platform and the rated load capacity or the maximum intended load.

Personnel platforms must be used only for employees, their tools, and the materials necessary to do their work, and must not be used to hoist materials or tools only.

Materials and tools for use during a personnel lift must be secured to prevent displacement. These items must be evenly distributed within the confines of the platform while the platform is suspended.

7.2.0 Personnel Platform Rigging

When a wire-rope bridle sling is used to connect the personnel platform to the load line, each bridle leg shall be connected to a master link or shackle in such a manner as to ensure that the load is evenly divided among the bridle legs (*Figures 30* and *31*).

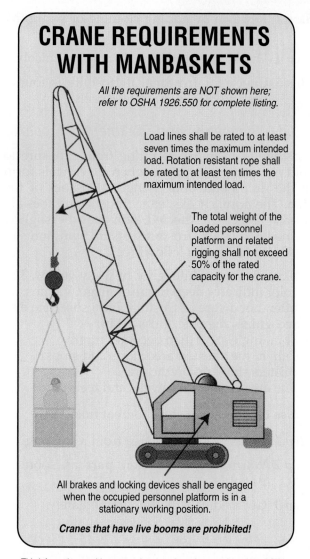

CRANE REQUIREMENTS WITH MANBASKETS

All the requirements are NOT shown here; refer to OSHA 1926.550 for complete listing.

Load lines shall be rated to at least seven times the maximum intended load. Rotation resistant rope shall be rated to at least ten times the maximum intended load.

The total weight of the loaded personnel platform and related rigging shall not exceed 50% of the rated capacity for the crane.

All brakes and locking devices shall be engaged when the occupied personnel platform is in a stationary working position.

Cranes that have live booms are prohibited!

This information provides a generic, non-exhaustive overview of the OSHA standard on suspended personnel platforms. Standards and interpretations change over time; you should always check current OSHA compliance requirements for your specific requirements.

29 CFR 1926.550 addresses the use of personnel hoisting in the construction industry, and *29 CFR 1910.180* addresses the use of personnel hoisting in general industry.

302F28.EPS

Figure 28 ◆ Crane requirements with manbaskets.

Hooks on headache ball assemblies, lower load blocks, or other attachment assemblies shall be of a type that can be closed and locked, eliminating the hook throat opening. Alternatively, an alloy anchor type shackle with a bolt, nut, and retaining pin may be used.

Wire rope, shackles, rings, master links, and other rigging hardware must be capable of supporting, without failure, at least five times the maximum intended load applied or transmitted to that component. Where rotation-resistant rope is used, the slings shall be capable of supporting

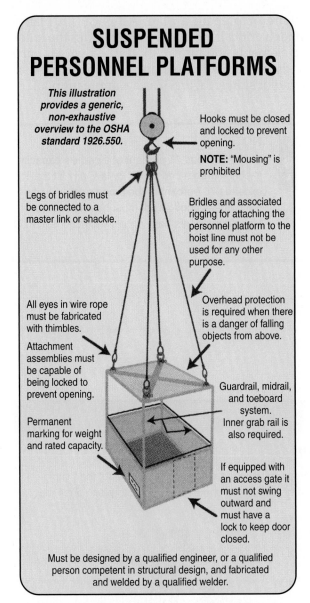

SUSPENDED PERSONNEL PLATFORMS

This illustration provides a generic, non-exhaustive overview to the OSHA standard 1926.550.

Hooks must be closed and locked to prevent opening.

NOTE: "Mousing" is prohibited

Legs of bridles must be connected to a master link or shackle.

Bridles and associated rigging for attaching the personnel platform to the hoist line must not be used for any other purpose.

All eyes in wire rope must be fabricated with thimbles.

Overhead protection is required when there is a danger of falling objects from above.

Attachment assemblies must be capable of being locked to prevent opening.

Guardrail, midrail, and toeboard system. Inner grab rail is also required.

Permanent marking for weight and rated capacity.

If equipped with an access gate it must not swing outward and must have a lock to keep door closed.

Must be designed by a qualified engineer, or a qualified person competent in structural design, and fabricated and welded by a qualified welder.

The OSHA rules on crane suspended personnel platforms contain many specifics that are not covered in this book. Refer to *29 CFR 1926.550* for the current OSHA compliance requirements.

302F29.EPS

Figure 29 ◆ Suspended personnel platforms.

without failure at least ten times the maximum intended load. All eyes in wire rope slings shall be fabricated with thimbles.

Bridles and associated rigging for attaching the personnel platform to the hoist line shall be used only for the platform and the necessary employees, their tools, and required materials, and they shall not be used for any other purpose.

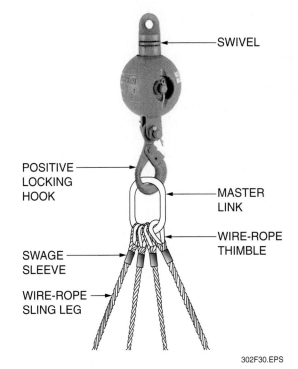

SWIVEL

POSITIVE LOCKING HOOK

MASTER LINK

WIRE-ROPE THIMBLE

SWAGE SLEEVE

WIRE-ROPE SLING LEG

302F30.EPS

Figure 30 ◆ Bridle sling using a master link.

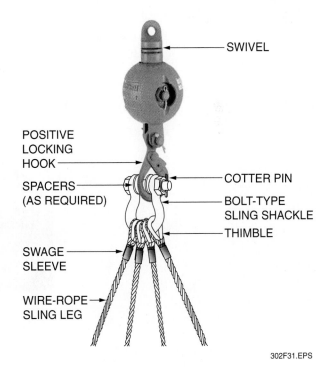

SWIVEL

POSITIVE LOCKING HOOK

COTTER PIN

SPACERS (AS REQUIRED)

BOLT-TYPE SLING SHACKLE

THIMBLE

SWAGE SLEEVE

WIRE-ROPE SLING LEG

302F31.EPS

Figure 31 ◆ Bridle sling using a shackle.

8.0.0 ◆ LIFT PLANNING

Before conducting a lift, most construction sites or companies require that a lift plan be completed and signed by competent personnel. Lift plans are mandatory for steel erection and multiple-crane lifts. A lift plan contains information relative to the crane, load, and rigging, and it lists any special instructions or restrictions for the lift. Remember that any deviation from the original lift plan, no matter how small, requires a new lift plan.

8.1.0 Lift Plan Data

Critical lifts always require a lift plan. As a matter of policy, all personnel involved in a lift should require or prepare a plan. A typical lift plan for either a critical or ordinary lift includes the following elements and information. The rigger is particularly concerned with crane placement, rope, and sizing of slings. *Figure 32* is a sample lift plan.

NOTE

If a lift exceeds 75 percent of a crane's capacity, it is considered a critical lift. By law, any lift that exceeds 75 percent of the crane's capacity, as the crane is configured, must be engineered. Many companies have tighter restrictions than 75 percent.

INSIDE TRACK

Tilt-Up Construction

Tilt-up construction is done by preparing concrete wall panels on a slab, then lifting them into place. Cranes are used to raise tilt-up concrete panels into place once they have been cast.

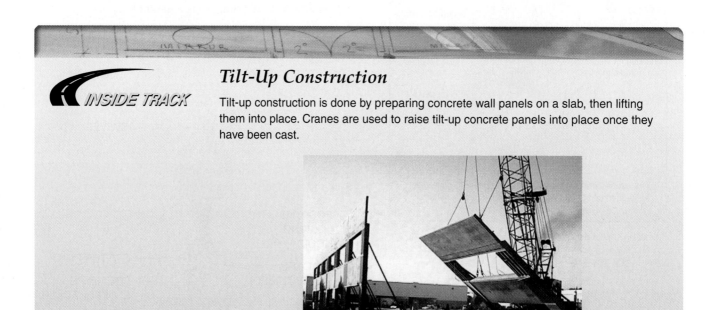

302SA02.EPS

PRE-LIFT CHECKLIST
USE FOR LIFTS EXCEEDING 75% OF CRANE'S RATED CHART CAPACITY
LAND BASED CRANES ONLY. CRANE APPROPRIATELY SUPPORTED AND LEVEL WITHIN 1%.

1. Crane Type: _____
2. Load Description:_____
3. Operating Radius:_____ Boom Length:_____ Boom Tip Elevation:_____
4. Loaded Boom Angle:_____ Minimum Boom Length:_____
5. Elevation of Lift:_____
6. Crane Capacity at Working Radius: (6)_____
   What is the Maximum Radius with total load? _____
7. Weight of Load: (7) – (_____)
                                                                       Subtotal _____
8. Crane Deductions:
   a. Block Capacity _____   Block WT. +_____
   b. Ball(s) Capacity _____   Ball WT. +_____
   c. Jib Effective WT   +_____
   d. Wire Rope # of parts Required: _____
   e. Other+_____   +_____
      WT/Ft. x # of ft. x parts being used ____ x ____ x____ = +_____

9. Total Crane Deductions: (9) – (_____)
                                                                       Subtotal _____

10. Rigging Deductions:
    a. Slings: Qty.____ Type ____ Size ____ Cap. ____ WT. +_____
                    Qty.____ Type ____ Size ____ Cap. ____ WT. +_____
    b. Shackles: Qty.____ Type ____ Size ____ Cap. ____ WT. +_____
                    Qty.____ Type ____ Size ____ Cap. ____ WT. +_____
    c. Lifting Beam(s) Qty.____   Cap. ____ WT. +_____
    d. Softeners: Qty.____ Type ____ Size ____   WT. +_____
    e. Misc. Rigging: (Snatch Blocks, Turn Buckles, etc.)   WT. +_____

                                                                       (11) – (_____)
11. Total Rigging Deductions:
12. For Total Load (add 7 + 9 + 11) = (12)_____
    To double check safety margin subtract total load # 12 from line # 6 _____
    This number and line # 13 should match.
13. Safety Margin   (13) _____

Lifting Information

14. # of Cranes in lift: _____ Use additional checklist for each crane.
15. Ground conditions: _____ Use appropriate blocking mats required. Y____ N____
16. Weather conditions: _____ Wind speed _____ Direction _____
17. Tag lines required: Y_____ N_____ Size_____ Length _____ No. of lines_____
18. Designated Signal Person: Name _____ Spotter (s) Y____ N____ No. of _____
19. Signal Method: Hand ____ Radio _____
20. Has matching Activity Plan been done and reviewed by crew? Y____ N____

Sign – off
Crane Operator: _____   Competent Rigger: _____
Crew: _____   _____   _____

                _____   Date: _____ Time: _____
Superintendent: _____

302F32A.EPS

Figure 32 ◆ Sample lift plan (1 of 2).

ADDED INFORMATION:

WIRE ROPE— IWRC –EIPS 6 X 19 & 6 X 37
MECHANICAL SPLICE SLINGS CAPACITY IN TONS

Diameter (inches)	Weight (lbs/ft)	Vertical	Choker	Vertical Basket
1⅜	0.26	1.4	1.1	2.9
½	0.46	2.5	1.9	5.1
⅝	0.72	3.9	2.9	7.8
¾	1.04	5.6	4.1	11
⅞	1.42	7.6	5.6	15
1	1.85	9.8	7.2	20
1⅛	2.34	12	9.1	24
1¼	2.89	15	11	30
1⅜	3.50	18	13	36
1½	4.16	21	16	42
1⅝	4.88	24	18	49
1¾	5.67	28	21	57
1⅞	6.50	32	24	64
2	7.39	37	28	73
2⅛	8.35	40	31	80
2¼	9.36	44	35	89
2⅜	10.4	49	38	99
2½	11.6	54	42	109
2¾	14.0	65	51	130

CROSBY SCREW PIN ANCHOR SHACKLES
(G-209, S-209)

Size	Capacity (t)	Weight (lbs)
¾	4¾	3
⅞	6½	4
1	8½	5
1⅛	9½	8
1¼	12	10
1⅜	13½	14
1½	17	18
1¾	25	28
2	35	45
2½	55	86

302F32B.EPS

Figure 32 ◆ Sample lift plan. (2 of 2)

9.0.0 ◆ CRANE LOAD CHARTS

One or more types of cranes may be used for a job site. These can include truck- or crawler-mounted lattice or hydraulic boom cranes, rough-terrain cranes, or tower cranes. In order to give or receive directions or calculate load capacities, the correct terms for the crane components must be understood.

NOTE

Load charts are specific to a given crane and must be kept on board that crane.

9.1.0 Crane Component Terminology

Figures 33, 34, and *35* show the components of most wheel- or crawler-mounted lattice boom cranes.

Crane component terminology varies in different locations and sometimes between manufacturers. The following describes common crane components and identifies some of the alternate terms used for components. Some of the components are described in more detail later in this module.

- *Base mounting* – This structure consists of the carbody, swing circle, crawler frames, axles and track, and the propelling mechanism that forms the lowest element of a crane. It transmits loads to the ground. It is the crawler mounting for mobile cranes.
- *Base section* – The base section of a telescopic boom is attached to the base mounting of a crane. It does not telescope, but contains the boom-foot, pin-mountings, and the boom-hoist cylinder upper-end mountings.
- *Boom* – A boom is a crane member used to project the upper end of the hoisting tackle in reach or in combination of height and reach. The boom supports the weight of the load and gives the crane its lift and reach capabilities. Boom sections can be added to extend the boom length. The capacity of a boom decreases as it is lowered from a vertical position.
- *Boom base* – The boom base is the lowest section of a sectional-latticed boom having the attachment (boom-foot pins) mounted at its lower end. It is also called the boom butt or butt section.
- *Boom sheaves* – Boom sheaves are the pulleys that the load lines pass over.
- *Carbody* – A carbody is the part of a crawler crane base mounting that carries the upper structure. The crawler side frames are attached to it.
- *Counterweights* – Counterweights are weights added to a crane to counteract the weight of a load and to achieve lifting capacity.
- *Falls of line* – See *parts of line.*

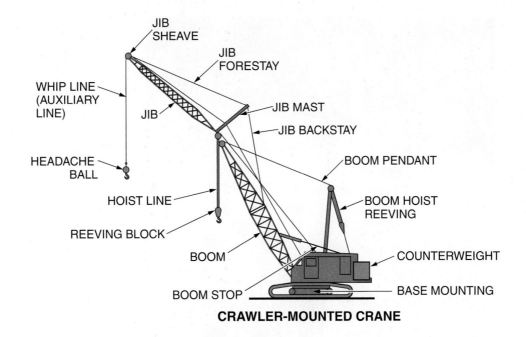

CRAWLER-MOUNTED CRANE

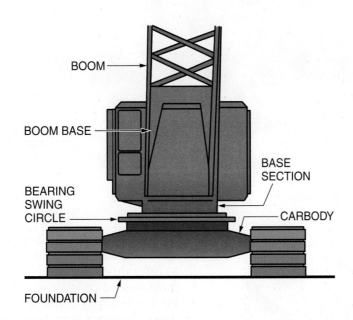

Figure 33 ◆ Crawler-mounted crane components.

302F33.EPS

- *Headache ball* – A headache ball is a weight added to a load fall to overcome resistance and to permit unspooling at the rope drum when no live load is being supported. A headache ball is usually equipped with a hook.
- *Hoist line reeving* – Hoist reeving is a method used to multiply the pulling or lifting capability of a rope (line) by using multiple pulleys in sheaves. Single-line reeving is used for a whip line, and multiple-line reeving is used for main load, boom, and jib lines. Also see *parts of line*.

- *Jib* – A jib is an extension that is added to the boom and mounted at the boom tip. It may be in line with the boom long axis, or it may be off-set from it. It is equipped with its own fixed wire rope suspensions (pendants) that are fastened to a mast at the boom tip. A fixed jib is supported by jib pendants, called a jib backstay and forestay.

LUFFING JIB

LUFFING JIB PENDANTS

LUFFING BOOM

LUFFING BOOM PENDANTS

JIB HOIST REEVING

WHIP LINE AND HEADACHE BALL

BOOM HOIST REEVING

HYDRAULIC OUTRIGGERS

302F34.EPS

Figure 34 ◆ Wheel-mounted crane components.

UPPERWORKS COUNTERWEIGHTS

CRAWLER FRAME COUNTERWEIGHTS

302F35.EPS

Figure 35 ◆ A heavy-lift crane with counterweights.

- *Jib mast or jib strut* – The jib mast or strut is a short strut or frame mounted on the boom head to provide an attachment for the jib pendants. It may also be called a gantry, horse, or A-frame. With a luffing jib, the pendants and associated masts together may be called the forestay and backstay.
- *Jib sheaves* – Jib sheaves serve the same function as boom sheaves.
- *Latticed boom or conventional boom* – This boom is constructed of four longitudinal corner members called chords, assembled with transverse and/or diagonal members called lacing, to form a trusswork in two directions. The chords carry the axial (perpendicular) boom forces and bending moments, while the lacings resist shear forces.
- *Load block* – A load block is the lower block in a crane reeving system that moves with the load. The load block is sometimes called the travelling block.

- *Luffing jib* – This jib can have its angle to the boom changed by the crane operator via jib reeving.
- *Outriggers* – Outriggers are extendible arms attached to a crane base mounting that relieve the wheels of crane weight and increase stability.
- *Parts of line* – These are the number of wire ropes supporting a load block in a crane reeving system. They are also referred to as just parts or falls.
- *Pendant* – A pendant is a fixed-length rope or solid rod forming part of the boom or jib suspension system. It may be called the boom guy line, hog line, boom stay, standing line, forestay, or backstay.
- *Running line* – A running line is a wire rope that moves over sheaves or drums.
- *Standing line* – A standing line is a fixed line that supports loads without being spooled on or off a drum. It is a line on which both ends are dead. It is also referred to as a guy line, stay rope, or pendant.
- *Tag line* – A tag line is usually a fiber rope that is attached to the load and used for controlling load spin or alignment from the ground. When a tag line is used for clamshell operations, it consists of a wire rope needed to retard rotations and the pendulum action of the bucket.
- *Upperworks* – The upperworks is the entire rotating structure less the front end attachment. It may also be referred to as upper superstructure, revolving superstructure, or upper structure.
- *Whip line* – See *hoist line reeving*.

9.2.0 Load Chart Requirements

Load chart requirements explain the critical measurements and cautions that must be considered when calculating lifting capacities. *Figure 36* is an example of a load chart. The following sections explain notes found on a typical lifting capacity chart.

9.2.1   Operating Conditions

Operating conditions are the conditions that affect the machine lifting capacities. When the machine is operated in an unlevel condition, the boom is subjected to high side loads that can cause boom damage or tipping. The machine should be leveled to within 1 percent of grade. To check the level of the machine, place a spirit level on the roller path or use the cross level provided in or near the operator's cab. *Figure 37* shows a crane that is not level and a crane that is level.

Every attempt to verify soil conditions must be made before making a lift. If conditions cannot be verified, a support mat must be installed on the area under the crane. Crane operators must use judgment to allow for the effects of increased load caused by swinging, hoisting, lowering, traveling, adverse operating conditions, and machine wear.

9.2.2   Operating Radius

Load charts require the measurement of the operating radius. The operating radius is the horizontal distance, in feet, from the center line of rotation to the center of the vertical hoist line or load block. This measurement is taken with the load freely suspended.

9.2.3   Boom Angle and Length

The boom angle is the angle between the horizontal plane and the center line of the boom base, or boom butt, and inserts. Boom length is measured from the boom pivot point to the boom point sheave pin. These measurements are shown in *Figure 38*.

9.2.4   Boom Point Elevation

The boom point elevation is the vertical distance from ground level to the center line of the main boom point sheave (*Figure 38*). This distance is measured in feet and changes when the boom angle changes.

9.2.5   Hoist Reeving

The load chart instructions for hoist reeving the main load block must be followed to ensure that the proper parts of line are used. The maximum capacity of the reeving should be greater than or equal to the maximum load that will be hoisted. Use the corresponding parts of line for the maximum load selected. Parts of line are based on the catalogue breaking strength of the rope, with a recommended safety factor. *Figure 39* shows a typical chart for hoist reeving for the main load block taken from the example crane load chart. *Figure 40* shows an example of ten-part reeving.

9.2.6   Load and Whip Line Specifications

The load line and whip line are parts of the machine equipment. Their strength requirements must be met before the capacity chart can be used. The maximum whip line capacity for a given operating radius is limited by the maximum load per line noted in the specifications. The load cannot

MANITOWOC 4100 W-2

LIFTCRANE CAPACITIES

BOOM NO. 22C WITH OPEN THROAT TOP
146,400 LB. CRANE COUNTERWEIGHT
60,000 LB. CARBODY COUNTERWEIGHT
26'6" CRAWLERS EXTENDED

***WARNING:** This chart will apply only when two 12,000 lb. side ctwts. and two 30,000 lb. carbody ctwts. bear MEC registered Serial Numbers.*

LIFTING CAPACITIES: Capacities for various boom lengths and operating radii may be based on percent of tipping, strength of structural components, operating speeds and other factors.

Capacities are for freely suspended loads and do not exceed 75% of a static tipping load. Capacities based on structural competence are shown by shaded areas.

Capacities are shown in pounds. Deduct 1200 pounds from capacities listed when single sheave upper boom point is attached and 1500 pounds when two sheave upper boom point is attached. To comply with B30.5 requirements, upper boompoint cannot be used on the 260 ft. boom. Weight of jib, (see chart A), all load blocks, hooks, weight ball, slings, hoist lines beneath boom and jib point sheaves, etc., is considered part of the main boom load. Boom is not to be lowered beyond radii where combined weights are greater than rated capacity. Where no capacity is shown, operation is not intended or approved.

OPERATING CONDITIONS: Machine to operate in a level position on a firm surface with crawlers fully extended and gantry in working position and be rigged in accordance with and under conditions referred to in rigging drawing No. 190693 and load line specification chard No. 6592-A.

Crane operator judgement must be used to allow for dynamic load effects of swinging, hoisting or lowering, travel, as well as adverse operating conditions & physical machine depreciation.

OPERATOR RADIUS: Operating is the horizontal distance from the axis of rotation to the center of vertical hoist line or load block with the load freely suspended. Add 14" to boom point radius for radius of sheave when using single part hoist line.

Boom angle is the angle between horizontal and centerline of boom butt and inserts and is an indication of operating radius. In all cases, operating radius shall govern capacity.

BOOM POINT ELEVATION: Boom point elevation, in feet, is the vertical distance from ground level to centerline of boom point shaft.

MACHINE EQUIPMENT: Machine equipped with 26'6" extendible crawlers, 48" treads, 17' retractable gantry, 12 part boom hoist reeving, four 1 3/8" boom pendants, 1st ctwt. 41,900 lbs., 2nd ctwt. 41,500 lbs., 3rd ctwt. 39,000 lbs., two 12,000 lbs. side ctwt's. and two 30,000 lbs. carbody ctwt's.

LOAD AND WHIP LINE SPECIFICATIONS

LOAD LINE:	1-1/8" - 6 x 31 Warrington-Seale, Extra Improved Plow Steel, Regular Lay, IWRC. Minimum Breaking Strength 65 Ton. (Approx. Weight Per Ft. in Lbs. 2.34)
WHIP LINE:	1-1/8" - Warrington-Seale, Improved Plow Steel, Regular Lay, IWRC. Minimum Breaking Strength 56.5 Ton. Maximum Load - 28,300 Lbs. Per Line. (Approx. Weight Per Ft. in Lbs. 2.34)

HOIST REEVING FOR MAIN LOAD BLOCK

No. Parts Of Line	1	2	3	4	5	6
Max Load - Lbs.	32,500	65,000	97,500	130,000	162,500	195,000
No. Parts of Line	7	8	9	10	11	12
Max. Load - Lbs.	227,500	260,000	292,500	325,000	357,500	400,000
No. Parts of Line	13					
Max. Load - Lbs.	430,000					

MAXIMUM BOOM AND JIB LENGTH LIFTED UNASSISTED / DEDUCT FROM CAPACITIES WHEN JIB IS ATTACHED

OVER FRONT OF BLOCKED CRAWLERS		OVER SIDE OF EXTENDED CRAWLERS		DEDUCT FROM CAPACITIES WHEN JIB IS ATTACHED	
BOOM LENGTH	JIB NO. 123	BOOM LENGTH	JIB NO. 123	JIB LENGTH	JIB NO. 123
260'	--	260'	--	30'	3,000 lbs.
250'	--	250'	--	40'	3,600 lbs.
240'	40'	240'	40'	50'	4,200 lbs.
230'	60'	230'	60'	60'	4,900 lbs.

Load block, hook and weight ball on ground to start.

FOR JIB CAPACITIES, CONSULT JIB CHART.

BOOM LGTH FEET	OPER. RAD. FEET	BOOM ANG. DEG.	BOOM POINT ELEV.	CAPACITY: CRAWLERS EXTENDED
7 0	16.5	79.7	75.9	460,000
	17	79.3	75.8	400,000
	18	78.5	75.6	380,100
	19	77.6	75.4	363,000
	20	76.8	75.1	347,300
	22	75.1	74.6	319,600
	24	73.4	74.1	293,400
	26	71.7	73.5	266,100
	28	69.9	72.8	237,500
	30	68.2	72.0	214,300
	32	66.4	71.2	195,100
	34	64.6	70.2	178,900
	36	62.8	69.3	165,200
	38	60.9	68.2	153,300
	40	59.1	67.0	143,000
	45	54.1	63.7	122,100
	50	48.9	59.8	106,300
	55	43.2	54.9	93,900
	60	36.9	49.0	84,000
	65	29.4	41.3	75,800
	70	19.5	30.3	63,900

BOOM LGTH FEET	OPER. RAD. FEET	BOOM ANG. DEG.	BOOM POINT ELEV.	CAPACITY: CRAWLERS EXTENDED
8 0	17	80.6	85.9	392,800
	18	79.9	85.8	378,900
	19	79.2	85.6	361,800
	20	78.5	85.4	346,100
	22	77.0	84.9	318,400
	24	75.5	84.5	292,500
	26	74.0	83.9	265,600
	28	72.5	83.3	237,000
	30	71.0	82.7	213,800
	32	69.5	81.9	194,600
	34	68.0	81.2	178,500
	36	66.4	80.3	164,700
	38	64.8	79.4	152,800
	40	63.3	78.4	142,400
	45	59.2	75.7	121,500
	50	54.9	72.5	105,700
	55	50.4	68.6	93,300
	60	45.6	64.1	83,400
	65	40.3	58.8	75,200
	70	34.4	52.2	68,300
	75	27.4	43.9	52,500
	80	18.2	32.0	53,900

BOOM LGTH FEET	OPER. RAD. FEET	BOOM ANG. DEG.	BOOM POINT ELEV.	CAPACITY: CRAWLERS EXTENDED
9 0	18	81.1	95.9	355,400
	19	80.4	95.7	346,900
	20	79.8	95.6	336,900
	22	78.5	95.2	317,400
	24	77.2	94.7	291,700
	26	75.9	94.3	264,800
	28	74.5	93.7	236,600
	30	73.2	93.2	213,400
	32	71.9	92.5	194,200
	34	70.5	91.9	178,000
	36	69.2	91.1	164,200
	38	67.8	90.3	152,300
	40	66.4	89.5	142,000
	45	62.9	87.1	121,100
	50	59.3	84.4	105,200
	55	55.5	81.2	92,800
	60	51.5	77.5	82,900
	65	47.3	73.2	74,700
	70	42.8	68.2	67,800
	75	37.9	62.3	62,000
	80	32.4	55.2	57,000
	85	25.8	46.2	52,600
	90	17.1	33.5	45,900

BOOM LGTH FEET	OPER. RAD. FEET	BOOM ANG. DEG.	BOOM POINT ELEV.	CAPACITY: CRAWLERS EXTENDED
1 0 0	19	81.4	105.9	332,900
	20	80.8	105.7	327,100
	22	79.6	105.4	316,200
	24	78.5	105.0	290,800
	26	77.3	104.5	263,900
	28	76.1	104.1	236,200
	30	74.9	103.6	212,900
	32	73.7	103.0	193,700
	34	72.5	102.4	177,500
	36	71.3	101.7	163,700
	38	70.1	101.0	151,800
	40	68.9	100.3	141,400
	45	65.8	98.2	120,500
	50	62.6	95.8	104,700
	55	59.3	93.0	92,300
	60	55.9	89.8	82,300
	65	52.4	86.2	74,100
	70	48.7	82.1	67,200
	75	44.8	77.4	61,400
	80	40.5	72.0	56,400
	85	35.9	65.6	52,000
	90	30.7	58.0	48,200
	95	24.5	48.5	44,900
	100	16.3	35.0	39,300

CAUTION! CHECK AMOUNT OF COUNTERWEIGHT ON MACHINE BEFORE USE OF THIS CHART

© Manitowoc 1997

302F36.EPS

Figure 36 ◆ Load chart.

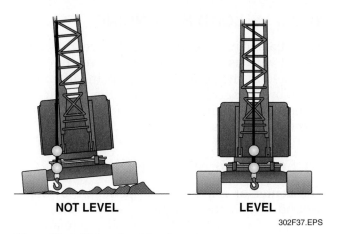

NOT LEVEL   **LEVEL**

302F37.EPS

Figure 37 ◆ Unlevel and level cranes.

exceed the capacities shown for the radius on the main boom capacity chart. The wire rope must meet the recommended requirements.

9.2.7 Maximum Boom and Jib Lengths Lifted Unassisted

The crane load chart also lists the maximum boom and the boom and jib lengths that can be lifted unassisted. Do not attempt to raise a longer boom or jib than is allowed under the conditions specified on the chart.

9.2.8 Deductions from Capacities

The weight of certain crane components must be deducted from the load charts to determine the maximum load capacity of the crane. These are

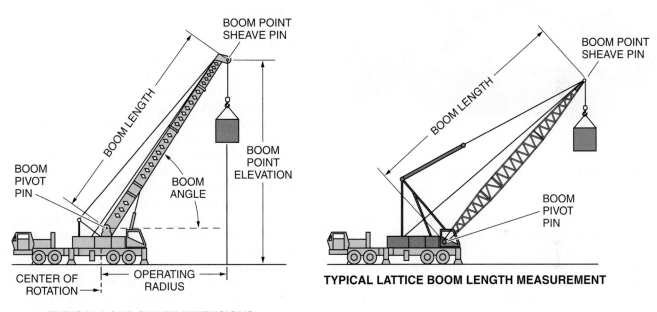

TYPICAL LOAD CHART DIMENSIONS

TYPICAL LATTICE BOOM LENGTH MEASUREMENT

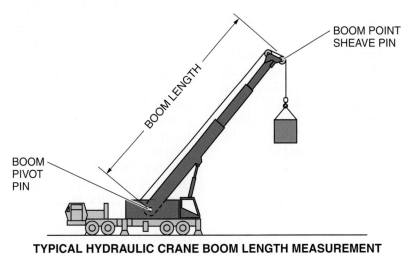

TYPICAL HYDRAULIC CRANE BOOM LENGTH MEASUREMENT

302F38.EPS

Figure 38 ◆ Boom length, boom angle, load operating radius, and boom point elevation measurements.

HOIST REEVING FOR MAIN LOAD BLOCK						
No. Parts Of Line	1	2	3	4	5	6
Max Load - Lbs.	32,500	65,000	97,500	130,000	162,500	195,000
No. Parts of Line	7	8	9	10	11	12
Max. Load - Lbs.	227,500	260,000	292,500	325,000	357,500	400,000
No. Parts of Line	13					
Max. Load - Lbs.	430,000					

302F39.EPS

Figure 39 ◆ Hoist reeving chart.

10-PART REEVING

302F40.EPS

Figure 40 ◆ Heavy-lift crane with ten-part reeving.

sometimes referred to as above-the-hook deductions. The deductions for a typical lattice boom crane are shown in *Figure 41*. These deductions are furnished as part of the load charts. Other deductions, sometimes called below-the-hook deductions, consist of the weight of all rigging equipment including spreader beams, cables, slings, rings, and clamps, exclusive of the load.

The lifting capacity of the machine changes when using different styles of boom tips or when adding a jib. A jib deduction chart lists the number of pounds to be deducted from the load chart when the jib is attached and not being used. The deduction depends on the length of the jib.

The jib offset angle must be determined before using the jib load chart. The jib offset angle is the angle from the center line of the boom top section to the center line of the jib. Make sure the chart being used is for the desired jib offset angle. *Figure 42* shows the jib offset angle.

10.0.0 ◆ LOAD BALANCING

Load balancing is equalizing the weight of the load at various lifting points. If the weight is concentrated at one point, the object being lifted may bend, break, or fall. Distributing the weight over several lifting points ensures that the load is balanced and lifted safely.

10.1.0 Center of Gravity

The center of gravity is the point on an object around which the weight is concentrated. The location of a crane's center of gravity in relation to its tipping fulcrum directly affects its leverage and stability.

To understand the relationship between a crane's center of gravity and stability, you must understand the principle of leverage. The principle of leverage can be illustrated with a simple teeter-totter (*Figure 43*). When the weight of the heavy load multiplied by the distance (X) from its center of gravity to the tipping fulcrum is equal to the weight of the lighter load multiplied by the distance (Y) from its center of gravity at its tipping fulcrum, a condition of balance has occurred.

This relationship is illustrated again with the long lever bent upwards in *Figure 44*.

A further example shows the relationship with the lighter load being suspended below the long lever in *Figure 45* like a crane. Note that in all three figures, the loads will remain balanced as long as the load weights remain the same and the horizontal distances X and Y remain the same.

The weight and center of gravity of various mobile crane members are determined by calculation or by weighing. This data then becomes the basis upon which stability ratings are calculated. The ratings and accuracy of the weight and center-of-gravity data are then confirmed by testing.

The center of gravity can change depending on the crane's quadrant of operation. When the crane is in over-the-side, over-the-front, or over-the-rear configurations, the center of gravity is shifted either closer or farther away from the tipping fulcrum. This, in turn, may increase or decrease the crane's leverage. For a rough-terrain crane, maximum true lifting capacity (greatest stability margin) is obtained when the crane boom is operated directly over the front. Maximum true lifting capacity of a truck crane is obtained when the boom is over the rear.

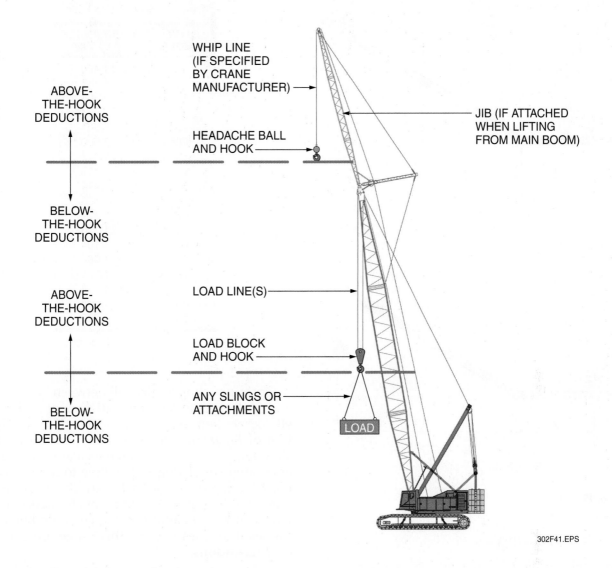

Figure 41 ◆ Typical deductions for a lattice boom crane.

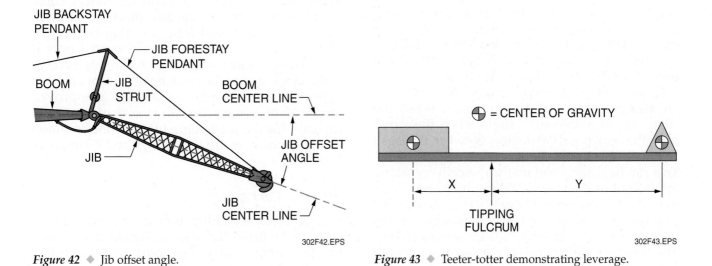

Figure 42 ◆ Jib offset angle.

Figure 43 ◆ Teeter-totter demonstrating leverage.

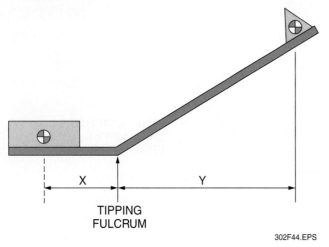

Figure 44 ◆ Bent lever.

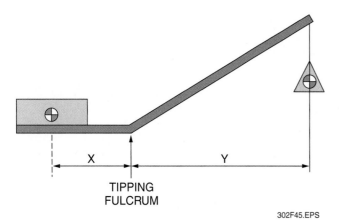

Figure 45 ◆ Crane-shaped lever.

10.2.0 Sling Angles

The angle formed by the legs of a sling with respect to the horizontal when tension is put upon the load is called the sling angle. The amount of tension on the sling is directly affected by the angle of the sling. For this reason, proper sling angles are crucial to safe rigging. *Figure 46* shows the effect of sling angles on sling loading. To actually determine the load on a sling, a factor table is used. *Table 2* shows a sling factor table.

In the example shown in *Figure 46*, two slings are being used to lift 2,000 pounds. When the slings are at a 45-degree angle when measured from the horizontal (90 degrees between the legs), there are 1,414 pounds of tension on each sling. This can be determined mathematically by taking the weight of the load (2,000 pounds) and dividing it by the number of slings (2); this equals 1,000 pounds. Then, multiply 1,000 pounds by the corresponding factor in *Table 2* for 45 degrees (1.414). The result is 1,414 pounds of tension on each sling based on the sling angle.

Table 2 Sling Factor Table

SLING ANGLE	LOAD ANGLE FACTOR
5°	11.490
10°	5.747
15°	3.861
20°	2.924
25°	2.364
30°	2.000
35°	1.742
40°	1.555
45°	1.414
50°	1.305
55°	1.221
60°	1.155
65°	1.104
70°	1.064
75°	1.035
80°	1.015
85°	1.004
90°	1.000

302T02.EPS

Optimum sling angles fall between 90 degrees and 60 degrees to horizontal (0 degrees and up to 60 degrees between sling legs). Further examination of *Figure 46* shows that the tension on the sling legs is higher when the legs are positioned at an angle of 30 degrees relative to the horizontal (120-degree angle between the legs) than when the legs are at an angle of 60 degrees relative to the horizontal (60-degree angle between the legs). Angles beyond this range are considered hazardous.

10.3.0 Lifting Connectors

Many pieces of equipment and machinery come with lifting connectors already attached at proper locations for balanced lifting. Lifting connectors may be manufactured or field-fabricated only if the lifting connectors have been engineered. Field-fabricated connectors must be fabricated of approved material and installed using approved methods to ensure that they are of adequate capacity for the load being lifted. Some common lifting connectors are lifting lugs and lifting eyebolts.

10.3.1 Lifting Lugs

Lifting lugs are welded, bolted, or pinned to the object to be lifted. They are designed and located to balance the load and support it safely. Unless angular lifts are specifically allowed by the

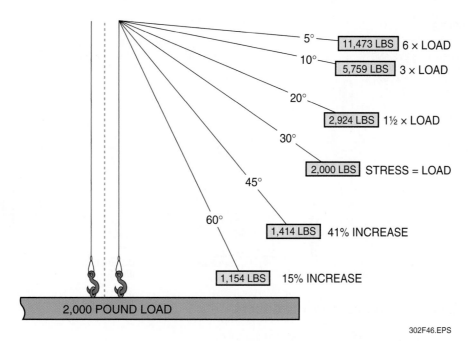

Angle	Load	Factor
5°	11,473 LBS	6 × LOAD
10°	5,759 LBS	3 × LOAD
20°	2,924 LBS	1½ × LOAD
30°	2,000 LBS	STRESS = LOAD
45°	1,414 LBS	41% INCREASE
60°	1,154 LBS	15% INCREASE

2,000 POUND LOAD

302F46.EPS

Figure 46 ◆ Sling angles.

manufacturer, lifting lugs should be used for straight, vertical lifting only, because they will bend if loaded at an angle. *Figure 47* shows two types of lifting lugs.

10.3.2 Lifting Eyebolts

Lifting eyebolts are also used to balance the weight of the load. There are three types of lifting eyebolts: the plain, or shoulderless, type; the forged alloy steel eyebolt with shoulders or collars; and the swivel eyebolt. The shoulderless eyebolt is used for straight, vertical lifts only, because it will bend when loaded at an angle.

Eyebolts with shoulders can be used for straight or slightly angled lifts. The shoulder of the bolt must be tight against the surface of the load and make full contact with the surface. Washers can be used under shoulder eyebolts to ensure that tight contact is made. The eyebolts must be aligned so that force is applied to the plane of the eye to prevent the eyebolt from bending during an angled pull. One type of shouldered eyebolt, called a ringbolt, is equipped with an additional lifting ring. The safe working load of shouldered eyebolts and ringbolts is reduced with angular loading. Swivel eyebolts allow lifting from any

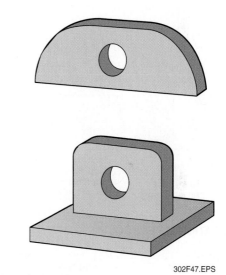

302F47.EPS

Figure 47 ◆ Lifting lugs.

angle and do not require load derating. *Figure 48* shows eyebolt and ringbolt installation and lifting criteria.

When lifting an object using eyebolts, always use a shackle for each eyebolt. Never use a hook in an eyebolt, because a hook may bend or disfigure the eye.

USE OF EYEBOLTS

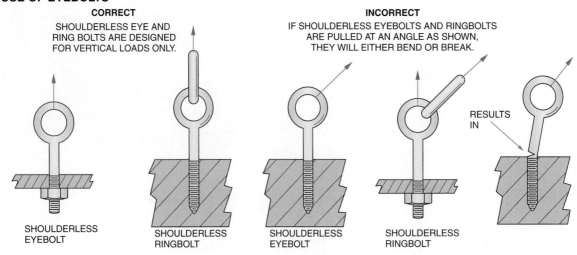

CORRECT
SHOULDERLESS EYE AND
RING BOLTS ARE DESIGNED
FOR VERTICAL LOADS ONLY.

INCORRECT
IF SHOULDERLESS EYEBOLTS AND RINGBOLTS
ARE PULLED AT AN ANGLE AS SHOWN,
THEY WILL EITHER BEND OR BREAK.

RESULTS
IN

SHOULDERLESS
EYEBOLT

SHOULDERLESS
RINGBOLT

SHOULDERLESS
EYEBOLT

SHOULDERLESS
RINGBOLT

USE OF SHOULDER TYPE EYEBOLTS AND RINGBOLTS

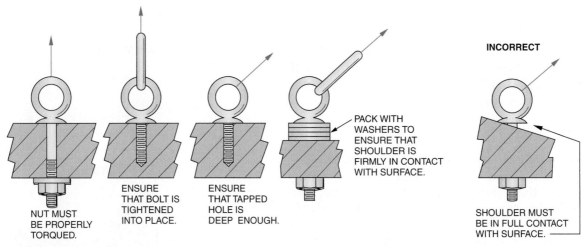

CORRECT
FOR SHOULDER TYPE EYEBOLTS AND RINGBOLTS
PROVIDING LOADS ARE REDUCED TO ACCOUNT FOR ANGULAR LOADING.

INCORRECT

PACK WITH
WASHERS TO
ENSURE THAT
SHOULDER IS
FIRMLY IN CONTACT
WITH SURFACE.

NUT MUST
BE PROPERLY
TORQUED.

ENSURE
THAT BOLT IS
TIGHTENED
INTO PLACE.

ENSURE
THAT TAPPED
HOLE IS
DEEP ENOUGH.

SHOULDER MUST
BE IN FULL CONTACT
WITH SURFACE.

ORIENTATION OF EYEBOLTS

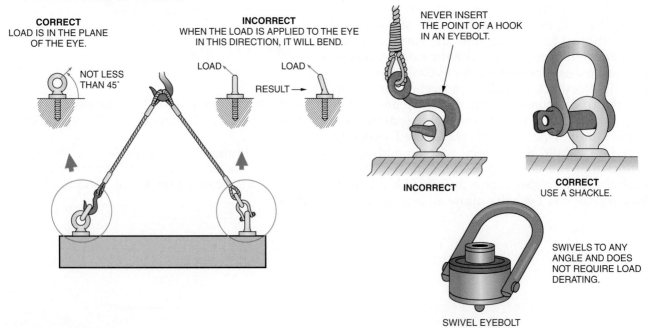

CORRECT
LOAD IS IN THE PLANE
OF THE EYE.

NOT LESS
THAN 45°

INCORRECT
WHEN THE LOAD IS APPLIED TO THE EYE
IN THIS DIRECTION, IT WILL BEND.

LOAD

LOAD

RESULT →

NEVER INSERT
THE POINT OF A HOOK
IN AN EYEBOLT.

INCORRECT

CORRECT
USE A SHACKLE.

SWIVELS TO ANY
ANGLE AND DOES
NOT REQUIRE LOAD
DERATING.

SWIVEL EYEBOLT

302F48.EPS

Figure 48 ◆ Eyebolt and ringbolt installation and lifting criteria.

11.0.0 ◆ RIGGING PIPE

The following sections explain how to determine the weight of a load of pipe, and how to block, choke, lift, and balance the load. Guidelines are also given for landing a load of pipe.

11.1.0 Determining the Weight of the Pipe

The weight of the pipe must be determined before it is lifted. Every foot of pipe weighs a given amount, depending on the wall thickness and nominal size of the pipe. Therefore, if you know the weight per foot and the total number of feet, the total weight of the lift can be determined. *Table 3* lists the weights of carbon steel pipe.

The numbers in the far left column represent nominal pipe size in inches. The designations and numbers across the top represent wall thickness, or schedule. To use the table, find the point at which the nominal size and wall thickness of the pipe being used meet. The number in this block is the weight of 1 foot of pipe. To find the total weight, multiply the total number of feet by the weight per foot.

For example, to find the weight of a 20-inch, Schedule 40 carbon steel pipe that is 10 feet long, read across the table from the 20 in the nominal pipe size column until you reach the Schedule 40 column. The number you find there is 123.1. This is the weight, in pounds, of 1 foot of pipe. Multiply this number by 10 to find the total weight of the pipe. The pipe weighs 1,231 pounds.

Table 3   Carbon Steel Pipe Weights

Nominal Pipe Size (Inches)	Wall Thickness								
	STD	XS	XXS	10	40	60	80	120	160
	Weight Per Foot in Pounds								
2	3.65	5.02	9.03	-	3.65	-	5.02	-	7.06
2.5	5.79	7.66	13.7	-	5.79	-	7.66	-	10.01
3	7.58	10.25	18.58	-	7.58	-	10.25	-	14.31
3.5	9.11	12.51	22.85	-	9.11	-	12.51	-	-
4	10.79	14.98	27.54	-	10.79	-	14.98	18.98	22.52
6	18.97	28.57	53.16	-	18.97	-	28.57	36.42	45.34
8	28.55	43.39	72.42	-	28.55	35.66	43.39	60.69	74.71
10	40.48	54.74	104.1	-	40.48	54.74	64.40	89.27	115.7
12	49.56	65.42	125.5	-	53.56	73.22	88.57	125.5	160.3
14	54.57	72.09	-	36.71	63.37	85.01	106.1	150.8	189.2
16	62.58	82.77	-	42.05	82.77	107.5	136.6	192.4	245.2
18	70.59	93.45	-	47.39	104.8	138.2	170.8	244.1	308.6
20	78.60	104.1	-	52.73	123.1	166.5	208.9	296.4	379.1
22	86.61	114.8	-	58.07	-	197.4	250.8	353.6	451.1
24	94.62	125.5	-	63.41	171.2	238.3	296.5	429.5	542.1
26	102.6	136.2	-	85.73	-	-	-	-	-
28	110.6	146.9	-	92.41	-	-	-	-	-
30	118.7	157.5	-	99.08	-	-	-	-	-
32	126.7	168.2	-	105.8	229.9	-	-	-	-
34	134.7	178.9	-	112.4	244.6	-	-	-	-
36	142.7	189.6	-	119.1	282.4	-	-	-	-
42	166.7	221.6	-	-	330.4	-	-	-	-

302T03.EPS

11.2.0 Blocking

Everything on the job site, including structural steel beams, machinery, and pipe, must be placed on blocking or dunnage. Blocks should be hardwood, preferably oak. They should be thick enough to protect the object from contact with the ground and to enable a rigger to slip a choker beneath the load.

Pipe placed on blocks requires wedges to keep the pipe from rolling off the blocking. Large diameter pipe requires chocks to keep it from rolling. The general rule regarding chocks is that there should be 1 inch of chock per 1 foot of diameter. Thus, a 42-inch pipe requires about a 3½-inch-thick chock.

11.3.0 Choking

When an item more than 12 feet long or a bundle of loose items such as rebar or pipe is being rigged, the general rule is to use two choker hitches spaced far enough apart to provide the stability required to transport the load (*Figure 49*).

To lift a bundle of short items, or to maintain the load in a certain position during transport, a double-wrap choker hitch (*Figure 50*) may be useful. A two-legged double-wrap choker hitch is preferred for bundles. The double-wrap choker hitch is made by wrapping the sling completely around

the load, and then wrapping the choke end around again and passing it through the eye like a conventional choker hitch. This enables the load weight to produce a constricting action that binds

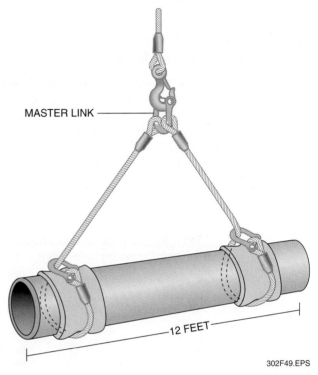

Figure 49 ◆ Double choker hitch.

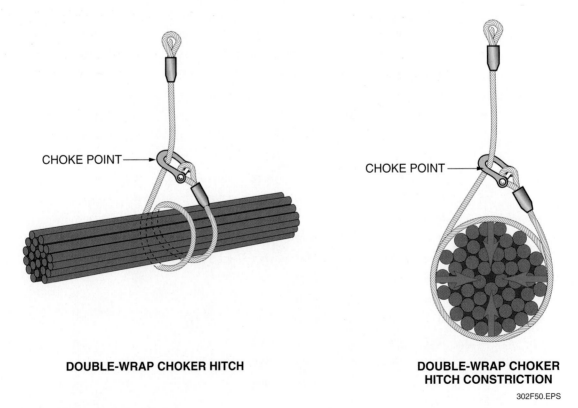

DOUBLE-WRAP CHOKER HITCH   **DOUBLE-WRAP CHOKER HITCH CONSTRICTION**

Figure 50 ◆ Double-wrap choker hitch.

the load into the middle of the hitch, holding it firmly in place throughout the lift.

Forcing the choke down will drastically increase the stress placed on the sling at the choke point. To gain gripping power, use a double-wrap choker hitch. The double-wrap choker uses the load weight to provide the constricting force, so there is no need to force the sling down into a tighter choke.

A double-wrap choker hitch is ideal for lifting bundles of items, such as pipes and structural steel. It will also keep the load in a certain position, which makes it ideal for equipment installation lifts. Lifting a load longer than 12 feet requires two of these hitches.

Use the following guidelines when choking a load of pipe:

- Pipe of the same length should be lifted together. If pipes of greatly different lengths must be lifted, lift each different length separately.
- Lay the pipe on blocks so the chokers can be wrapped around the load.
- Use two choker hitches to lift a load of pipe. This allows a level lift to be made and ensures that the pipe will not slip out of the sling. Make sure both chokers grab all pipes.
- Ensure that the open part of the hook is facing away from center when using slings with fixed or sliding hooks.
- Do not use carbon steel chokers on painted or stainless steel pipe because of cross-contamination of the metals. Use nylon web slings on stainless steel pipe.

11.4.0 Lifting

Follow these guidelines when lifting a load of pipe:

- Use the hook and lifting line of the crane as the center line with which to line up the load.
- Be sure to check the boom angle of the crane to make sure that the load will not be moved forward or backward when tension is put on the line.
- Stand clear of the load and where the operator can clearly see you, and signal any necessary adjustments, using the proper hand signals. Never stand underneath the load.
- As soon as the load clears the ground, check its orientation. If it is not level, signal the operator to stop lifting the load, and guide the load back onto the blocks to correct the position of the chokers.
- Handle all loads with a tag line.
- Keep the load as low to the ground as possible.

11.5.0 Landing

Follow these guidelines when landing the load:

- Store all pipe on level ground.
- Land the load on blocks that are long enough and thick enough to support the load.
- Stand to one side of the load, and guide it onto the blocks with a tag line. Move to the end of the load before the rigging is released.
- Ensure that the chokers can be removed once the load is placed on the blocks.
- Remember that a load of pipe will roll when tension is released. Keep away from pinch points, and do not stand in a position where the pipe may roll on you.
- Chock the sides of the pipe to keep it from rolling.
- Lay pipe side by side. If at all possible, do not stack pipe.

INSIDE TRACK

Demolition

Many projects involve demolition to remove old structures on a property before new construction can begin. Wrecking balls attached to cranes are often used for demolition work. When demolition is underway, the surrounding area must be barricaded to prevent injury due to flying debris.

302SA03.EPS

12.0.0 ◆ RIGGING VALVES

Rigging a valve correctly involves knowing how to place the sling, what kind of sling to use, and what kind of valve is being lifted. First, determine what the valve is made of. Do not use a carbon steel choker to rig a stainless steel valve. Use synthetic slings for rigging stainless steel valves.

To rig a valve correctly, place a synthetic sling on each side of the valve body between the bonnet and the flanges. If the valve is to be vertical, bring the slings up through the handwheel so that the valve cannot tilt from front to back and so that the weight of the valve is evenly supported by the body of the valve. Do not place a sling around the handwheel or through the valve. The handwheel is not built to support the weight of the valve. A valve rigged around the handwheel is unsafe, even if the valve is going to be moved a short distance. Placing a sling through the valve will destroy the inner workings of the valve, even if soft synthetic slings are used.

13.0.0 ◆ GUIDELINES FOR UNLOADING AND YARDING MATERIALS

Reinforcing bars and other structural steel components are ordered from the fabricator. Delivery of these materials is usually scheduled to coincide with the construction schedule. Structural and reinforcing steel usually arrives at the job site on flatbed trucks or tractor trailers. If a spur track is available at the job site, shipments may be received by flat or gondola railroad cars. Where delivery of steel is scheduled to meet daily placement requirements, truckloads are delivered to the points of placement. Workers should be aware of safety factors that are necessary to achieve safe, efficient handling, storage, and hoisting of structural materials.

Charts are available for most types of materials so that riggers can calculate the weight of a load. *Table 4* is an example of such a chart. By knowing the number of reinforcing bars and their lengths, the rigger can easily calculate the weight of the load. *Table 3* provides similar information for pipe.

13.1.0 Unloading

Trucks should be unloaded promptly to prevent job-site clutter and potential safety hazards. Structural materials that are stored on the ground must be placed on timbers or other suitable blocking to keep them free from mud and to allow safe and easy rehandling.

Bars and other structural stock are normally stored by size and shape, and by length within each size. Tags are kept at the same end of each piece for easy identification. When a bundle is opened and part of the stock removed, the unit with the tag should remain with the bundle, and a new number indicating the remaining inventory should be inserted. Machine oil or grease that collects on the stock must be removed using a solvent. All mud must be washed off before placement.

Table 4 ASTM Standard Metric and Inch-Pound Reinforcing Bars

		Nominal Characteristics*					
Bar Size		Diameter		Cross-Sectional Area		Weight	
Metric	[in.-lb.]	mm	[in.]	mm	[in.]	kg/m	[lbs./ft.]
#10	[#3]	9.5	[0.375]	71	[0.11]	0.560	[0.376]
#13	[#4]	12.7	[0.500]	129	[0.20]	0.944	[0.668]
#16	[#5]	15.9	[0.625]	199	[0.31]	1.552	[1.043]
#19	[#6]	19.1	[0.750]	284	[0.44]	2.235	[1.502]
#22	[#7]	22.2	[0.875]	387	[0.60]	3.042	[2.044]
#25	[#8]	25.4	[1.000]	510	[0.79]	3.973	[2.670]
#29	[#9]	28.7	[1.128]	645	[1.00]	5.060	[3.400]
#32	[#10]	32.3	[1.270]	819	[1.27]	6.404	[4.303]
#36	[#11]	35.8	[1.410]	1006	[1.56]	7.907	[5.313]
#43	[#14]	43.0	[1.693]	1452	[2.25]	11.380	[7.650]
#57	[#18]	57.3	[2.257]	2581	[4.00]	20.240	[13.600]

*The equivalent nominal characteristics of inch-pound bars are the values enclosed within the brackets.

302T04.EPS

A spreader bar may be necessary when unloading bundles of bars or similar stock. They are usually made from a fabricated truss, a piece of heavy-duty pipe, or an I-beam.

Tag lines are required on most loads. Tag lines guide the load as it is being hoisted. Fiber rope is normally used for this purpose. Safe hoisting requires a skilled crane operator and an authorized signal person. Operators take their directions from the signal person using hand signals, radios, or telephone headsets.

13.2.0 Using Slings

Never pick up a bundle by the wire wrappings that are used to tie the bundle together. Slings must be used to lift bundles. Choose a sling appropriate to the material being lifted. Check the weight of each bundle on the bill of lading, and ensure that the sizes of the wire rope slings, hooks, and shackles are safe. Chokers and slings of sufficient strength must be selected to lift the load.

The load on each sling depends on the number of slings or chokers, the angle of the choker, and the total load. Although the total weight lifted can be divided between the supporting slings, the force of the load is down. The greater the angle of the sling, the greater the tension on the sling. If the hoisting line and the slings are the same material and size, the tension on each sling must be less than or equal to the tension in the hoist line. This means that the strength of the hoist line determines the maximum capacity of the combination.

If two slings are used to lift bundles of structural iron, always thread the loops in the same direction. If one sling is looped from the opposite side, the bundle will twist when being lifted, making it less safe and causing difficulty when the bars are removed from the bundle. If possible, double wrap the slings to help prevent slipping of the slings and items in the bundle.

Summary

One of the important tasks a rigger performs is guiding the crane operator during a lift. In some instances, radio communications will be used. In others, it will be necessary to use the *ASME B30.5 Consensus Standard* hand signals. Both the rigger and operator must know these signals by heart.

The selecting and setting up of hoisting equipment, hooking cables to the load to be lifted or moved, and directing the load into position are all part of the process called rigging. Performing this process safely and efficiently requires selecting the proper equipment for each hoisting job, understanding safety hazards, and knowing how to prevent accidents. Riggers must have the greatest respect for the hardware and tools of their trade because their lives may depend on them working correctly.

The size of a crane and the huge loads it handles create a large potential for danger to anyone in the vicinity of the crane. The crane operator and rigging workers must be vigilant to ensure that the crane avoids power lines and that site personnel are not endangered by the movement of the crane or the load. Because of tipping hazards, it is important to make sure a crane is on level ground with outriggers extended, if applicable, before lifting a load. Although using cranes to lift personnel was once a common practice, it is discouraged by OSHA, and can only be done in special situations, and under special conditions.

Notes

1. The main advantage of a hardwired communication system is _____.
   a. low cost
   b. portability
   c. less radio interference
   d. ease of use

2. What action is signaled by tapping your fist on your head, then using regular hand signals?
   a. Use main hoist.
   b. Lower.
   c. Use whip line.
   d. Raise boom and lower load.

3. Which of the following is a mode of non-verbal communication?
   a. Buzzer
   b. Portable radio
   c. Bullhorn
   d. Hardwired radio

4. When the signal person gives the dog everything signal, the operator is expected to _____.
   a. turn the machine
   b. travel the machine
   c. retract the boom sections
   d. make no machine movement

5. If it is apparent that the crane operator has misunderstood a hand signal, the signal person should _____.
   a. climb up on the cab and knock on the door
   b. find a supervisor
   c. signal the operator to stop
   d. get away from the crane as quickly as possible

6. A one-handed signal that is given with the fist in front of the body and the thumb pointing toward the signaler's body means _____.
   a. extend the boom
   b. move the crane toward me
   c. swing the load toward me
   d. I'm the signal person

7. When calculating the weight of the load, the rigging and related hardware should *not* be considered.
   a. True
   b. False

8. The most important rigging precaution is determining the weight of all loads before attempting to lift them.
   a. True
   b. False

9. The correct time to determine weight loads for rigging is after the load has been lifted.
   a. True
   b. False

10. When safe working loads are determined, they are based on _____ conditions.
    a. ideal
    b. average
    c. rare
    d. worst-case

11. A(n) _____ is used to allow controlled rotation of the load for position.
    a. tag line
    b. equalizer beam
    c. hoist line
    d. safe-load indicator

12. _____ lines are used when physical control of a load beyond the ability of the crane is required.
    a. Lockout
    b. Tag
    c. Lead
    d. Plumb

13. Tag lines are attached after the rigger verifies that the load is balanced.
    a. True
    b. False

14. When using two or more slings on a load, the rigger must ensure that _____.
    a. the sling angle is greater than 30 degrees relative to the horizontal
    b. all slings are made from the same material
    c. only chain slings are used
    d. only wire rope slings are used

15. The minimum safe distance from power lines of up to 50,000 volts (or 50kV) is _____ feet.
    a. 10
    b. 15
    c. 20
    d. 25

16. If a crane boom has come into contact with a power line, the operator should _____.
    a. immediately jump off the crane
    b. stop and turn off the crane
    c. try to back the crane away from the power line
    d. find out if the line is energized

17. High winds and lightning, which pose danger to cranes, often arrive without warning.
    a. True
    b. False

18. The amount of injury caused by exposure to abnormally cold temperatures depends on all of the following *except* _____.
    a. wind speed
    b. length of exposure
    c. temperature
    d. altitude

19. When cranes are used to lift people, the lift capacity of the crane is _____ percent as a safety factor.
    a. increased 10
    b. increased 20
    c. decreased 20
    d. decreased 50

20. Before a crane is used for a lift, it must be leveled to within _____ percent of grade.
    a. 1
    b. 2
    c. 5
    d. 10

21. The operating radius of a crane is _____.
    a. the length of the boom plus the distance from the end of the boom to the ground
    b. the distance from the center line of rotation to the center of the load block
    c. always the same regardless of the boom position
    d. the distance from the center line of rotation to the top of the boom or jib

22. When two slings positioned at a sling angle of 60 degrees are being used to lift a 1,000-pound load, what is the tension on each sling? Assume a sling angle load factor of 1.155.
    a. 577.5 pounds
    b. 652.5 pounds
    c. 777.5 pounds
    d. 1,000 pounds

23. Shoulderless eyebolts *cannot* be used for angled lifts.
    a. True
    b. False

24. Using the rule of thumb for sizing chocks, a 24-inch diameter pipe would require a chock that is _____ inches thick.
    a. 1.5
    b. 2
    c. 2.5
    d. 3.5

25. The correct way to rig a valve is to _____.
    a. lift it by the handwheel
    b. run the choker through the valve body
    c. place a synthetic sling on each side of the valve body
    d. bolt lifting eyes to the valve flanges

Trade Terms
Introduced in This Module

Anti-two-blocking devices: Devices that provide warnings and prevent two-blocking from occurring. Two-blocking occurs when the lower load block or hook comes into contact with the upper load block, boom point, or boom point machinery. The likely result is failure of the rope or release of the load or hook block.

Blocking: Pieces of hardwood used to support and brace equipment.

Center of gravity: The point at which an object is perpendicular to and balanced in relation to the earth's gravitational field.

Cribbing: Timbers stacked in alternate tiers. Used to support heavy loads.

Powerline Awareness Permit

Today's Date _____ **Job Number** _____

Contractor Name	
Job Address	
Telephone Number	**Fax Number**

Emergency Contact Number	

Survey

Before beginning any project, you must first survey your work area to find power lines at the job site. (See job-site sketch on reverse side.)

Identify

After finding all of the power lines at your site, identify the activities you'll be doing that may put you or your workers at risk. Mark one or more of the following:

☐ Cranes (mobile or truck mounted) ☐ Aerial lifts
☐ Drilling rigs   ☐ Dump trucks
☐ Backhoes/excavators   ☐ Ladders
☐ Long-handled tools   ☐ Material handling & storage
☐ Other tools/high-reaching equipment ☐ Scaffolding
☐ Concrete pumper   ☐ Other_____

Eliminate or Control

After identifying the power line and high-risk activities on the job site, determine how to eliminate or control the risk of electrocution (a successful determination is often reached only after consultation with the utility).

Mark one or more of the following:

☐ Move the activity   ☐ Use barrier protection (insulated sleeves)
☐ Change the activity   ☐ Use an observer
☐ Have the utility de-energize the power line ☐ Use warning lines with flags
☐ Have the utility move the power line   ☐ Use non-conductive tools
                                          ☐ Use a protective technology:
                                             ☐ Insulated link
                                             ☐ Boom cage guard
                                          ☐ Proximity device

Always maintain your minimum safe clearance distance from the power line, except when the utility has de-energized and visibly grounded the power line.

Voltages	Distance from Power Line
Less than 50 kV	10 Feet
More than 50 kV	10'+(0.4")(# of kV over 50 kV)

WARNING!
It is unlawful to operate any piece of equipment within 10' of energized lines

CONSTRUCTION SAFETY COUNCIL

302A01.EPS

Job-Site Sketch

(Draw in location of power lines and their proximity to construction site, including such things as proposed excavations, location of heavy equipment, scaffolding, material storage areas, etc.)

Completed by_____Date_____

Title_____

Approved by_____Date_____

Title_____

CONSTRUCTION SAFETY COUNCIL

302A02.EPS

This module is intended to be a thorough resource for task training. The following reference works are suggested for further study. These are optional materials for continued education rather than for task training.

Crane Safety on Construction Sites, 1998. Task Committee on Crane Safety on Construction Sites. Reston, VA: ASCE.

Rigging Handbook, 2003. Jerry A. Klinke. Stevensville, MI: ACRA Enterprises, Inc.

NCCER makes every effort to keep these textbooks up-to-date and free of technical errors. We appreciate your help in this process. If you have an idea for improving this textbook, or if you find an error, a typographical mistake, or an inaccuracy in NCCER's Contren® textbooks, please write us, using this form or a photocopy. Be sure to include the exact module number, page number, a detailed description, and the correction, if applicable. Your input will be brought to the attention of the Technical Review Committee. Thank you for your assistance.

Instructors – If you found that additional materials were necessary in order to teach this module effectively, please let us know so that we may include them in the Equipment/Materials list in the Annotated Instructor's Guide.

Write: Product Development and Revision
National Center for Construction Education and Research
3600 NW 43rd St., Bldg. G, Gainesville, FL 32606

Fax: 352-334-0932

E-mail: curriculum@nccer.org

Craft _____ Module Name _____

Copyright Date _____ Module Number _____ Page Number(s) _____

Description _____

_____

_____

_____

(Optional) Correction _____

_____

_____

(Optional) Your Name and Address _____

_____

_____

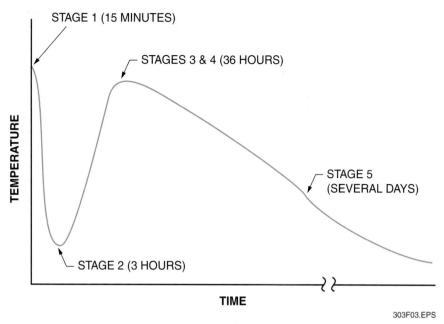

STAGE 1 (15 MINUTES)

STAGES 3 & 4 (36 HOURS)

STAGE 5 (SEVERAL DAYS)

STAGE 2 (3 HOURS)

TEMPERATURE

TIME

303F03.EPS

Figure 3 ◆ Typical heat of hydration rate curve during hydration of portland cement.

2.1.2 Types of Portland Cement

Manufacturers use their own brand names, but nearly all portland cements are manufactured to meet ASTM International or ANSI specifications. Various types of common portland cements are briefly described below. These portland cements, as well as some other less common cements, are explained in more detail in *Appendix A*.

The *ASTM C150* specifications for cement are as follows:

- *Type I, Normal* – A general-purpose cement suitable for all uses where it is not subject to attack by sulfates or to an undesired temperature rise due to hydration.
- *Type II, Modified* – A cement with moderate sulfite resistance and usually with a low heat of hydration. This cement is used in concrete for piers, large structures, and structures exposed to seawater. Today, it is the most commonly specified cement.
- *Type III, High Early Strength* – A cement used in concrete when forms must be removed as soon as possible. Because of finer grinding and different content proportions, the cement reaches a strength about equal to the 28-day strength of Types I and II within only seven days.
- *Type IV, Low Heat* – A cement used in very massive structures, such as dams, where low heat buildup from hydration is required to prevent expansion and cracking.
- *Type V (or C452, Type V), Sulfate Resistant* – A **sulfate-resistant cement** that is generally used only in concrete exposed to severe sulfate action caused by high-alkali content water and/or soil.

- *Types IA through IIIA, Air Entraining* – An **air-entraining cement** with materials added that create many tiny air bubbles when water is added and concrete is mixed. This improves the concrete's workability as well as its ability to resist freezing and thawing, but may also reduce its final strength.
- *White* – A finely ground cement that has a controlled manufacturing process that causes the final product to be white instead of gray. It is used for architectural purposes such as stucco, facing panels, cement paint, and terrazzo, or when truer concrete coloring is required.

 WARNING!

Working with dry cement or wet concrete is hazardous. Dry cement dust can enter open wounds and cause blood poisoning. The cement dust, when it comes in contact with body fluids, can cause chemical burns to the membranes of the eyes, nose, mouth, throat, or lungs. It can also cause a fatal lung disease known as silicosis. Wet cement or concrete can also cause chemical burns to the eyes and skin. Make sure that appropriate personal protective equipment is worn when working with dry cement or wet concrete. If wet concrete enters waterproof boots from the top, remove the boots and rinse your legs, feet, boots, and clothing with clear water as soon as possible. Repeated contact with cement or wet concrete can also cause an allergic skin reaction known as cement dermatitis.

Type I and Type II Cement

Portland Type I and Type II cements account for about 90 percent of all the cements that are produced. A portland cement designated as Type I/II means that the cement meets the specifications of both portland cement Types I and II.

2.1.3 Types of Blended Cements

The *ASTM C595* or *C1157* specifications include several classes of blended cement as follows:

- *Type IS, portland blast furnace slag cement* – It is produced by mixing portland cement with 25–70 percent granulated blast-furnace slag by weight. It typically is used in general construction applications. When suffixes A, MS, or MH follow the IS designation, they indicate an IS cement with air entrainment, moderate sulfate resistance, or moderate heat of hydration, respectively.
- *Type IP and P, portland pozzolan cement* – It is produced by mixing portland cement with 15–40 percent of a pozzolan by weight. Pozzolans are described in more detail later in this module. Type IP can be used for general construction. Type P is typically used in large structures such as dams, footings, and piers. Suffixes A, MS, or MH following after the IP or P designation indicate a cement with air entrainment, moderate sulfate resistance, or moderate heat of hydration, respectively.
- *Type I(PM), pozzolan-modified portland cement* – It is produced by mixing portland cement or portland blast furnace cement with a fine pozzolan of less than 15 percent by weight. It is used for general construction. Suffixes of A, MS, or MH following the I(PM) designation indicate an I(PM) cement with air entrainment, moderate sulfate resistance, or moderate heat of hydration, respectively.

- *Type S, slag cement* – It is produced by mixing portland cement with a minimum of 70 percent ground blast-furnace slag by weight when making concrete for general construction. When making mortar, the ground blast-furnace slag is mixed with lime, instead of portland cement. The suffix A used after the S designation indicates an S cement with air entrainment.
- *Type I(SM), slag-modified portland cement* – It is produced by mixing portland cement with less than 25 percent granulated blast-furnace slag by weight. It is used for general construction. Suffixes of A, MS, or MH following the I(SM) designation indicate an I(SM) cement with air entrainment, moderate sulfate resistance, or moderate heat of hydration, respectively.

2.2.0 Aggregates Used In Concrete

Aggregates used to make concrete are solid, chemically inert materials. They can range in size from small particles of sand to large, coarse rocks. Aggregates constitute about 60 percent to 80 percent of the volume of concrete. Some commonly used aggregates are natural sand, gravel, crushed stone, and blast-furnace slag. The selection of a particular aggregate for use depends on the desired characteristics of the concrete. Aggregates used for making concrete must be hard and strong, and must be processed to ensure that they are clean of coatings of clay or other materials and free of absorbed chemicals.

Oil Well Cements

There are special cements made for sealing oil wells. These cements have the properties of being slow setting and resistant to high temperatures and pressures. Oil well cements are generally made from portland cement clinker or from blended cements. Nine classes of oil well cement, designated A through J, are specified by the American Petroleum Institute. Each class is specified for use with wells having different depths, temperatures, and sulfate environments.

Today, recycled concrete is also being used as an aggregate in new concrete. Use of recycled concrete helps save natural materials and eliminates the need to dispose of old concrete in landfill areas. Old pieces of concrete are processed to remove contaminants, crushed into suitable aggregate sizes, and screened. Some typical applications for new concrete made using recycled concrete aggregate include: pavement, shoulders, median barriers, sidewalks, curbs, and bridge foundations. After processing, both new and recycled aggregates must be handled and stored in a manner that prevents contamination. Some important considerations when making new concrete include the strength, size, shape, and the cleanliness of the aggregate material selected for use.

2.2.1 Strength

Cement only binds the aggregates together in concrete. Much of the strength of cured concrete depends on the strength of the pieces of aggregate as well as the binding of the cement. High-strength concrete cannot be made from aggregates that are structurally weak, such as soft sandstone, shale, or coal. Aggregates that readily split, crack, flake, or are soft must not be used in normal concrete.

2.2.2 Size

Fine aggregates are defined by *ASTM C33* as 0.19" (4.75 mm) in diameter or smaller. Washed natural or manufactured sand is normally used as a fine aggregate. Fine aggregates are necessary for workability and smooth surfaces. The fine particles help fill the spaces between the larger particles. However, an excess of fine aggregates requires more cement-water mixture to attain the right strength, and thus increases the cost.

Coarse aggregates are larger than 0.19" (4.75 mm) in diameter and are usually washed gravel, crushed stone, or slag. For average concrete, the largest aggregate generally used is approximately 1½" (37.5 mm) in diameter. As a rule of thumb, the largest size aggregate used should never be greater than one-fifth the thickness of a finished wall section, one-third the thickness of a slab, or three-fourths the width of the narrowest space through which the concrete will be required to pass during placement. Use of the maximum allowable aggregate size usually results in less drying shrinkage and lower cost, but does not necessarily increase the strength of the concrete. Data from the National Sand and Gravel Association has indicated that for a given cement factor and **slump**, the compressive strength of rich concrete mixtures increases as aggregate size decreases from 2½" (63.5 mm) to ⅜" (9.5 mm) and that no significant strength improvement occurs from the use of aggregates larger than ¾".

Normal concrete uses fine and coarse aggregates in the ranges defined above and weighs 140 to 160 pounds per cubic foot. In certain special concrete mixes, much lighter or much larger and heavier aggregates are used.

Aggregates that are randomly proportioned often produce inferior concrete because they pack so tightly that the binding mixture of cement and water cannot flow freely and coat all surfaces of the aggregate. Fairly precise amounts of fine and coarse aggregates must be used to obtain the desired concrete characteristics.

2.2.3 Shape

Natural gravel and stone or crushed gravel and stone produce concrete of approximately the same strength. In fact, some high-strength concrete is made using only crushed rock. However, the use of crushed materials creates a harsher concrete mix with a greater number of large voids between the coarse aggregate particles than between rounder aggregates of the same size. This, in turn, requires the use of more sand and consequently more cement and water to produce a given consistency of concrete. In these cases, a water-reducing additive may also be used to increase strength. Coarse aggregate content of elongated or thin pieces of crushed aggregate are sometimes limited to a maximum of 10 to 15 percent by weight to minimize harsh concrete mixes whose surfaces may be subject to tearing during finishing.

2.2.4 Cleanliness

Aggregates that are contaminated by the presence of dirt, clay, chert (a splintery, flint-like rock), coal, lignite (a type of soft, brown coal), oil, or other organic impurities should not be used. In most cases, the presence of these materials will interfere with the strength and/or appearance of the cured, finished concrete.

2.3.0 Water for Concrete

Generally, any potable water (unless it is extremely hard or contains too many sulfates) may be used to make concrete. If the quality of the water is unknown or questionable, the water should be analyzed, or mortar cubes should be made and tested against control cubes made with potable water. If the water is satisfactory, the test cubes should show the same compressive strength as the control cubes after a 28-day cure time.

High concentrations of chlorides, sulfates, alkalis, salts, and other contaminants have corrosive effects on concrete and/or metal reinforcing rods, mesh, and cables. Sulfates can cause disintegration of concrete, while alkalis, sodium carbonate, and bicarbonates may affect the hardening times as well as the strength of concrete.

It is the water mixed with concrete that causes the chemical reactions of hydration in cement to form a paste that hardens and gains strength as it surrounds the aggregates. The strength of the concrete depends on the water-cement ratio. The water-cement ratio (w/c) is defined as the weight of the water used in the mix divided by the weight of the cement used in the mix. For example, a mix made with 235 pounds of water and 470 pounds of cement has a w/c ratio of 0.5 (235 ÷ 470 = 0.5). The less water used, the lower the w/c ratio, and the stronger the concrete, provided the ratio is not so low that it sacrifices the workability of the fresh concrete. As the w/c ratio increases, the porosity of the cement paste in the concrete increases, which causes the strength of the concrete to decrease.

2.4.0 Admixtures of Concrete

Admixtures are materials other than the main ingredients of concrete. Most are added to the concrete mix in small quantities typically ranging between 2 percent and 5 percent of cement weight before or during the mixing process in order to modify the properties of the concrete while it is in the plastic state and/or hardened state. Samples of concrete that contain admixtures should be fully tested and evaluated using ASTM test methods for slump, air content, setting time, compressive strength, flexural strength, resistance to freezing and thawing, and volume change before deciding that the admixture(s) are suitable for the application at hand. Before using an admixture, it should also be determined if it will cause corrosion of reinforcement or embedded metals or an undesirable color change of the cured concrete. It should also be determined that suitable and accurate dispensing equipment is available and whether any special handling, mixing, or finishing conditions are required.

Admixtures are of two types: chemical and mineral.

2.4.1 Chemical Admixtures

Chemical admixtures are used to reduce the cost of construction, modify the properties of hardened concrete, and ensure the quality of concrete during mixing, transportation, placing, and curing. They function to affect the hydration and/or are absorbed by the particles of cement. There are several categories of commonly used chemical admixtures.

- *Air-entraining agents* – These agents produce millions of minuscule air bubbles or cells in the cement paste. These air cells act to relieve internal pressures in the concrete by providing room for the expansion of water when it freezes, thereby preventing the concrete from cracking and scaling. The air cells also improve durability, workability, and reduce bleed water and segregation of the aggregate before the concrete can set. These agents impart the same qualities to concrete as **air-entraining cement**. The advantage is that they can be varied at the time the concrete is mixed to match local conditions or requirements. These agents are commonly used in cold weather environments, but they are generally not used for structural concrete. Entrapped air in concrete is air that was not able to escape from voids in the pour. This is a weak place, and may also show up as holes or dips at the surface while the concrete is setting. Entrained air consists of tiny bubbles intentionally distributed throughout the mix, allowing room for expansion of water that may freeze while the pour is setting.

- *Accelerating agents* – These agents are commonly used to modify the properties of concrete in cold weather. They speed up the setting time and early strength of the concrete, allowing finishing operations to begin earlier. They also reduce the time needed for proper curing and protection.
- *Normal water-reducing/water retarding agents* – Various types of water-reducing or water-reducing/water-retarding agents are available that will allow water reduction of 5 to 10 percent and still result in the same consistency of concrete. The reduction of water allows very high-strength concrete to be produced. If the water is not reduced, very high workability (flowing concrete) can be achieved. Water-reducing agents also cause retarded curing. In these cases, accelerators such as calcium chloride are sometimes used to counteract this effect.
- *High range water reducing agents* – These agents, also called superplasticizers or plasticizers, are used to reduce water content by 12 percent to 30 percent, thereby increasing the strength by decreasing the water needed for workable concrete. They are typically used on very large projects that require high levels of workability. Concrete made with superplasticizers is highly fluid and flows easily so that it can be placed with little vibration or compaction. The period of easy workability typically lasts for about 30 to 60 minutes after which it fast becomes unworkable.
- *Coloring agents* – Coloring agents are used for decorative, warning, or identification purposes. Integrally colored concrete is made by adding a liquid or powder colorant agent during the mixing process. This produces uniform coloring throughout the mixture. Colored hardeners are another type of coloring agent. These are finely ground cement-like aggregates that are sprinkled onto freshly placed concrete. Moisture from the concrete activates and bonds

the agent to produce a denser, colored finished surface. Colored stains are also made that chemically react with the lime in concrete. These lightly etch and bond color into the concrete surface.

2.4.2 Mineral Admixtures

Mineral admixtures, commonly called supplementary cementing materials, are used primarily to reduce the amount of cement used in making concrete, thus making the concrete cheaper. Mineral admixtures also are used in some applications to reduce permeability, increase strength, or affect other properties of concrete. Mineral admixtures are either hydraulic or pozzolanic in nature. Hydraulic mineral admixtures, such as ground granulated blast-furnace slag, react directly with water to form cement-like compounds. In their natural state, pozzolanic materials, called pozzolans, have no cementing properties. However, when ground finely and used in a concrete mix, they react with the alkalis and calcium hydroxide, a product of hydration in portland cement, to produce cement-like compounds.

Pozzolanic materials contain reactive silicates or alumino-silicates. Some commonly used pozzolans include fly ash, silica fume, metakaolin, and rice husk ash. Fly ash is produced as a by-product of combustion of ground coal in coal-burning electric utilities. Silica fume is produced as waste product of the silicon metal industry. It is widely used when making very high strength concretes such as used in high-rise buildings. It is also used where the concrete is exposed to abrasive or corrosive environments. Metakaolin is made from thermally activated high-purity kaolin containing clay. Rice husk ash is a natural byproduct derived from the processing of rice. Pozzolans are widely used in **mass concrete** applications, such as dams or very large structures, where reduced hydration heat is required and reduced cement content can be tolerated.

Hydraulic Cement

INSIDE TRACK

Roman structures still standing today, such as the Appian Way and the Colosseum, were built with a hydraulic cement made from a mixture of hydraulic lime and fine volcanic ash (a pozzolan) obtained from Mount Vesuvius. The name pozzolan originated from the town of Pozzuoli, which was located near a major source of Mount Vesuvius volcanic ash used by the Romans.

There are a number of special admixtures available that are not commonly used. These include gas-forming, grouting, expansion-producing or expansion-reducing, bonding, corrosion-inhibiting, fungicidal, germicidal, and insecticidal admixtures. Products are available for hardening and sealing concrete surfaces. Some such products, under various proprietary names, employ a reaction between silicon compounds and the calcium hydroxide in concrete to form very hard surfaces. These are a treatment after the pour is completed, which produces a denser and more liquid-repellant surface. Epoxy and polyurethane compounds are used to seal and fill cracks in concrete. Included in such coatings are many colorant options, allowing for geometric designs, or even artwork floors. Specialized admixtures such as these are generally used under the supervision of the manufacturer or a specialist. The commonly used admixtures briefly described above along with selected special admixtures are more fully described in *Appendix B*.

3.0.0 ◆ NORMAL CONCRETE MIX PROPORTIONS AND MEASUREMENTS

The desirable properties of concrete—workability when fresh and strength and durability when hardened—depend on the careful selection, proportioning, and mixing of its ingredients. Different proportions of materials are used when making concrete depending on the intended application. A typical concrete mix consists of 10 percent to 15 percent portland cement, 60 percent to 75 percent fine and/or coarse aggregates, and 15 percent to 20 percent water. When entrained air is used in concrete mixes it typically ranges from 5 percent to 8 percent. The percentage of admixtures when used is about 2 percent to 5 percent. Proportions used in a mixture should be measured by weight, rather than volume. Some considerations about the proportion of specific materials in a concrete mix are as follows:

- *Cement* – As the cement content in the mix is increased, the strength and durability of the concrete is increased. Conversely, as it is decreased, the strength and durability of the concrete is decreased.
- *Water* – The more water used, the weaker the hardened concrete. Ideally, use as little water as possible, only enough to make the mix workable. The water must not contain excessive amounts of impurities such as sulfates, chlorides, alkalis, and solids. These impurities can

cause efflorescence, staining, volume instability, and reduced durability of the concrete. Some can also cause corrosion of rebar and other reinforcement materials. The amount of water used in a concrete mixture must be adjusted to take into account any moisture conditions of the aggregate in the mix. For example, the moisture content of any wet sand used in the mixture must be taken into consideration.

- *Aggregates* – Using too much fine aggregate yields a mix that can result in no coarse aggregate in the top layer of the concrete after compaction, thereby making the concrete less durable. Using too much coarse aggregate yields a mix that can result in aggregate protruding from the top surface of the concrete after compaction.

In the mixing process the cement and water initially combine to form a cement paste that coats each particle of aggregate in the mix. Because of hydration, the cement paste hardens over time and gains strength. As described earlier, the strength of the cement paste depends on the water-cement ratio. Higher quality concrete is produced when the lowest water-cement ratio possible is used that will not affect the workability of the fresh concrete. Most concrete is made with a water-cement ratio between 0.35 and 0.71. *Figure 4* shows an example of the typical strength range of a concrete made with a Type I portland cement at various water-cement ratios. As shown, a 0.44 water-cement ratio yields compressive strengths ranging between 4,800 and 6,400 pounds per square inch (psi): a ratio of 0.53 yields strengths ranging between 4,000 and 5,400 psi. Concretes having strengths up to 7,000 psi are considered conventional concretes. Those with strengths of 7,000 psi up to 14,500 psi are considered high-strength concretes. The strength of the concrete for any given water-cement ratio varies over a certain range because of variations in the cementitious materials, along with variations caused by the quality of the aggregates.

CAUTION

Because the water-cement ratio is critical in determining the strength of concrete, never add more water to the premixed concrete delivered to the job site. Adding water will lower the strength of the concrete below that specified for the job.

Project specifications for the proportioning of concrete mixtures are of two general types:

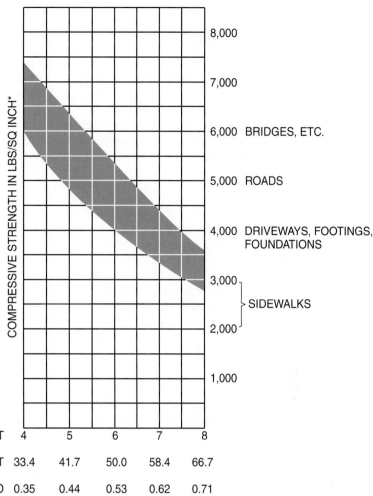

Figure 4 ◆ Typical concrete strength for various water-cement ratios using Type I portland cement.

U.S. GAL WATER/BAG (94 LB) CEMENT	4	5	6	7	8
EQUIVALENT LBS WATER/BAG (94 LB) CEMENT	33.4	41.7	50.0	58.4	66.7
EQUIVALENT WATER-CEMENT RATIO	0.35	0.44	0.53	0.62	0.71

303F04.EPS

prescription specifications and performance specifications. With prescription specifications, volume-proportion requirements are typically given as 1:2:3, meaning one part cement, two parts sand, and three parts aggregate by volume with water only limited by the maximum amount of slump allowed. Prescription specifications are usually stated by weight, such as kilograms per cubic meter or pounds per cubic yard, and often cover only minimum cement content along with the water-cement ratio, usually by weight. The American Concrete Institute (ACI) has developed numerous prescription-type tables. The data presented in these tables can be used to produce a concrete mix that will be on the side of safety in both strength and durability.

Performance specifications place the responsibility for the strength and durability of the concrete on the concrete producer or contractor. The specifications usually state the strength required,

The Rule of Sixes

One general rule for mixing concrete is called the rule of sixes. It states that a minimum of six bags of cement and six gallons of water be used per cubic yard of concrete. If air-entrained concrete is being mixed because the concrete will be subjected to freezing and thawing, it is recommended that the air content be 6 percent. The rule also states that the curing period during which the concrete is kept moist should be a minimum of six days.

the minimum cement content or maximum water-cement ratio, consistency as measured by slump, air-entrainment (if required), and usually some limitation on aggregate sizes and properties. By keeping the limitations to a minimum, concrete producers or contractors can use prescription tables as a starting point to design (with laboratory assistance) the most effective concrete mix based on local conditions. These types of specifications usually require that the concrete producer or contractor test a number of cured samples of the proposed concrete mixes to determine and demonstrate strength and durability.

4.0.0 ◆ SPECIAL TYPES OF CONCRETE

In addition to normal concrete mixes, there are a number of specialized types of concrete for specific applications. A few of these special types of concrete do not look anything like normal concrete during placement. Many special types of concrete were briefly covered earlier in *Carpentry Level One, Introduction to Concrete, Reinforcing Materials, and Forms* and are explained in more detail in *Appendix C*. These include the following:

- Mass concrete
- High-strength and/or high-performance concrete
- Roller-compacted concrete
- Lightweight concrete
- Preplaced aggregate (prepacked) concrete
- Heavyweight (high-density) concrete

Some other special concretes you may encounter include:

- *Refractory concrete* – A concrete composed of calcium aluminate cement and refractory (heat resistant) aggregate. It is used in high-temperature applications such as space program vehicle launch pads.
- *Self-consolidating concrete* – Self-consolidating concrete is also commonly called self-compacting, self-leveling, or self-placing concrete. It is a high-performance concrete made with super-plasticizer admixtures. It is used in applications that require the concrete to flow into tight areas without segregating and without requiring vibration.
- *No-fines concrete* – A concrete made using only coarse aggregate in the mix. As a result, when hardened it is porous and has a much lower density than conventional concrete. It is used mainly for drainage layers under reservoirs, basement floors, and similar applications.

- *Sprayed concrete* – Sprayed concrete, commonly called shotcrete, is a type of concrete that is sprayed onto a structure. Two methods are used: wet-mix or dry-mix. In the wet mix method, previously mixed concrete, including the water needed for hydration, is pumped from a holding hopper to the nozzle of a spray hose where compressed air is used to propel the ready-mixed concrete at high-velocity onto the structural surface. In the dry mix method, the dry mixed ingredients only are moved from a holding hopper to the spray hose nozzle. There, water is added to the dry mix and then propelled by high-velocity compressed air onto the structural surface. The mixing process of the dry material and water is not totally completed at the nozzle, but is finalized as the mixture strikes and coats the structural surface. Some in the trade refer to the concrete produced by the dry-mix method as gunite. However, the term shotcrete is more commonly used for concrete produced by both methods. Shotcrete is widely used in tunneling, in-ground swimming pools, and erosion control.

5.0.0 ◆ CURING OF CONCRETE

After new concrete is placed and finished, it must be cured by maintaining it at a satisfactory moisture content and temperature for a specific time period, typically 5 to 7 days for conventional concrete. This process aids the chemical reaction of hydration between the cement and water in the concrete. Any appreciable loss of water by evaporation will delay or prevent the hydration process. For this reason, the surface of new concrete must be kept moist. To prevent the premature evaporation of the moisture in new concrete, it can be kept moist by covering it with waterproof curing paper or plastic sheeting. Wet curing can be done by wetting the concrete with soaking hoses or sprinklers or by using moistened cotton mats or blankets like those shown in *Figure 5*. Another commonly used method coats the concrete surface with commercially available curing compounds, which seal in moisture. In cold weather, where it is necessary to prevent the concrete from freezing, commercial insulating blankets, fiberglass batts, or expanded plastic cell slabs can be used provided they are protected from snow or water penetration. The methods and materials used to achieve proper curing are covered in more detail in *Appendix D*.

Figure 5 ◆ Curing of a concrete floor using moistened curing blankets.

6.0.0 ◆ CONCRETE TESTING

Some of the most common standards that are widely accepted for determining the characteristics/properties of concrete are published by the ASTM and described below.

- *Slump* – *ASTM C143* describes the method for the slump testing of portland cement concrete.
- *Air content* – *ASTM C231* describes the test of air content of freshly mixed concrete by the pressure method.
- *Time of setting* – *ASTM C403* describes the time-of-set test of a concrete mixture by penetration resistance.
- *Compressive strength* – *ASTM C31* describes making and curing cylinder specimens for concrete compression tests and beam specimens for flexure tests. *ASTM C39* describes the method of test for compressive strength of molded concrete cylinders.
- *Flexural strength* – *ASTM C78* describes the method of test for the flexing strength of concrete.

- *Resistance to freezing and thawing* – *ASTM C666* describes the method of test for concrete resistance to freezing and thawing.
- *Volume change* – *ASTM C157* describes the method of test for volume change of cement mortar and concrete.

There are a number of other ASTM standards used to test the properties and characteristics of aggregate, cement, and concrete. Some of the additional standards cover tests for such things as tensile strength, unit weight and yield, uniformity of mixing, coarse-aggregate content, and modulus of elasticity. In addition to ASTM test methods, other agencies have various applicable cement and concrete evaluation methods. These agencies include the American Association of State Highway and Transportation Officials, the American Concrete Institute, the Federal Bureau of Reclamation, and the Army Corps of Engineers.

Some of the tests provided in the ASTM standards are divided into those that can usually be performed in the field and those that are usually performed in the laboratory. In this module, only the field methods for slump testing and the casting of a cylinder for compression tests will be covered. However, it should be noted that testing of concrete for only one or two properties such as workability or compressive strength may lead to the erroneous conclusion that a particular concrete mix, including any admixtures, is suitable for the intended application. For example, a high-compressive strength concrete with poor resistance to freezing and thawing would be undesirable for highway construction. Likewise, a high-compressive strength concrete with a high drying shrinkage would be unsuitable for most structures. It is important that the characteristics of a concrete mix, especially those containing admixtures, be completely evaluated in relation to the ultimate use of the concrete.

THINK ABOUT IT

Concrete Testing

Shown here is an example of a form used to record the results of concrete testing. Can you give two or more reasons why you think testing of concrete is important?

Client _____

Project _____

Field Data	**Concrete Data**

Date Sampled _____   Specified 28 Day Strength PSI _____

Sampled By _____   Design Mix _____

Plant _____   Gallons Water _____

Truck No. _____ Ticket# _____   Admixture _____

Time (Batched) _____ (Sampled) _____   % Air By Volume _____

Unit Wt. _____ % Air _____   Cement _____

Temp. (Air) _____ (Mix) _____   Fine Aggregate _____

Date Received _____ Age (Days) _____   Coarse Aggregate _____

Data Submitted By _____   Remarks: _____

LAB No. _____

Compressive Strength Test Results

CYL. I.D.	SLUMP INCHES	CURING	DATE TESTED	AGE (DAYS)	FAILURE PLANE	COMPRESSIVE STRENGTH (PSI)

Location of Concrete Placement _____

_____

_____

_____

303SA01.EPS

6.1.0 Sampling Concrete

The procedures for taking a sample of concrete depend on the equipment from which the sample is taken. *ASTM C172* describes proper sampling methods. Conformance to proper methods is essential for reliable results and is considered the most important single factor in concrete testing.

WARNING!

Concrete is toxic. Chemicals in wet concrete can be absorbed through the skin or an open wound and cause blood poisoning. Wet concrete can also cause chemical burns to the eyes and skin. Appropriate personal protective equipment must be worn. If concrete enters waterproof boots from the top, remove the boots and rinse legs, feet, boots, and clothing with clear water as soon as possible. Repeated contact with wet concrete can also cause an allergic skin reaction (cement dermatitis).

The following is a summary of the *ASTM C172* sampling procedures.

- For trucks or stationary mixers, proceed as follows:
  - Obtain concrete samples at two or more regularly spaced intervals during discharge of the middle portion of the batch. Obtain the samples within 15 minutes of each other.
  - Make sure the rate of discharge of the batch from the mixer is regulated by the rate of rotation of the drum and not by the size of the gate opening.
  - Using a suitable nonabsorbent receptacle such as a wheelbarrow, obtain each portion either by totally intercepting the concrete stream or by diverting the stream completely into the receptacle.
  - Move concrete samples to the place where the test specimens are to be molded. Make sure samples are protected from the effects of sun, wind, and contamination.
  - If necessary, sift out aggregate particles over 1½" (38 mm). Then thoroughly mix individual samples for uniformity before testing, and start testing within the required time frame. Begin slump and/or air content testing within 5 minutes and cylinder or beam casting within 15 minutes.
- For paving mixers, the entire batch should be discharged and the samples collected from at least five different portions of the pile. Compacting, protection, and time limits are the same as above.

- For open-top truck mixers, agitators, and non-agitating equipment, take samples by whichever of the procedures described above is most appropriate.

6.2.0 Concrete Slump Testing

A slump test is used to determine the workability of concrete. The test is the distance, in inches, that the top of a conical pile of fresh concrete will sag after a standardized cone mold is removed. If the slump is too low, it can cause poor flow of the concrete, resulting in improper consolidation of the concrete. If too high, the free flowing concrete can cause mortar loss through the formwork, excessive pressures in the formwork, segregation, and delays in finishing the concrete. Concrete slump must conform to the structure specifications. Typical ranges of slump for various types of construction are given in *Table 1*.

NOTE

The entire slump test from the start of filling to the completion of the cone lift should be accomplished within 2½ minutes. If concrete falls away or a portion shears away from the cone in two consecutive tests, the concrete lacks the necessary plasticity and cohesiveness for the slump test to be applicable. *ASTM C31* requires that concrete having a slump of less than 1" (25 mm) must be vibrated for consolidation; for slumps of 1" to 3" (25 to 75 mm), vibration or rodding may be used; and for slumps greater than 3" (75 mm), rodding must be used.

Table 1 Typical Slump Ranges

| | Slump (inches)* | |
Type of Construction	Maximum	Minimum
Reinforced foundation walls and footings	4	2
Unreinforced footings, caissons, and substructure walls	3	1
Reinforced slabs, beams, and walls	5	2
Building columns	5	3
Pavements	2	1
Sidewalks, driveways, and slabs on ground	4	2
Heavy mass construction	2	1

303T01.EPS

*When high-frequency vibrators are *not* used, the values may be increased by about 50 percent, but in no case should the slump exceed 6".

ASTM C143 details the procedures for making a slump test and is summarized as follows:

Step 1 A moistened cone (*Figure 6*) is placed on a firm, level, moistened, nonabsorbent surface and is held in place by standing on the foot pieces.

Step 2 The cone is filled with fresh concrete, one-third full by volume, and vibrated or rodded evenly over the surface area 25 times with a standard steel ⅝" smooth tamping rod with a rounded end (*Figure 7*).

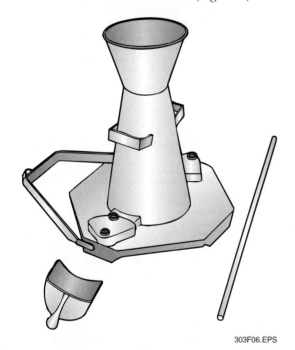

Figure 6 ◆ Slump cone mold.

303F06.EPS

Step 3 The next layer of fresh concrete is added until the cone is two-thirds full by volume. This layer is vibrated or rodded evenly 25 times with the rod just penetrating the first layer (*Figure 8*).

Step 4 The cone is then heaped to overflowing, and the third layer is vibrated or rodded evenly 25 times with the rod just penetrating the second layer (*Figure 9*). If the concrete sags below the top of the cone, more concrete is added to keep the concrete above the top of the cone.

Step 5 After rodding or vibration, the excess concrete is scraped off the top of the cone with the rod (*Figure 10*) and any spilled concrete is cleaned from around the base of the cone.

Step 6 Using the hand grips, the cone is then lifted vertically. This must be done slowly and carefully within 3 to 7 seconds, while avoiding rotational movement or bumping of the molded concrete. The cone is then placed upside down next to, but not touching, the slumped concrete, and the rod is laid across the cone over the concrete.

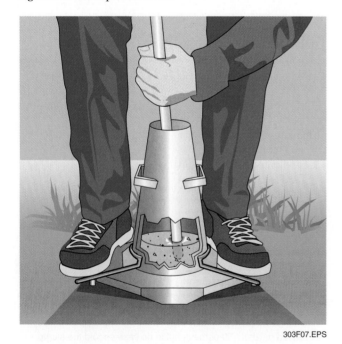

303F07.EPS

Figure 7 ◆ Cone mold one-third full.

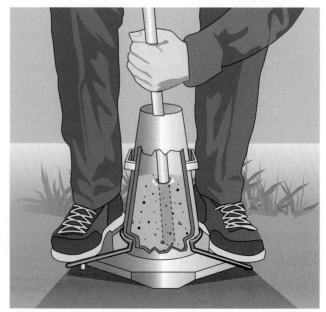

303F08.EPS

Figure 8 ◆ Cone mold two-thirds full.

Figure 9 ◆ Cone mold full and overflowing.

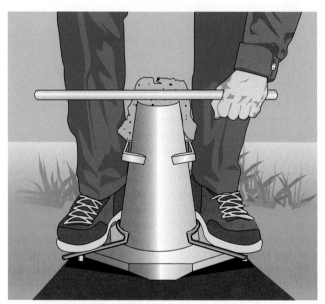

Figure 10 ◆ Leveling top of cone mold.

Step 7 The distance from the bottom of the tamping rod to the sagged top of the concrete at the original center of the concrete cone is immediately measured to the nearest ¼" (6 mm) to determine the concrete slump (*Figure 11*). Record the slump and discard the test sample of concrete.

6.3.0 Concrete Compression Testing

The compression test measures the strength of the concrete in the hardened state. The actual testing

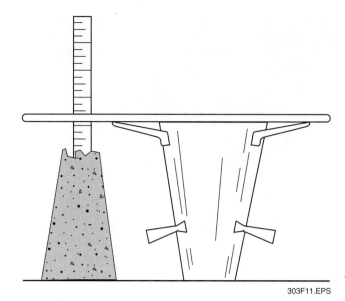

Figure 11 ◆ Measurement of concrete slump.

of the concrete compression strength is performed on a laboratory off site. The only work done on site is to prepare one or more concrete cylinders of the sampled concrete for the compression test. Sampling of the concrete and preparation and handling of the cylinders must be done carefully and properly as wrong results can be costly.

Concrete samples taken for at least two compressive strength specimens are generally required by specifications for each 150 cubic yards, or fraction thereof, of each class of concrete placed in any one day. However, some job specifications may require more frequent testing. The samples for the specimens are taken as described earlier. The cylindrical specimens are cast and then are usually laboratory-cured as described in *ASTM C31* and laboratory-tested as described in *ASTM C39*. The casting of standard 6" × 12" (150 mm × 300 mm) cylindrical specimens is completed as follows:

Step 1 The cylindrical molds used for strength testing can be either reusable or single-use cardboard (*Figure 12*). They must be checked for compliance with *ASTM C470*.

Step 2 The molds are placed on a smooth, firm, and level surface.

Step 3 The molds are filled in three equal layers with concrete mixed just prior to the start of sampling, and rodded or vibrated in the same way as during the slump test. See *Figures 13, 14*, and *15*. When making multiple specimens, each mold should have the same layers placed and rodded or vibrated at the same time. An excess of concrete should be on top of the mold.

303F12.EPS

Figure 12 ◆ Cylindrical molds used for strength testing.

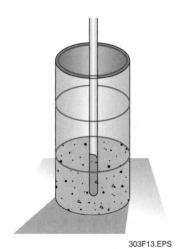

303F13.EPS

Figure 13 ◆ Cylindrical mold one-third full.

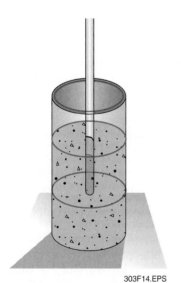

303F14.EPS

Figure 14 ◆ Cylindrical mold two-thirds full.

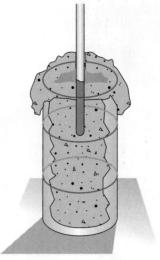

303F15.EPS

Figure 15 ◆ Cylindrical mold full and overflowing.

WARNING!

Concrete is toxic. Chemicals in wet concrete can be absorbed through the skin or an open wound and cause blood poisoning. Wet concrete can also cause chemical burns to the eyes and skin. Appropriate personal protective equipment must be worn. If concrete enters waterproof boots from the top, remove the boots and rinse legs, feet, boots, and clothing with clear water as soon as possible. Repeated contact with wet concrete can also cause an allergic skin reaction (cement dermatitis).

Step 4 After rodding or vibration, the excess concrete is scraped off with a straightedge (*Figure 16*). The concrete specimens must be identified (tagged) with consecutively numbered metal tags or equivalent. The tags should be marked with the project name, mix proportions, date, slump, air content, temperature, location in structure, and ages at which the samples are to be tested, along with the identity of the person making the cylinder. Tag wires are usually buried in the concrete specimens at the edge of the cylinder.

Step 5 Cap all specimen containers to prevent moisture loss, then allow 24 hours for the concrete to set before moving the specimens. It is important not to move the specimens before 24 hours have elapsed because movement can cause the aggregates in the specimen to settle to the bottom, resulting in an inaccurate test result.

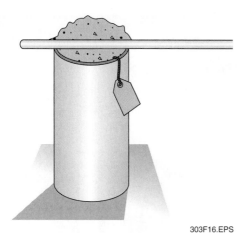

Figure 16 ◆ Leveling top of cylindrical mold after tag wires are inserted.

303F17.EPS

Figure 17 ◆ Laboratory compression-strength testing machine.

Step 6 After 24 hours have elapsed, the concrete specimens may be sent to a lab for curing. Their cylindrical molds are usually removed, then they are placed in warm, moist conditions to cure for the designated period (typically 28 days). Other specimens may be kept at the job site so that they can cure under actual job conditions. Molds kept at the job site are placed in a **curing box**. The cylindrical molds for these specimens are usually removed at the same time that the forms for the related wall, column, or slab are being removed. A batch of concrete may also be cured at both a lab and at the job site in order to compare the characteristics of specimens cured under ideal lab conditions versus those cured under actual conditions.

Step 7 Once the cylinder specimens have cured for the desired length of time, they are compression-tested on a machine (*Figure 17*) in accordance with *ASTM C39*.

7.0.0 ◆ ESTIMATING CONCRETE VOLUME

Estimating the volume of concrete needed for a job was briefly covered in *Carpentry Level One*. Because accurate measuring and estimating of concrete quantities is required to accomplish cost-effective concrete work, the subject is covered in more detail here. You will recall that most concrete structures can be divided into two or more rectangular, circular, or other shapes. The volume of concrete for each shape can then be individually estimated, and the results obtained for each shape added together to obtain the required total volume of concrete for the structure.

Blueprints for a project will provide the dimensions for the various portions of a concrete structure, and these dimensions are used to calculate the volume of concrete required for the structure. For reference purposes, *Appendix E* provides area or volume formulas for various geometric shapes and a table for conversion of inches to fractions of a foot or a decimal equivalent.

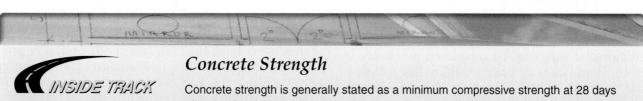

INSIDE TRACK

Concrete Strength

Concrete strength is generally stated as a minimum compressive strength at 28 days of curing for concrete in various structural elements. Compressive strength depends mainly on the type of cement-water ratio and aggregate quality. The most important is the cement-water ratio. Generally, the lower the cement-water ratio, the greater the compressive strength of the concrete. The 28-day compressive strength for standard mixes of commercial ready-mix concrete is typically in the range of 3,000 to 4,000 psi.

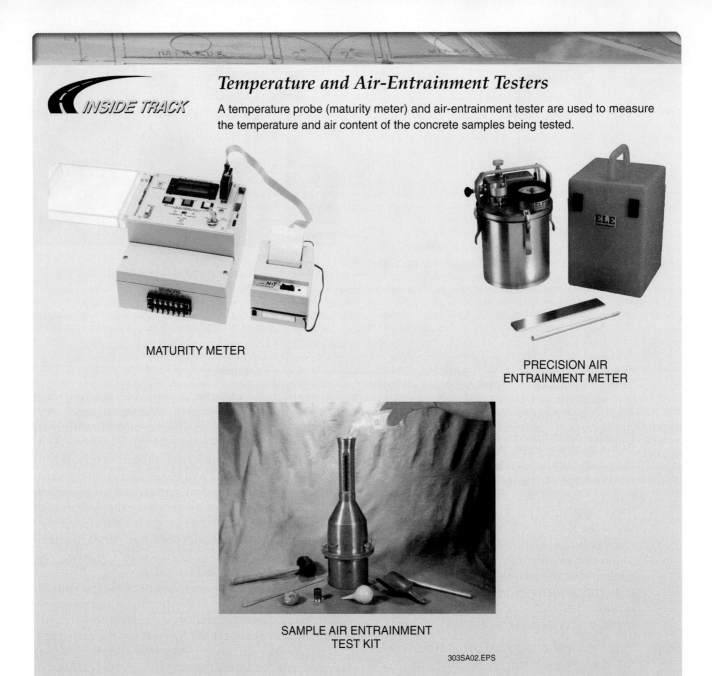

Temperature and Air-Entrainment Testers

A temperature probe (maturity meter) and air-entrainment tester are used to measure the temperature and air content of the concrete samples being tested.

MATURITY METER

PRECISION AIR
ENTRAINMENT METER

SAMPLE AIR ENTRAINMENT
TEST KIT

303SA02.EPS

7.1.0 Rectangular Volume Calculations

Determining the concrete volumes for rectangular structures can be done using concrete volume calculators, or they can be calculated manually by using formulas and concrete tables. Regardless of the method used, all require that the length, width, and thickness of the concrete rectangular structure be known. Normally, the dimensions used for the length and width (or height) of the structure are expressed in feet. Depending on the calculator or other method used, the thickness is expressed either in feet or inches.

7.1.1 Calculating Concrete Volume by Formula and Concrete Tables

Manually calculating rectangular concrete volume by formula and with concrete tables is described here first because both methods provide background information and tasks common to both manual and concrete calculator methods of calculation.

The formula method uses the following formula:

$$\text{Cubic yards of concrete (rounded up to next } \tfrac{1}{4} \text{ yard)} = \frac{\text{width or height (ft)} \times \text{length (ft)} \times \text{thickness (ft)}}{27 \text{ (cubic ft/yard)}}$$

To use the formula, all dimensions in inches must be converted to feet and/or fractions of a foot and then into a decimal equivalent. For example:

$$7" = \tfrac{7}{12}' \text{ or } 7 \div 12 = 0.58'$$
$$8" = \tfrac{8}{12}' \text{ or } \tfrac{2}{3}' \text{ or } 2 \div 3 = 0.66'$$
$$23" = \tfrac{23}{12}' \text{ or } 23 \div 12 = 1.92'$$

An example volume calculation using the formula method is given here to determine the amount of concrete required for the partial wall, footing, and floor slab plan shown in *Figure 18*.

Step 1 The entire footing and wall length must be determined. Since the wall is centered on the footing, the wall length is 8" less than the footing length. Taking the long side of the wall and footing gives us 25' in length. So that we won't double count the footing, we subtract the 2' of the footing

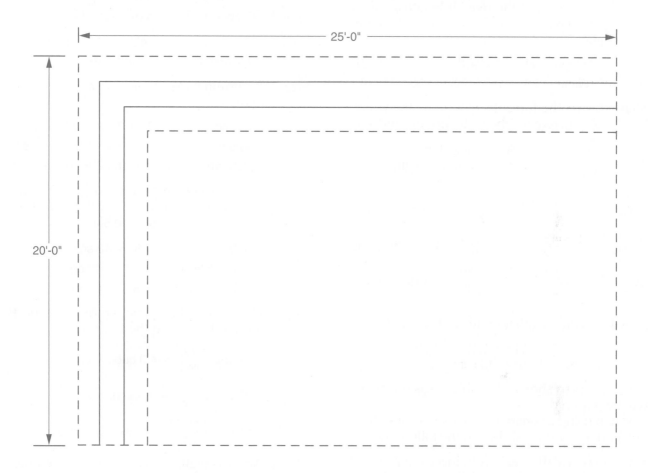

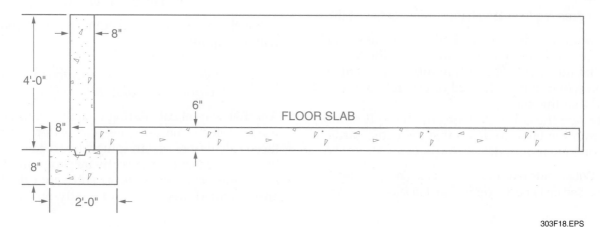

Figure 18 ◆ Partial wall, footing, and floor slab plan.

303F18.EPS

and wall from the other length, which is 20' to the outside corner of the footing. That gives us the following:

Footing/wall length = 25' + (20' − 2') = 43' each of wall and footing

Step 2 Determine the floor slab length and width. The slab overlaps the footing by 8", so it is 16" from the outside corner in both directions. That means that we can subtract 16" from each of the overall lengths, and we will have the length and width of the floor slab:

Length = 25' − 16" = 25' − 1.33' = 23.67'
Width = 20' − 16" = 20' − 1.33' = 18.67'

Step 3 Using the formula, determine the volume of concrete for the wall, footing, and slab:

$$\text{Volume} = \frac{\text{width or height (ft)} \times \text{length (ft)} \times \text{thickness (ft)}}{27 \text{ (cubic ft/yard)}}$$

$$\text{Wall} = \frac{4 \times 43 \times 0.67}{27} = \frac{115.24}{27} = 4.27 \text{ cubic yards}$$

$$\text{Footing} = \frac{2 \times 43 \times 0.67}{27} = \frac{57.62}{27} = 2.13 \text{ cubic yards}$$

$$\text{Slab} = \frac{18.67 \times 23.67 \times 0.5}{27} = \frac{221.0}{27} = 8.18 \text{ cubic yards}$$

Step 4 Add the wall, footing, and slab volumes:

4.27 + 2.13 + 8.18 = 14.58
rounded up to 15 cubic yards

For the plan shown, 15 cubic yards of concrete will be required.

When using a concrete table like the one shown in *Figure 19*, you must first do the following:

- Convert any dimensions in inches to feet and/or fractions of a foot and then into a decimal equivalent, then calculate the area:

Area (sq ft) = length (ft) × width or height (ft)

- Locate the desired thickness (in inches) in the table and note the sq ft number in the table for that thickness. The sq ft number represents the area that one cubic yard of concrete will cover at that thickness.
- Divide the calculated area by the sq ft number from the table to determine the cubic yards of concrete required.

$$\frac{\text{Cubic yards required}}{\text{(rounded up to next ¼ yard)}} = \frac{\text{area (in square feet)}}{\text{sq ft (number from table)}}$$

An example volume calculation using the concrete table is given here to determine the amount of concrete required for the partial wall, footing, and floor slab plan shown in *Figure 18*.

Step 1 The entire footing and wall length must be determined. Since the wall is centered on the footing, the wall length is the same as the footing length:

Footing/wall length = 25' + (20' − 2') = 43'

Step 2 Determine the area of the footing and wall:

Wall area = 4' × 43' = 172 sq ft
Footing area = 2' × 43' = 86 sq ft

Step 3 Determine the floor slab length, width, and area:

Length = 25' − 16" = 25' − 1.33' = 23.67'
Width = 20' − 16" = 20' − 1.33' = 18.67'
Slab area = 23.67' × 18.67' = 441.92 sq ft

Step 4 From the concrete table in *Figure 19*, determine the sq ft number for the thicknesses of the wall, footing, and slab:

Wall thickness = 8" = 40 sq ft
Footing thickness = 8" = 40 sq ft
Slab thickness = 6" = 54 sq ft

Step 5 Determine the cubic yards of concrete required by using the formula:

$$\text{Wall} = \frac{172}{40} = 4.3 \text{ cubic yards}$$

$$\text{Footing} = \frac{86}{40} = 2.15 \text{ cubic yards}$$

$$\text{Slab} = \frac{441.92}{54} = 8.18 \text{ cubic yards}$$

Step 6 Add the wall, footing, and slab volumes:

4.3 + 2.15 + 8.18 = 14.63
rounded up to 15 cubic yards

For the plan shown, 15 cubic yards of concrete will be required.

7.1.2 *Determining Concrete Volume Using a Concrete Calculator*

Another way of calculating concrete volume is to use an electronic concrete calculator. Some of these calculators are an integral part of construction-oriented computer software programs. Other easy-to-use concrete volume software calculators are provided free by most ready-mix concrete

ONE CUBIC YARD OF CONCRETE WILL PLACE:					
THICKNESS	SQ FT	THICKNESS	SQ FT	THICKNESS	SQ FT
1"	324	5"	65	9"	36
1¼"	259	5¼"	62	9¼"	35
1½"	216	5½"	59	9½"	34
1¾"	185	5¾"	56	9¾"	33
2"	162	6"	54	10"	32.5
2¼"	144	6¼"	52	10¼"	31.5
2½"	130	6½"	50	10½"	31
2¾"	118	6¾"	48	10¾"	30
3"	108	7"	46	11"	29.5
3¼"	100	7¼"	45	11¼"	29
3½"	93	7½"	43	11½"	28
3¾"	86	7¾"	42	11¾"	27.5
4"	81	8"	40	12"	27
4¼"	76	8¼"	39	15"	21.5
4½"	72	8½"	38	18"	18
4¾"	68	8¾"	37	24"	13.5

303F19.EPS

Figure 19 ◆ Portion of a typical concrete table.

suppliers on their websites. All of these calculators are basically the same. An example is shown in *Figure 20*. To use these calculators for rectangular volume calculations requires that you know the same dimensions (length, width or height, and thickness) for the walls, footing, and slabs that were needed to perform manual calculations by the formula or concrete table methods. Once the dimensions are known, you simply enter the width and length of the structure in feet and the thickness, either in feet or inches, into the calcula-

tor. Following this you click on the calculate button and read the answer expressed in the cubic yards required. *Figure 20* shows the calculated volume results for the same wall, footing, and slab structures shown in *Figure 18* and manually calculated above.

Handheld calculators like the one shown in *Figure 21* are also widely used. Calculation of concrete volume when using these devices is done in accordance with the calculator manufacturer's instructions.

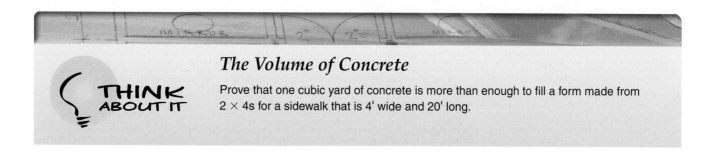

The Volume of Concrete

Prove that one cubic yard of concrete is more than enough to fill a form made from 2 × 4s for a sidewalk that is 4' wide and 20' long.

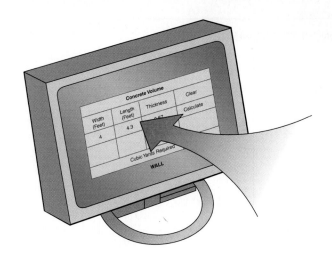

Concrete Volume			
Width (Feet)	Length (Feet)	Thickness	Clear
4	4.3	0.67	Calculate
		○ Inches ● Feet	
Cubic Yards Required			4.26815

WALL

Concrete Volume			
Width (Feet)	Length (Feet)	Thickness	Clear
2	43	0.67	Calculate
		○ Inches ● Feet	
Cubic Yards Required			2.13407

FOOTING

Concrete Volume			
Width (Feet)	Length (Feet)	Thickness	Clear
18.67	23.67	0.5	Calculate
		○ Inches ● Feet	
Cubic Yards Required			8.18368

SLAB

Concrete Volume		
Height (Feet)	Diameter (Inches)	Clear
30	48	Calculate
Cubic Yards Required		13.9626

COLUMN

303F20.EPS

Figure 20 ◆ Website concrete volume calculator.

Slide Rule Concrete Calculators

Before the widespread use of electronic calculators to calculate concrete volume, slide rule concrete calculators typical of the one shown here were often used. Their use was limited to volume calculations greater than one-half cubic yard. Also, the results of the calculator had to be estimated by sight between rule marks, which made the results subject to some variation.

Using the calculator requires:

- Location of the thickness in inches of the rectangular object on Scale A and the width (or height) in feet on Scale B.
- Moving the sliding part of the calculator to align the desired thickness value on Scale A with the desired width (or height) value on Scale B.
- Locating the length of the object on Scale C and reading the required concrete volume in cubic yards on Scale D directly opposite the length on Scale C.

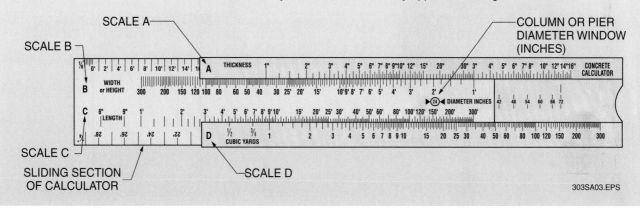

303SA03.EPS

7.2.0 Circular Concrete Volume Calculations

The volume of concrete required for a circular column or pier can be calculated by using the following formula:

$$\text{Cubic yards of concrete} = \frac{\pi \times \text{radius}^2 \text{ (sq ft)} \times \text{height (ft)}}{27 \text{ (cubic ft/yard)}}$$

Where:

$\pi = 3.14$

Radius = diameter (ft) of column ÷ 2

Inches are expressed as fractions or decimal equivalents

An example circular volume calculation is given here to determine the volume of concrete required for the circular column plan shown in *Figure 22*.

Step 1 Determine the radius of the column:

$$4' \div 2 = 2.0'$$

Step 2 Calculate the volume using the formula:

$$\text{Cubic yards of concrete} = \frac{\pi \times \text{radius}^2 \text{ (sq ft)} \times \text{height (ft)}}{27 \text{ (cubic ft/yard)}}$$

$$\text{Column} = \frac{3.14 \times (2)^2 \times 30}{27} = \frac{376.8}{27} = \frac{13.96 \text{ rounded}}{\text{up to 14 cubic yards}}$$

For the plan shown, 14 cubic yards of concrete will be required.

As with rectangular volume measurements, the same calculation for our example column can be made using an electronic concrete calculator. The result for our example column using an online calculator is shown in *Figure 20*. Note that the dimension for the column diameter is entered in inches rather than feet when using this calculator.

303F21.EPS

Figure 21 ◆ Typical handheld electronic concrete calculator.

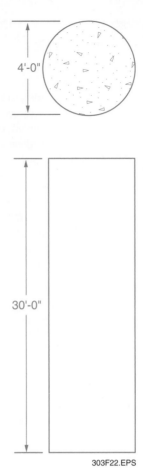

4'-0"

30'-0"

303F22.EPS

Figure 22 ◆ Typical circular column plan.

NOTE

When using any of the three methods for calculating the volume of concrete needed for a job, a factor for waste must be taken into consideration. Typically, about 5 percent of the calculated volume is added to account for waste. For larger jobs, experienced carpenters order the required number of full truckloads (typically 12 cubic yards per load), then specify the required amount needed for the last truckload once the total volume of concrete needed is known.

Summary

Concrete consists of portland cement, fine aggregates, coarse aggregates, and water. These ingredients are mixed in specific proportions as defined by engineers for each project. Many concrete mixtures also contain admixtures. There are many kinds of admixtures used to modify the properties of concrete. For example, they can accelerate or retard the setting-up time of concrete to compensate for weather conditions. Special care must be taken in the use of water, because adding water to a mixture can reduce its strength. All concrete is not the same. Over the years, engineers have developed many different types of concrete for specific applications. Concrete must be tested as it is delivered to the job site in order to make sure that it meets the project specifications. Testing methods include the slump test and compression test.

Notes

Review Questions

1. The basic materials used to make concrete are _____.
   a. portland cement, water, and admixtures
   b. sand, water, and aggregates
   c. aggregates, water, and portland cement
   d. admixtures, aggregates, and water

2. In the United States a bag of portland cement weighs _____ pounds.
   a. 85
   b. 94
   c. 100
   d. 105

3. The strength and initial set of concrete during the first seven days is caused mainly by the hydration of the _____ in the portland cement.
   a. tricalcium silicate
   b. tricalcium aluminate
   c. tetracalcium aluminoferrite
   d. dicalcium silicate

4. Low-heat cement is used when _____.
   a. low placement temperatures are encountered
   b. forms must be removed as soon as possible
   c. high ground sulfate concentrations are encountered
   d. it is necessary to prevent expansion and cracking

5. Air-entraining cement is used to _____.
   a. increase freezing/thawing resistance
   b. increase strength
   c. increase sulfate resistance
   d. decrease workability

6. Aggregates make up about _____ percent of the volume of concrete.
   a. 15 to 20
   b. 30 to 40
   c. 40 to 50
   d. 60 to 80

7. A cubic foot of normal concrete using fine and coarse aggregate weighs _____ pounds.
   a. 130 to 150
   b. 140 to 160
   c. 150 to 170
   d. 160 to 180

8. Water-reducing admixtures are used in concrete to _____.
   a. decrease workability
   b. decrease curing time
   c. increase strength
   d. increase resistance to freezing/thawing

9. High-strength concrete is defined as concrete with a compressive strength above _____ psi.
   a. 4,000
   b. 5,400
   c. 6,000
   d. 7,000

10. Wet curing of concrete can be accomplished with _____.
    a. curing compounds
    b. curing paper
    c. plastic sheeting
    d. cotton mats

11. Slump testing of concrete is described in _____.
    a. *ASTM C31*
    b. *ASTM C78*
    c. *ASTM C143*
    d. *ASTM C157*

12. When collecting plastic concrete samples for testing, aggregates over _____ must be wet-sieved out.
    a. 1½"
    b. 1¾"
    c. 2¼"
    d. 2½"

13. A slump test, from start to finish, should be accomplished within _____ minutes.
    a. 1½
    b. 2⅛
    c. 2¼
    d. 2½

14. Cylindrical molds for strength testing must comply with _____.
    a. *ASTM C290*
    b. *ASTM C403*
    c. *ASTM C470*
    d. *ASTM C666*

15. When calculated using the formula method, the volume of concrete needed for a slab having a width of 15', a length of 18', and a thickness of 6" is _____ cubic yards.
    a. 4
    b. 5
    c. 6
    d. 7

Trade Terms
Introduced in This Module

American Concrete Institute (ACI): An organization that studies and furthers the use of concrete.

Air-entraining cement: A cement with an added agent that creates many tiny air bubbles when water is added and the concrete is mixed. This improves both the workability of the concrete and its resistance to freezing and thawing, but it may also reduce the final strength of the concrete.

Bleed water: A form of segregation in which some of the water in a mix tends to rise to the surface of freshly placed concrete.

Clinker: The material that is produced in a cement kiln after burning. Clinkers are dark, porous nodules that are ground with a small amount of gypsum to make cement.

Compressive strength: The measured resistance of a concrete specimen to axial loading, expressed as pounds per square inch (psi), of cross-sectional area. The maximum compressive stress that the concrete is capable of sustaining.

Cured concrete: Concrete that has hardened and gained its structural strength.

Curing box: An insulated chest designed to maintain concrete test samples at a constant temperature and humidity.

Ettringite: Rod-like crystals produced from the reaction of gypsum and tricalcium aluminate (C_3A) in the early stages of cement hydration that act as a coating over the surfaces of cement grains while concrete is in the plastic stage. This reaction allows for normal setting. Without ettringite, concrete would set and harden almost instantaneously.

Green concrete: Concrete that has hardened but has not yet gained its structural strength.

Heat of hydration: The heat generated when portland cement is mixed with water. It is the result of exothermic chemical reaction between cement and water. Generation of this heat raises the temperature of concrete.

Hydration: The catalytic action water has in transforming the chemicals in portland cement into a hard solid. The water interacts with the chemicals to form calcium silicate hydrate gel.

Mass concrete: Concrete used in dams, spillways, and other large structures. It is basically the same as normal concrete except that aggregate up to 6" or more in diameter is used. Admixtures such as water-reducing/water-retarding agents and pozzolans are widely used to decrease heat and cement content and to increase strength.

Plastic concrete: Concrete when it is first mixed and is in a semiliquid and moldable state.

Post-stressed concrete: Concrete placed around steel reinforcement such as steel rods or cables that are isolated from contact with the concrete by encasement and/or a lubricant. After the concrete has cured, tension is applied to the rods or cables to provide great structural strength.

Pozzolans: A siliceous or siliceous and aluminous mineral admixture that in itself has little or no cementing property. Pozzolans are not cements, but when the particles are very fine and mixed with the calcium hydroxide in concrete and water, they behave like cement, and speed the setting and curing of concrete.

Pre-stressed concrete: Concrete that is placed around pre-tensioned reinforcement steel in a casting bed. When the concrete has cured, the casting bed is removed and the pre-stressed reinforcement applies compression to the concrete that results in great structural strength. Pre-stressed concrete must never be cut without consulting a structural engineer.

Reinforced concrete: Concrete that has been placed around some type of steel reinforcement material. After the concrete cures, the reinforcement provides greater tensile and shear strength for the concrete. Almost all concrete is reinforced in some manner.

Objectives

When you have completed this module, you will be able to do the following:

1. Describe the applications of reinforcing bars, the uses of reinforced structural concrete, and the basic processes involved in placing reinforcing bars.
2. Recognize and identify the bar bends standardized by the American Concrete Institute (ACI).
3. Read and interpret bar lists and describe the information found on a bar list.
4. List the types of ties used in securing reinforcing bars.
5. State the tolerances allowed in the fabrication of reinforcing bars.
6. Demonstrate the proper use of common ties for reinforcing bars.
7. Describe methods by which reinforcing bars may be cut and bent in the field.
8. Use the tools and equipment needed for installing reinforcing bars.
9. Safely use selected tools and equipment to cut, bend, and install reinforcing materials.
10. Explain the necessity of concrete cover in placing reinforcing bars.
11. Explain and demonstrate how to place bars in walls, columns, beams, girders, joists, and slabs.
12. Identify lapped splices.

Trade Terms

Abutment	Inserts
Band	Lapped splice
Bar list	Light bending
Beam	Near face
Bent	Pile cap
Bundle of bars	Pitch
Caissons	Placing drawings
Column	Reinforced concrete
Column horses	Retaining wall
Column spirals	Schedule
Column ties	Simple beam
Concrete cover	Single-curtain wall
Contact splice	Sleeve
Continuous beam	Span
CRSI	Special bending
Double-curtain wall	Staggered splices
Dowel	Stirrups
Far face	Strips
Flat slab	Support bars
Girder	Temperature bars
Header	Template
Heavy bending	Tie
Hickey bar	Tie wire
Hook	Weep hole

CARPENTRY LEVEL THREE

27310-07 Tilt-Up Wall Systems	
27309-07 Horizontal Formwork	
27308-07 Vertical Formwork	F
27307-07 Foundations and Slab-on-Grade	O
27306-07 Trenching and Excavating	R
27305-07 Handling and Placing Concrete	M
27304-07 Reinforcing Concrete	S
27303-07 Properties of Concrete	
27302-07 Rigging Practices	
27301-07 Rigging Equipment	

CARPENTRY FRAMING & FINISHING

CARPENTRY FUNDAMENTALS

CORE CURRICULUM:
Introductory Craft Skills

304CMAP.EPS

Required Trainee Materials

1. Pencil and paper
2. Appropriate personal protective equipment
3. A copy of American Society for Testing and Materials (ASTM) standards
4. A copy of ACI standards

Before you begin this module, it is recommended that you successfully complete *Core Curriculum; Carpentry Fundamentals Level One; Carpentry Framing and Finishing Level Two;* and *Carpentry Forms Level Three,* Modules 27301-07 through 27303-07.

1.0.0 ◆ INTRODUCTION

Concrete is arguably our most important construction material. Properly installed and reinforced, it can safely serve as the supporting structures for large buildings, bridges, roads, and dams. Without proper reinforcing, however, concrete structures are accidents waiting to happen. Skilled, knowledgeable workers are required to select, place, and tie steel reinforcing rods (rebar) and welded wire mesh in concrete formwork for foundations, walls, floors, beams, columns, and pilings.

Concrete has good compressive strength, but it is relatively weak in tension or if subjected to lateral or shearing forces. Many kinds of proprietary reinforcement have been used for concrete in the past. Today, steel is generally the material used. This is because it has nearly the same temperature expansion and contraction rate as concrete. Additionally, modern reinforcement conforms to ASTM standards that govern both its form and the types of steel used. As an alternative to steel reinforcement, fibers made from steel, fiberglass, or plastics such as nylon are sometimes added to concrete mixes to provide reinforcement.

This module presents the basics of reinforcing materials, along with various tasks related to placing reinforcing materials. There are many special trade terms used in this area of construction. Study the definitions of these trade terms, located in the glossary, and refer to them often while reading this module.

2.0.0 ◆ OVERVIEW OF REINFORCED CONCRETE

Concrete is a mixture of cement, fine aggregate (sand), coarse aggregate (stone), water, and possibly one or more admixtures. By varying the proportions of the mixture, concrete with different compression strengths can be obtained. These strengths typically vary from about 2,000 to 6,000 pounds per square inch (psi). Concrete is also available in higher strengths. Concrete will usually set firm in a matter of hours and will typically attain design strength in about 28 days.

INSIDE TRACK

Reinforcing Bars

These are bundles of reinforcing bars used to reinforce concrete.

304SA01.EPS

Reinforced concrete is a combination of concrete and steel. It combines the compression resistance of concrete with the tension (or pull) resistance of steel.

The adhesion of concrete to the surface of steel reinforcing bars and/or wire mesh and the resistance provided by the bar deformation, or lugs, keep the bars from slipping through the concrete. It makes the two materials act as one. This adhesion is called the concrete bond.

One of the primary purposes of reinforcing steel is to control cracking caused by tension and shear loads on the concrete, as well as by expansion and contraction due to temperature changes and concrete shrinkage. Concrete has a high compressive strength, but a low tensile strength, so shrinking of concrete as it cures, along with bending or shear forces, can cause cracking. To avoid this, concrete is reinforced with steel, which has a very high tensile strength, so that in combination the final product can resist forces from any direction. Although some cracking is inevitable, the use of reinforcing steel results in small cracks, rather than large ones. Unreinforced concrete is likely to develop large cracks, which can lead to failure of the concrete.

In some instances, reinforcing steel is used strictly to control cracking in a slab, and does not provide any structural support. Wire mesh reinforcing is often used for this purpose, but #3 rebar on 12" centers may be used instead. In that application, the rebar is referred to as temperature steel.

Only the correct amount and type of reinforcement, placed in the correct locations, can serve the intended purpose. Concrete reinforcement must always be selected and placed according to the engineer's drawings and specifications.

2.1.0 Resistance of Forces by Reinforcing Bars

Reinforcing bars are most effectively used in the following applications:

- *Simple beams* (slabs, joists, and **girders**) – *Figure 1* shows that the top half of the **beam** is in compression and the bottom half is in tension, so the steel is placed in the lower half far enough from the bottom to achieve the proper amount of **concrete cover** (discussed later). To resist diagonal tension, **stirrups** are placed vertically across the beam, as shown in *Figure 2*. The stirrups are spaced more closely near the support and farther apart near the middle of the **span**.

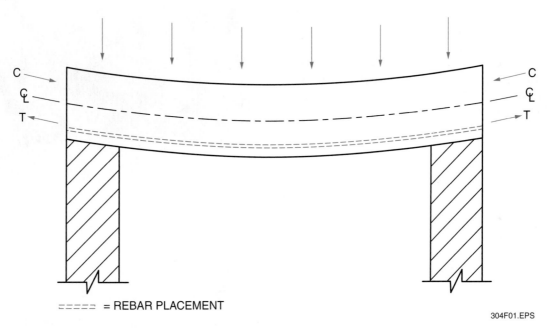

===== = REBAR PLACEMENT

304F01.EPS

Figure 1 ◆ Rebar placement.

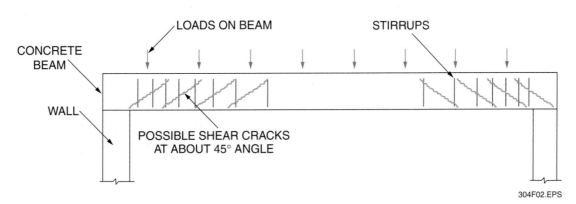

304F02.EPS

Figure 2 ◆ Stirrup placement.

- *Continuous beams over more than one span* – These are beams that deflect downward between supports and have an upward thrust over the supports. Steel is required at the bottom between supports and at the top over supports, as shown in *Figure 3*.
- *Overhang, interior support, and cantilever beams* – Tension bars must be placed in the top of the overhang and cantilever and carried back into the main span or support, as shown in *Figure 4*.
- *Cantilever retaining walls* – Main bars are required on the side toward the earth. See *Figure 5*.

NOTE

The deflection shown in *Figures 1*, *3*, and *4* has been exaggerated for illustration purposes.

- *Combined footings* – These carry column loads at two or more points. Straight bars are placed near the top of the slab between the columns. Truss bars are placed under the column ends. Bottom cross bars prevent curling of the concrete. See *Figure 6*.

- *Rectangular footings* – Bars are placed in two directions (at right angles to each other) and located a prescribed distance from the bottom of the footing, as shown in *Figure 7*. (Note that the deflection is exaggerated.)

INSIDE TRACK

Welded-Wire Fabric Mesh

These are rolls of welded-wire fabric mesh used to reinforce concrete.

304SA02.EPS

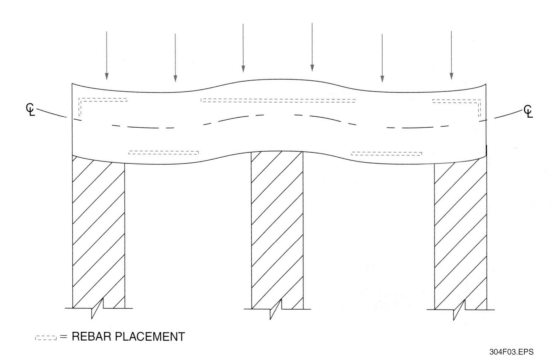

= REBAR PLACEMENT

304F03.EPS

Figure 3 ◆ Continuous beam.

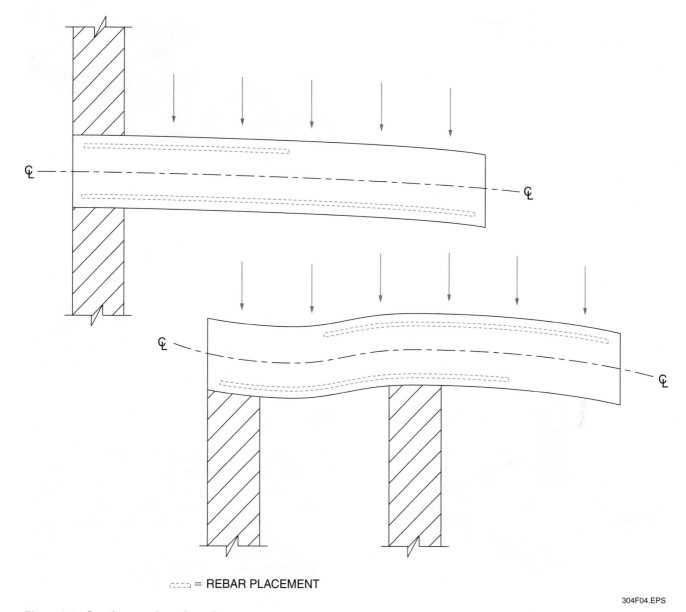

= REBAR PLACEMENT

304F04.EPS

Figure 4 ◆ Cantilever and overhang beams.

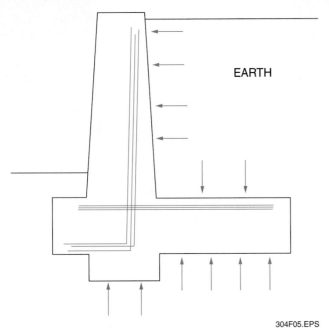

EARTH

Figure 5 ◆ Cantilever wall.

304F05.EPS

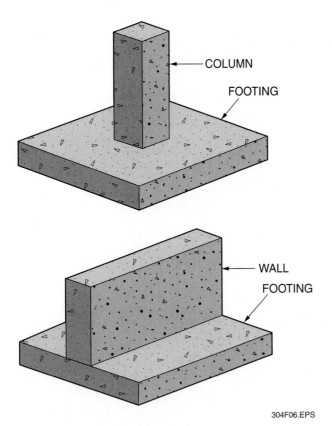

COLUMN

FOOTING

WALL

FOOTING

304F06.EPS

Figure 6 ◆ Combined footings.

- *Inside corners* – Reinforcing bars extend past the corner from each direction and are **hooked** for anchorage, if necessary.
- *Stairs and landings* – Bars continue across the tension point and are bent into the stair and landing slabs. See *Figure 8*.

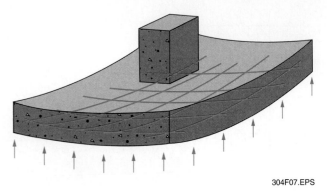

304F07.EPS

Figure 7 ◆ Rectangular footing.

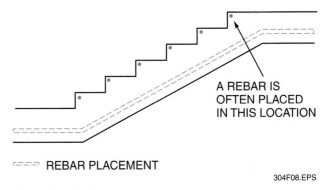

A REBAR IS OFTEN PLACED IN THIS LOCATION

⌐˭˭˭˭ REBAR PLACEMENT

304F08.EPS

Figure 8 ◆ Stairway.

- *Columns* – Reinforcing steel for compression forces is most commonly used in columns. If concrete alone were used, the column height would be very limited. Reinforcing bars are about 20 times stronger than an equivalent area of concrete, so they are used to carry part of the column load. Vertical column bars are in compression and will buckle if not restrained. **Column ties** (*Figure 9*) or **column spirals** act to prevent this.

2.2.0 Use of Reinforced Structural Concrete

Reinforced structural concrete has various applications in multistory building frames and floors, walls, shell roofs, folded plates, bridges, and prestressed or precast elements of all types. The architectural expression of form combined with functional design can be readily achieved with structural reinforced concrete. Architects, engineers, and contractors recognize that there are inherent economic and production values in the use of reinforced structural concrete, as evidenced by the many structures in which it is used.

2.3.0 Buildings

Building frames and floors of reinforced concrete are constructed using the joist floor depicted in

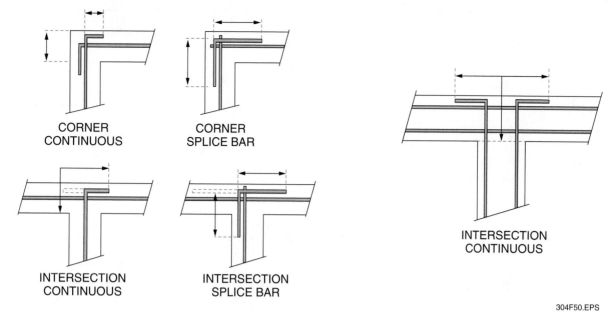

CORNER CONTINUOUS

CORNER SPLICE BAR

INTERSECTION CONTINUOUS

INTERSECTION CONTINUOUS

INTERSECTION SPLICE BAR

304F50.EPS

Figure 50 ◆ Corner details.

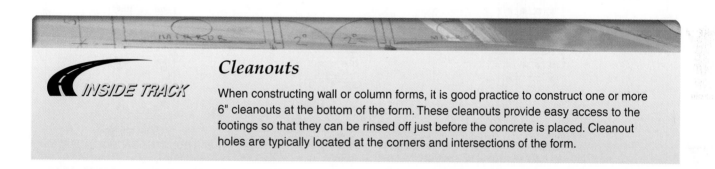

Cleanouts

When constructing wall or column forms, it is good practice to construct one or more 6" cleanouts at the bottom of the form. These cleanouts provide easy access to the footings so that they can be rinsed off just before the concrete is placed. Cleanout holes are typically located at the corners and intersections of the form.

6.5.1 Column Ties

The bands wrapped around the vertical bars are called column ties. They must be placed outside the vertical bars. These ties can be square, rectangular, U-shaped, circular, or any other shape designated by the engineers. Standards have been developed concerning the placing of column ties. *Figure 51* shows the standard placing of column ties in columns containing an even number of vertical bars. The information in *Figure 51* applies to those cages that are either preassembled or erected in place on freestanding, butt-spliced vertical bars.

Figure 52 shows the standard placing of column ties for lap-spliced preassembled cages only. The dotted lines indicated in *Figure 52* for the 6-, 8-, and 10-bar columns show how the column ties are to be tied if the distance between the centers of the bars is over 6".

Each pattern consists of an outside closed tie with pairs of U-shaped bars that are lap-spliced and hooked at each end.

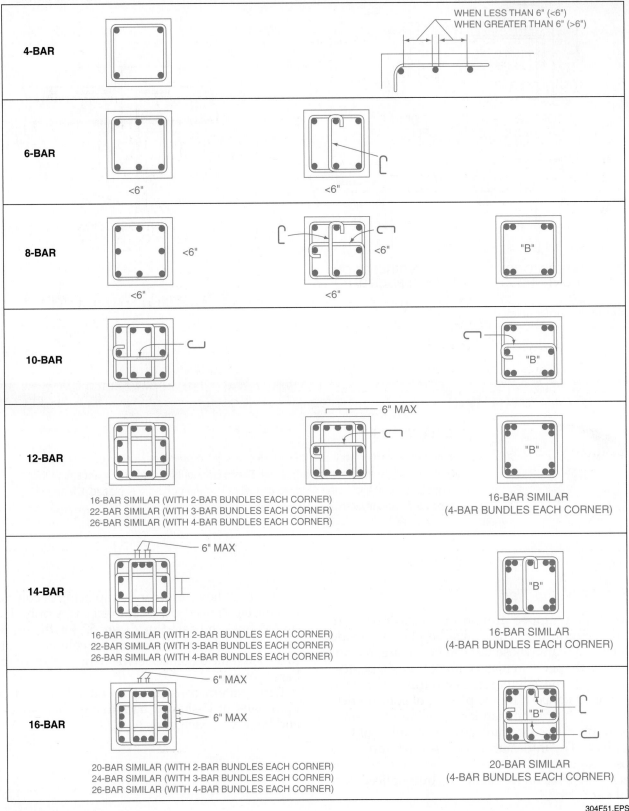

Figure 51 ◆ Standing column ties.

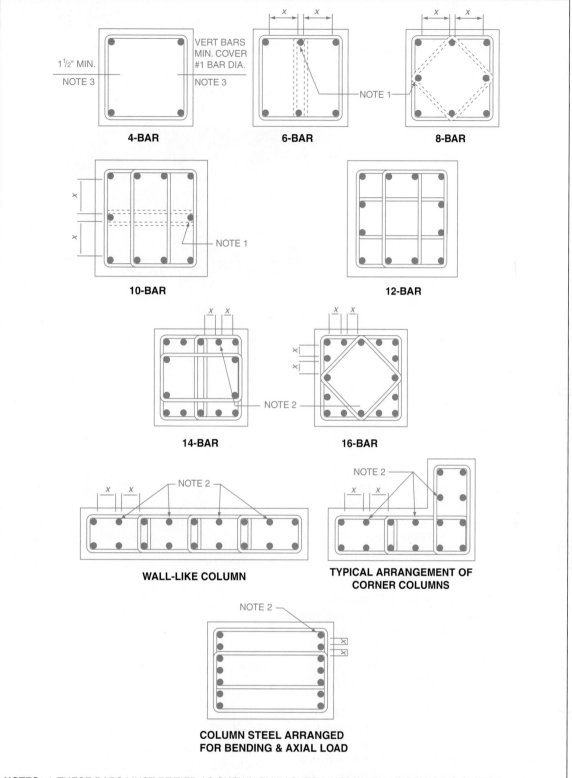

NOTES: 1. THESE BARS MUST BE TIED AS SHOWN BY DASHED LINES WHEN *x* DISTANCE IS OVER 6".

2. THESE BARS NEED NOT BE TIED WHEN *x* DISTANCE EQUALS 6" OR LESS.

3. APPLICABLE TO ALL TIED COLUMNS.

A DIFFERENT PATTERN OF TIES MAY BE SUBSTITUTED PROVIDED THAT DETAILS OF THE REQUIREMENTS ARE SHOWN ON THE CONTRACT DRAWINGS.

* APPLICABLE ONLY FOR LAP-SPLICED PREASSEMBLED CAGES.

304F52.EPS

Figure 52 ◆ Closed column ties.

Reinforcing Steel Framework

This is an example of preassembled reinforcing steel framework for a column that will eventually be raised into place. For ease of construction, rebar is often installed horizontally and then raised and placed into forms.

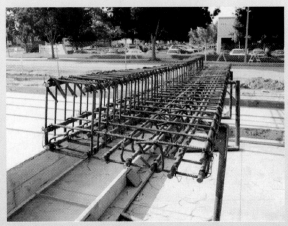

304SA11.EPS

6.5.2 Tying Columns

The usual procedure for tying preassembled reinforcing column steel is to first lay out all the verticals for one side across supports, called **column horses**, as shown in *Figure 53*. Then the vertical column ties are laid out on the verticals and spaced according to the placing drawings. It is generally acceptable to alternate the position of the hooks of the column ties when placing them in sets. The column ties are then wired to the vertical bars using a saddle tie or a wrap-and-saddle tie for heavy bars. The remaining vertical bars are put in place and wired to the column ties. When tying columns, it is extremely important to make sure all vertical bars are lined up and even on the bottom end so that all bars of the finished column cage will sit firmly on the footing. On 4- and 6-bar columns, every tie should be wired to every vertical at every intersection to achieve good stability. On columns of 67 bars or more, tie 100 percent of the column-corner bars using saddle ties.

Large square or rectangular units may require diagonal wire bracing for greater stability. The bracing should be twisted with pliers until a sufficient amount of tension is obtained.

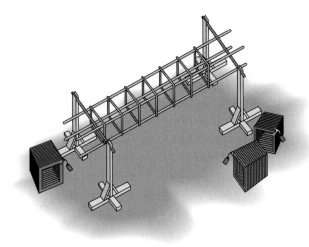

304F53.EPS

Figure 53 ◆ Column horse.

6.5.3 Spirals

In terms of strength, a column using spirals is generally stronger than a column using square or rectangular column ties.

Spirals are made of smooth bar or wire shaped like a coil spring. They have spacers attached on opposite sides that keep the turns of the spiral at equal distances. Center-to-center spacing of the turns of a spiral is known as pitch.

Spirals are usually shipped collapsed and must be opened or knocked down at the job site prior to assembly. They should be broken (that is, opened up), straightened, and bent over flat in the opposite direction to make sure they remain straight. After this is done, the spacers should be arranged to provide equal pitch around the spiral column.

To preassemble spirals, two vertical bars are placed inside the spiral and supported at either end by column horses. See *Figure 54*. These bars should be flush with one end of the spiral. This allows the bars at the other end to serve as dowels. After two bars are placed, the remaining number of verticals called for by the placing drawings are inserted and spaced according to the specifications. The bars are then wired to the spiral to achieve the necessary stability and rigidity.

6.5.4 Column Supports

Columns should be supported at three or four points, if possible. The supports should be placed as near to the bottom, midsection, and top of the column as possible. Columns may be supported with nails driven into the inside of the forms in much the same way nails are used to support wall reinforcing. However, precast concrete blocks with embedded tie wires are more commonly used.

If precast blocks are used, they should be wired to the column at intersections of the column ties and vertical bars. This will prevent the blocks from spinning when the column is lowered into place within the form.

6.6.0 Placing Bars in Beams and Girders

There is no standard sequence that can be listed concerning the placing of bars in beams and girders due to the individual differences in beam height and bar arrangement in any given structure. This section is intended to provide a general overview of bar placing methods and sequences. As in all steel reinforcing work, the placing drawings will dictate the best sequence. They must be studied carefully so that an efficient plan of placing may be developed.

A beam is a horizontal structural member used to carry loads from a floor to columns, walls, and girders. A girder is a principal beam. The main difference between the two is that beams support other parts of a structure, while girders support beams. This difference becomes important when placing reinforcing steel in beams and girders because it affects the sequence of bar placing.

In general, girders will be lower than the beams they support, so all bottom horizontal bars, truss bars, and stirrups must be placed in girders before any reinforcement is placed in beams. The actual placing procedures, however, are similar for both beams and girders. The placing of reinforcing steel in beams and girders begins after column verticals are positioned and concrete has been poured to the bottom of the lowest beam or girder. Steel is generally placed from bottom to top; that is, first in girders, then in beams, and, finally, in slabs and joists. This sequence usually minimizes the need to thread bars under one another at the points of intersection.

6.6.1 Placing Bars in Beams

Figure 55 illustrates the general procedure for placing reinforcing steel in beams within the formwork. To place reinforcing steel in beams, proceed as follows:

Step 1 The beam bolsters are placed in the forms on centers not to exceed 5'.

Step 2 The stirrups and stirrup **support bars** are then placed in the forms. The forms should be marked with the proper spacing as found in the placing drawings.

Step 3 The bottom straight bars are placed next. In order to prevent these bars from moving during the concrete pour, they are often wired to the beam bolsters.

Step 4 If more than one layer of bars is required, the upper beam bolsters or bar separators are placed in the forms.

Step 5 The truss bars are placed last. A truss bar is a bar that has been bent in such a way that it serves as both top and bottom reinforcement. If truss bars are used in beams that require reinforcing placed in two layers, the truss bars should be placed directly over those in the lower layer, not in the spaces between the bars.

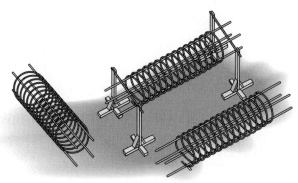

304F54.EPS

Figure 54 ◆ Spirals.

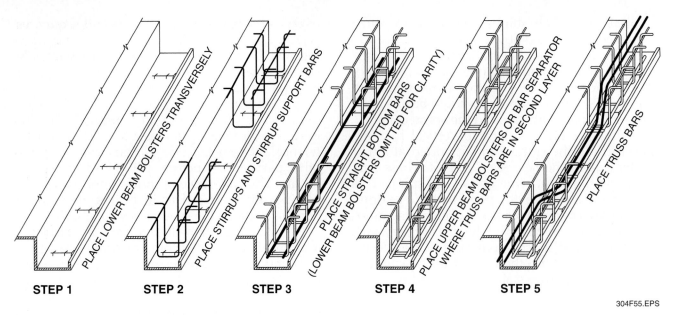

STEP 1 — PLACE LOWER BEAM BOLSTERS TRANSVERSELY

STEP 2 — PLACE STIRRUPS AND STIRRUP SUPPORT BARS

STEP 3 — PLACE STRAIGHT BOTTOM BARS (LOWER BEAM BOLSTERS OMITTED FOR CLARITY)

STEP 4 — PLACE UPPER BEAM BOLSTERS OR BAR SEPARATOR WHERE TRUSS BARS ARE IN SECOND LAYER

STEP 5 — PLACE TRUSS BARS

304F55.EPS

Figure 55 ◆ Beam placing sequence.

The reinforcing steel for beams and girders may also be preassembled. The sequence is usually as follows:

Step 1 Two straight bars are used as templates and marked with keel (marking crayon) or soapstone using the spacings found on the placing drawings.

Step 2 The template bars are placed on column horses.

Step 3 Stirrups are placed on the marks and tied in place using saddle ties.

Step 4 A side bar is tied to the stirrups.

Step 5 At this point, the beam may be taken off the column horses and placed flat on the deck or ground. Diagonal wire braces may be tied to it to provide added rigidity.

Step 6 The bars may then be placed into the form and the bottom layers of reinforcing may be added.

6.6.2 Closed Ties

Occasionally, the placing drawings will require closed ties instead of open, U-shaped stirrups. See *Figure 56*. Closed ties may be one piece with hooks in a corner or two pieces, known as cap ties, as shown in *Figure 57*.

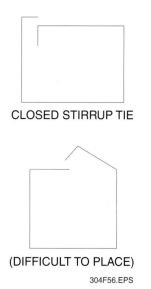

CLOSED STIRRUP TIE

(DIFFICULT TO PLACE)

304F56.EPS

Figure 56 ◆ Closed stirrup.

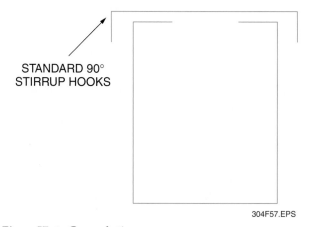

STANDARD 90°
STIRRUP HOOKS

304F57.EPS

Figure 57 ◆ Capped stirrup.

The easier tie to use is, of course, the cap tie, because the bottom piece can be placed in the same way as a stirrup. After all other bars have been placed, the top piece of the cap tie may be placed and wired to the lower piece. If the drawings call for one-piece closed ties, these ties must be used. They can sometimes be slipped into place over the lengthwise bars. Usually, however, they must be sprung open enough so that they can be worked around the bars running lengthwise. This tends to twist the reinforcing steel out of shape and is also time consuming.

6.6.3 *Placing Bars in Joists*

A joist is a small beam that is placed parallel between the main beams in floor construction. When joists are joined at the top to make a continuous structure, this structure is called a joist slab. Joist slabs are used in situations where high loads are anticipated.

Placing reinforcing steel in joists begins when all the beam reinforcement has been placed. In general, the sequence for placing reinforcing steel in joists is as follows:

Step 1 Place joist chairs in the form, beginning 1" from the edge of each support. If possible, joist chairs should be spaced as close as 5', or as specified.

Step 2 Place the straight bottom bars on the joist chairs. If necessary, thread the bars between the beam stirrups and under the top beam bar. The bottom bars must extend into the supports at each end according to the specifications found in the placing drawings.

Step 3 Place the truss bars on the joist chairs next to the straight bottom bars. The bent-up ends of the truss bars must cross over all top bars in the beam and extend into the adjoining section by the amount required by the placing drawings. If no truss bars are required, two bottom straight bars are generally used. Likewise, one or two top bars are generally extended into the adjoining section. The extended ends of the truss bars or straight bars are supported on individual chairs placed on support bars. They may also rest on upper-joist chairs. The placing drawings will indicate the proper method of support.

Step 4 Place the distribution ribs next in one or two lines. These are also called continuous **header** joists or bridging ribs. They extend the full length of the joist bay, are as deep as the joists, and are placed at right angles to the main joists. They provide lateral bracing for long spans of joists. Generally, there will be one rib placed at mid-span for spans ranging from 18' to 24'. Bars in these ribs are usually shown on the floor joist plans.

Step 5 Place the **temperature bars** last. Their purpose is to minimize cracks due to changes in temperature and the normal shrinkage of concrete. Temperature bars are either #3 bars or welded-wire fabric. If welded-wire fabric is used, it should be unrolled so that it arches upward and then bends straight. Welded-wire fabric is laid across the joists.

6.6.4 *Placing Bars in Slabs*

According to the direction of the main reinforcing run, slabs can be classified into two types. As its name indicates, a one-way slab contains reinforcement that runs in one direction between supports. A two-way slab contains reinforcement that runs in two directions between supports.

Reinforcement in one-way slabs consists of alternating straight bars and truss bars, or straight top and bottom bars running in one direction (*Figure 58*). Temperature bars are placed at right angles to the main reinforcing bars. Reinforcement is placed in one-way slabs in the same direction as the slab distributes the load applied to it.

The general procedure for placing and tying reinforcing steel in one-way slabs with straight bars and truss bars is as follows:

Step 1 Place slab bolsters so that they will lie at right angles to the main reinforcing. The placing drawings provide the proper spacing.

Step 2 Place main reinforcing according to the placing drawings. Each group of steel is tied in place as it is set.

Step 3 Place high chairs at right angles to the main reinforcing.

Step 4 Place temperature bars at right angles to the main reinforcing.

Step 5 Place truss bars on high chairs. Ensure the truss bars are parallel with the main reinforcing.

Reinforcement is placed in a two-way slab in the same direction as the slab distributes the load applied to it. See *Figure 59*. The reinforcement usually consists of straight and truss bars or straight top and bottom bars arranged in **strips** called column strips and middle strips.

The width of each strip is generally one-half the distance between the centers of the columns. Column strips usually receive more reinforcement than middle strips. A proper placing sequence

must be followed to avoid threading the bars. Study the placing drawings very closely.

A general sequence for placing reinforcing steel in a two-way **flat slab** with straight and truss bars is as follows:

Step 1 Place continuous lines of slab bolsters in an east-west direction. Proper spacing is found on the placing drawings.

Step 2 Place the required lengths of slab bolsters in the east-west column strips at right angles to the slab.

Step 3 Place bottom straight bars running north-south in column and middle strips.

Step 4 Place bottom straight bars running east-west in column strips.

Step 5 Place three rows of #4 support bars on high chairs in an east-west direction at the head of each column. Tie the middle support bar to the column verticals.

Step 6 Place truss bars running north-south in column strips.

Step 7 Place straight top bars. These bars are usually placed within the bend-down point of the truss bars running east-west.

Step 8 Place truss bars running east-west in column strips. Usually, the east-west truss bars that rest upon the north-south, straight, middle-strip, and bottom bars are tilted sideways so that they rest upon the top bars running north-south.

Step 9 Place three more rows of #4 support bars on high chairs in north-south and east-west column strips. Two rows should be placed at all slab edges.

Step 10 Place truss bars running north-south in the middle strip.

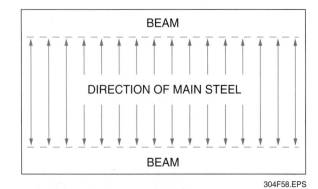

Figure 58 ◆ One-way reinforced slab.

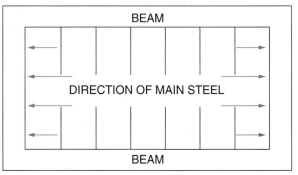

Figure 59 ◆ Two-way reinforced slab.

Reinforcing bars must be fabricated to conform to the designs drawn by the engineers for the particular structure. Most of the fabrication is done in shops, but a certain amount must always be done in the field. Fabrication of reinforcing bars includes the cutting, bending, and splicing of bars in accordance with certain tolerances and codes established by the American Concrete Institute.

7.0.0 ◆ POST-TENSIONED CONCRETE

When a load is applied to a conventional concrete slab such as an elevated parking garage deck, the concrete will tend to sag and may develop cracks. The use of rebar in the slab tends to combat this problem, but is not enough to prevent cracking under heavy load.

The solution is post-tensioning, in which a steel tendon is placed in the form with the ends protruding. The tendon is placed in accordance with a post-tensioning profile drawing developed by a qualified engineer. *Figure 60* is an example of post-tensioning profiles for post-tensioned beams. The multi-span beam profile diagram shows how the tendons go across the top of a column. A tendon

consists of a bar or strand, along with the anchoring hardware and sheathing. The strand is typically made from seven ½" diameter steel wires twisted together. Once the concrete has hardened around the tendon, one end of the tendon is anchored off, and the other end is tensioned using a special hydraulic jack. When the desired tension has been reached, the other anchor is secured.

There are two types of post-tensioning: bonded and unbonded. In bonded post-tensioning, a steel or plastic duct is inserted in the form. After the concrete is poured and has hardened, the strand is threaded through the duct. Tensioning is applied, and then the duct is filled with grout.

Figure 61 shows post-tensioning tendons protruding from recently poured concrete. Once the tendons are anchored, they are cut, and the openings are sealed (*Figure 62*).

In an unbonded system, the strand is covered with a corrosion-inhibiting grease and encased in a waterproof plastic sheath. The entire assembly is placed into the form before the concrete is poured.

The twisted-wire strand is used in large structures. The threaded bar is more common in smaller structures. A bearing plate and nut are used to anchor the bar.

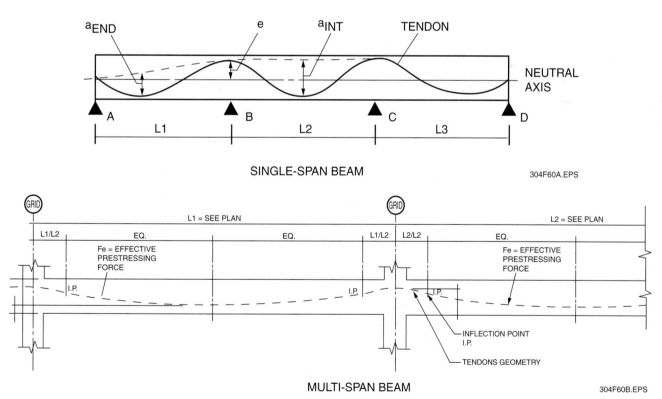

Figure 60 ◆ Examples of tendon profiles.

304F61.EPS

Figure 61 ◆ Post-tensioning tendons.

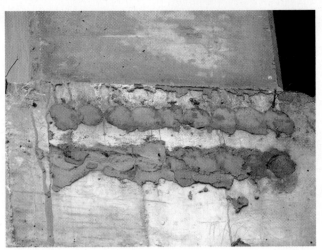

304F62.EPS

Figure 62 ◆ Sealed tendon openings.

Summary

Concrete used in structures must be properly reinforced with steel bars or wire mesh. Workers who place and tie rebar must be able to identify the various rebar types and sizes, as well as the various types of supports used to suspend rebar in the concrete.

In addition to concrete reinforcing materials and accessories, this module provides general information on cutting, bending, placing, splicing, and tying reinforcing steel for reinforced concrete members. Even though there are general methods of placing reinforcing steel in various types of structural components, the placing drawings provide the exact specifications and locations governing the reinforcing steel. The most efficient system of bar placement should be determined from the placing drawings.

Notes

1. The adhesion of concrete to reinforcement bars is called the _____.
   a. compression resistance
   b. tension resistance
   c. cohesive bond
   d. concrete bond

2. Column ties are used primarily to _____.
   a. prevent vertical slippage of horizontal bars
   b. prevent buckling of vertical bars
   c. secure vertical bars to forms
   d. space horizontal bars used in columns

3. The marking on a rebar reveals all of the following information about the bar *except* its _____.
   a. weight
   b. grade
   c. manufacturer
   d. type of steel

4. A keel holder is used for holding a _____.
   a. bolt cutter
   b. striker
   c. soapstone
   d. tip cleaner

5. The A and G dimensions for bar fabrication on a bar list refer to the _____.
   a. bends
   b. saddles
   c. stirrups
   d. hooks

6. On a bar list, up to _____ types of bars could be specified.
   a. three
   b. four
   c. five
   d. six

7. There are _____ types of hooks in general use, each defined by the size of the angle the hook encompasses.
   a. three
   b. four
   c. five
   d. six

8. The fabrication tolerance for the length of a hooked #7 bar is _____.
   a. ±¼"
   b. ±½"
   c. ±¾"
   d. ±1"

9. Steel wire bar supports may be available in up to _____ classes.
   a. three
   b. four
   c. five
   d. six

10. Welded-wire mesh is designed by a four-part code. The first two parts identify the _____.
    a. manufacturer
    b. gauge of the wire
    c. strength
    d. size of the mesh

11. The typical concrete cover for spirals and ties in columns is _____.
    a. ¾"
    b. 1"
    c. 1¼"
    d. 1½"

12. A hickey bar can be used to bend rebar sizes up to # _____.
a. 4
b. 5
c. 8
d. 10

13. A tie used to prevent horizontal bars from shifting during concrete placement is called a _____ tie.
a. snap
b. saddle
c. wrap-and-saddle
d. wrap-and-snap

14. The tying of rebar in horizontal formwork is best accomplished in a _____ position.
a. stiff-legged
b. squatting
c. kneeling
d. sitting

15. A rule of thumb for tied lap splices is that the bar overlap should be a minimum of 12" or _____ times the bar diameter, whichever is greater.
a. 20
b. 25
c. 30
d. 35

Trade Terms
Introduced in This Module

Abutment: The supporting substructure at each end of a bridge.

Band: A group of bars placed in a column tie or an area with a given amount of steel placed within it.

Bar list: A bill of materials for a job site that shows all bar quantities, sizes, lengths, grades, placement areas, and bending dimensions to be used.

Beam: A horizontal structural member.

Bent: A self-supporting frame having at least two legs and placed at right angles to the length of the structure it supports, such as the columns and cap supporting the spans of a bridge.

Bundle of bars: A bundle consisting of one size, length, or mark (bent) of bar, with the following exceptions: very small quantities may be bundled together for convenience, and groups of varying bar lengths or marks that will be placed adjacent to one another may be bundled together.

Caissons: Piers usually extending through water or soft soil to solid earth or rock; also refers to cast-in-place, drilled-hole piles.

Column: A post or vertical structural member supporting a floor beam, girder, or other horizontal member and carrying a primarily vertical load.

Column horses: Wood or metal supports that are used in groups of two or more to hold main reinforcing in a convenient position for placing ties while prefabricating column, beam, or pile cages.

Column spirals: Columns in which the vertical bars are enclosed within a spiral that functions like a column tie.

Column ties: Bars that are bent into square, rectangular, U-shaped, circular, or other shapes for the purpose of holding vertical column bars laterally in place and that prevent buckling of the vertical bars under compression load.

Concrete cover: The distance from the face of the concrete to the reinforcing steel; also referred to as fireproofing, clearance, or concrete protection.

Contact splice: A means of connecting reinforcing bars by lapping in direct contact.

Continuous beam: A beam that extends over three or more supports (including end supports).

CRSI: Concrete Reinforcing Steel Institute.

Double-curtain wall: A concrete wall that contains a layer of reinforcement at each face.

Dowel: A bar connecting two separately cast sections of concrete. A bar extending from one concrete section into another is said to be doweled into the adjoining section.

Far face: The face farthest from the viewers (as of a wall); may be the outside or inside face, depending on whether one is inside looking out or outside looking in.

Flat slab: A concrete slab reinforced in two or more directions, with drop panels but generally without beams, and with or without column capitals.

Girder: The principal beam supporting other beams.

Header: A short reinforced beam, joist, or slab edge generally used at floor openings to support similar members terminating at the opening.

Heavy bending: Bar sizes #4 through #18, which are bent in no more than six points in one plane; also referred to as single-radius bending.

Hickey bar: Hand tool with side-opening jaw used in developing leverage for making in-place bends on bars or pipes.

Hook: A 180-degree (semicircular) or 90-degree turn at the free end of a bar to provide anchorage in concrete. For stirrups and column ties only, turns of either 90 degrees or 135 degrees are used.

Inserts: Devices that are positioned in concrete to receive a bolt or screw to support shelf angles, machinery, etc.

Lapped splice: The joining of two reinforcing bars by lapping them side by side, or the length of overlap of two bars; similarly, the side and end overlap of sheets or rolls of welded-wire fabric.

Light bending: All #3 bars, all stirrups and ties, and all #4 through #18 bars that are bent at more than six points in one plane; all single-plane radius bending with more than one radius in any bar (three maximum); or a combination of radius and another type of bending on one plane (radius bending being defined as all bends having a radius of 12" or more to the inside of the bar).

Near face: The face nearest the viewer, which may be inside or outside, depending on whether one is inside looking out or outside looking in.

Pile cap: A structural member placed on the tops of piles and used to distribute loads from the structure to the piles.

Pitch: The center-to-center spacing between the turns of a spiral.

Placing drawings: Detailed drawings that give the bar size, location, spacing, and all other information required to place the reinforcing steel.

Reinforced concrete: Concrete that has been placed around some type of steel reinforcement material. After the concrete cures, the reinforcement provides greater tensile and shear strength for the concrete. Almost all concrete is reinforced in some manner.

Retaining wall: A wall that has been reinforced to hold or retain soil, water, grain, coal, or sand.

Schedule: A table on placing drawings that lists the size, shape, and arrangement of similar items.

Simple beam: A beam supported at each end (two points) and not continuous.

Single-curtain wall: A concrete wall that contains a single layer of vertical or horizontal reinforcing bars in the center of the wall.

Sleeve: A tube that encloses a bar, dowel, anchor bolt, or similar item.

Span: The horizontal distance between supports of a member such as a beam, girder, slab, or joist; also, the distance between the piers or abutments of a bridge.

Special bending: All bending to special tolerances; all radius bending in more than one plane; all multiple-plane bending containing one or more radius bends; and all bending for precast units.

Staggered splices: Splices in bars that are not made at the same point.

Stirrups: Reinforcing bars used in beams for shear reinforcement; typically bent into a U shape or box shape and placed perpendicular to the longitudinal steel.

Strips: Bands of reinforcing bars in flat-slab or flat-plate construction. The column strip is a quarter-panel wide on each side of the column center line and runs from column to column. The middle strip is half a panel in width, filling in between column strips, and runs parallel to the column strips.

Support bars: Bars that rest upon individual high chairs or bar chairs to support top bars in slabs or joists, respectively. They are usually #4 bars and may replace a like number of temperature bars in slabs when properly lap spliced; also used longitudinally in beams to provide support for the tops of stirrups. Also called raiser bars.

Temperature bars: Bars distributed throughout the concrete to minimize cracks due to temperature changes and concrete shrinkage.

Template: A device used to locate and hold dowels, to lay out bolt holes and inserts, etc.

Tie: A reinforcing bar bent into a box shape and used to hold longitudinal bars together in columns and beams. Also known as stirrup ties.

Tie wire: Wire (generally #16, #15, or #14 gauge) used to secure rebar intersections for the purpose of holding them in place until concreting is completed.

Weep hole: A drainage opening in a wall.

This module is intended to be a thorough resource for task training. The following reference works are suggested for further study. These are optional materials for continued education rather than for task training.

Placing Reinforcing Bars, 2005. Concrete Reinforcing Steel Institute (CRSI).

Manual of Standard Practice, Latest Edition. Concrete Reinforcing Steel Institute (CRSI).

This module is intended to be a thorough resource for task training. The following reference works are suggested for further study. These are optional materials for continued education rather than for task training.

American Concrete Institute (ACI). www.concrete.org.

Cement Association of Canada. www.cement.ca.

Portland Cement Association. www.cement.org.

CONTREN® LEARNING SERIES – USER UPDATE

NCCER makes every effort to keep these textbooks up-to-date and free of technical errors. We appreciate your help in this process. If you have an idea for improving this textbook, or if you find an error, a typographical mistake, or an inaccuracy in NCCER's Contren® textbooks, please write us, using this form or a photocopy. Be sure to include the exact module number, page number, a detailed description, and the correction, if applicable. Your input will be brought to the attention of the Technical Review Committee. Thank you for your assistance.

Instructors – If you found that additional materials were necessary in order to teach this module effectively, please let us know so that we may include them in the Equipment/Materials list in the Annotated Instructor's Guide.

Write: Product Development and Revision
National Center for Construction Education and Research
3600 NW 43rd St., Bldg. G, Gainesville, FL 32606

Fax: 352-334-0932

E-mail: curriculum@nccer.org

Craft _____ Module Name _____

Copyright Date _____ Module Number _____ Page Number(s) _____

Description _____

_____

_____

_____

(Optional) Correction _____

_____

_____

(Optional) Your Name and Address _____

_____

_____

Trenching and Excavating

27306-07
Trenching and Excavating

Topics to be presented in this module include:

Overview

The safety, stability, and durability of a building depend on its foundation. A foundation supports the structure and distributes its weight to the ground. The type and size of the structure, as well as the type of soil at the site, determine the type of foundation required for the building. Large commercial or industrial projects need large foundations that normally require deep excavations, so it is vital for carpenters working on these jobs to be familiar with trenching and excavating techniques. Of greater importance, carpenters need to know how to keep themselves and their co-workers safe when working in or near an excavation.

This module is intended to be a thorough resource for task training. The following reference work is suggested for further study. These are optional materials for continued education rather than for task training.

Boston Groundwater Trust Report. Aldrich & Lambrecht. *Civil Engineering Practices Journal of the Boston Society of Civil Engineers Section/ASCE,* Fall 1986 Volume 1, Number 2, http://www. bostongroundwater.org/ceprep.html.

NCCER makes every effort to keep these textbooks up-to-date and free of technical errors. We appreciate your help in this process. If you have an idea for improving this textbook, or if you find an error, a typographical mistake, or an inaccuracy in NCCER's Contren® textbooks, please write us, using this form or a photocopy. Be sure to include the exact module number, page number, a detailed description, and the correction, if applicable. Your input will be brought to the attention of the Technical Review Committee. Thank you for your assistance.

Instructors – If you found that additional materials were necessary in order to teach this module effectively, please let us know so that we may include them in the Equipment/Materials list in the Annotated Instructor's Guide.

Write: Product Development and Revision
          National Center for Construction Education and Research
          3600 NW 43rd St., Bldg. G, Gainesville, FL 32606

Fax: 352-334-0932

E-mail: curriculum@nccer.org

Craft   Module Name

Copyright Date   Module Number   Page Number(s)

Description

(Optional) Correction

(Optional) Your Name and Address

Foundations and Slab-on-Grade
27307-07

27307-07
Foundations and Slab-on-Grade

Topics to be presented in this module include:

Overview

Every structure requires a foundation to support the structure and distribute its weight. Large structures such as high-rise buildings require large foundations supported by piles or caissons that are embedded deep into the earth. A carpenter working on large commercial or industrial projects is likely to be involved in building these foundations, and therefore must be familiar with the different types and the methods used in forming, reinforcing, and placing them.

Objectives

When you have completed this module, you will be able to do the following:

1. Establish elevations.
2. Identify various types of footings and foundations.
3. Select the appropriate footing for a foundation.
4. Lay out and construct a selected footing and foundation using an established gridline.
5. Install templates, keyways, and embedments.
6. Form and strip pier foundation forms and prepare for resetting at another location.
7. Identify the different classes of slabs-on-grade.
8. Identify edge forms and explain their purpose.
9. Construct and disassemble edge forms.
10. Install vapor barrier, reinforcement, and control joints.
11. Establish finish grade and fill requirements.

Trade Terms

Backsight (BS)
Blockout
Caissons
Cross braces
Density
Fill
Foresight (FS)
Foundation
Height of instrument (HI)
Mat foundation (raft foundation)
Pilings
Settlement
Skeleton
Slab-on-grade (slab-at-grade)
Voids
Water table

Required Trainee Materials

1. Pencil and paper
2. Appropriate personal protective equipment

Prerequisites

Before you begin this module, it is recommended that you successfully complete *Core Curriculum*; *Carpentry Level One*; *Carpentry Level Two*; and *Carpentry Level Three*, Modules 27301-07 through 27306-07.

This course map shows all of the modules in the third level of the *Carpentry* curriculum. The suggested training order begins at the bottom and proceeds up. Skill levels increase as you advance on the course map. The local Training Program Sponsor may adjust the training order.

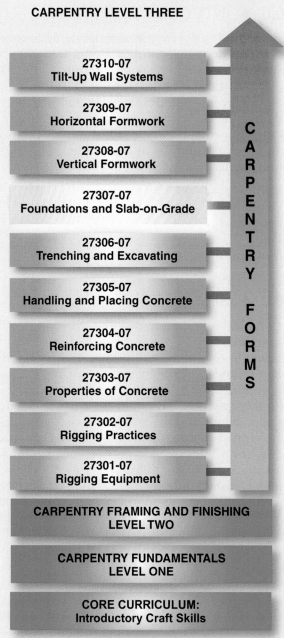

CARPENTRY LEVEL THREE

27310-07
Tilt-Up Wall Systems

27309-07
Horizontal Formwork

27308-07
Vertical Formwork

27307-07
Foundations and Slab-on-Grade

27306-07
Trenching and Excavating

27305-07
Handling and Placing Concrete

27304-07
Reinforcing Concrete

27303-07
Properties of Concrete

27302-07
Rigging Practices

27301-07
Rigging Equipment

CARPENTRY FORMS

CARPENTRY FRAMING AND FINISHING
LEVEL TWO

CARPENTRY FUNDAMENTALS
LEVEL ONE

CORE CURRICULUM:
Introductory Craft Skills

307CMAP.EPS

1.0.0 ◆ INTRODUCTION

This module is the first in a series of three modules about concrete forming systems. It focuses on formwork for commercial job site **foundation** elements and **slab-on-grade (slab-at-grade)** installations, including equipment used for placement and finishing as well as formwork for curbing and paving. Information on establishing foundation layout and elevation is also provided. The foundation elements covered are as follows:

- **Pilings**
- **Caissons**
- Footings
- Walls
- **Mat foundations (raft foundations)**

2.0.0 ◆ SITEWORK

For a typical foundation, once the structure design is complete, the job site must be laid out and the building lines established by surveying methods. This is followed by the installation of any excavation support system and **water table** mitigation equipment required. Then the foundation, including any elevator pits, machine base pits, and sumps, must be excavated and prepared. As necessary, any pilings or caissons must be placed and subsurface drainage, utility, and sewage piping systems installed, backfilled, and compacted. Once these items are completed, concrete formwork for the foundation can begin. Forms for any interior pits are installed first along with reinforcement steel. Concrete is placed and cured, and the exterior forms are stripped. Then, the structure footing forms are installed with reinforcement steel along with any required conduit or piping, and any embedded items such as castings for machinery bases, sumps, and manholes. The concrete is placed and cured, and the forms are stripped. Then any foundation wall forms, if required, are installed along with steel reinforcement and any required conduit and piping. The concrete is placed, cured, and the forms are stripped. As required, the soil within the remaining foundation area is prepared and compacted. The forms for the concrete foundation slab over, or between, the footings or foundation walls are installed along with any required reinforcement steel. Lastly, the concrete is placed and cured, and the slab forms are stripped.

2.1.0 Establishing Formwork Locations and Elevations

When working at a job site, carpenters must be able to establish the location and levelness of forms. To accomplish this, survey control points along with measuring and leveling equipment are used. The following sections briefly cover the equipment and the methods used for this purpose.

2.1.1 Control Points

Site plans show the locations of property corners and the direction and length of property lines or control lines. In most states, any layout work that establishes legal property lines or boundaries must be done by a registered surveyor. This is because the surveyor assumes the liability for any mistake in the surveying work. The surveyor is legally responsible if the building ends up on the wrong property or at some location that violates setback requirements, easements, or other regulations. Because of the tremendous liability involved, carpenters should never make any layout measurements that relate to property lines or boundaries. This is a task for the professional land surveyor.

Site layout involves establishing a network of control points on a site that serve as a common reference for all construction. The exact locations of these control points are marked at the site and recorded in a surveyor's field notes as they are made. Annotating control point location reference data in the field notes is important for two reasons. First, it makes it possible to locate a point should it become covered up or otherwise hidden. Second, it makes it possible to reestablish a point accurately if the marker is damaged or removed. On many larger job sites, a survey crew may establish all the following control points. In some cases, however, carpenters may be required to establish the secondary control points and/or the working control points. There are three basic categories of control points:

- *Primary control points* – These points are used as the basis for locating secondary control points and other points on the site. Primary control points are located where they are accessible and protected from damage for the duration of the job. Primary control points can be located and marked on many kinds of permanent and immovable objects such as fire hydrants and power poles. When no suitable permanent object is available for use as a primary control point marker, iron stakes driven into the ground, or a concrete monument dug and poured into the ground (*Figure 1*) can be used. If a poured

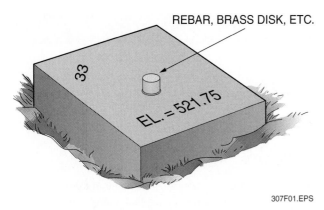

REBAR, BRASS DISK, ETC.

EL. = 521.75

33

307F01.EPS

Figure 1 ◆ Typical control point concrete monument (bench mark).

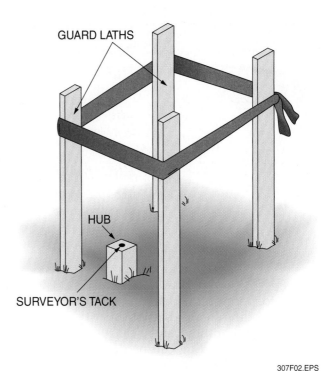

GUARD LATHS

HUB

SURVEYOR'S TACK

307F02.EPS

Figure 2 ◆ Typical secondary control point marker (TBM).

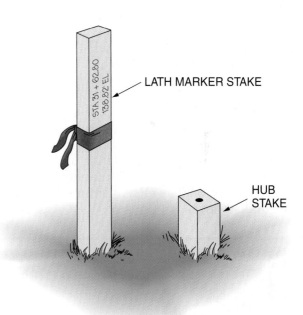

LATH MARKER STAKE

STA 3A + 62.80
138.82 EL

HUB STAKE

307F03.EPS

Figure 3 ◆ Typical working control point marker.

concrete monument is used, it must be dug a foot deeper than the frost line to prevent freezing and thawing from moving it. It must also have a distinct high point. This can be a rounded brass cap, rebar, etc., that sticks up out of the top of the concrete. Primary control point markers are typically established by a registered surveyor. They are commonly referred to as monuments or bench marks (BMs).

- *Secondary control points* – These are additional control points located within the job site to aid in the construction of the individual structures on the site. Secondary control points, also called temporary bench marks (TBMs), are typically marked by a hub stake surrounded by guard laths (*Figure 2*), posts, or fencing. The hub stake is typically a 1½" square piece of wood pointed on one end. Its length is normally determined by the hardness of the ground it must be driven into, with lengths between 8" and 12" being typical. The hub stake is driven into the ground until flush or nearly so. A surveyor's tack, with a depression in the center of the head, is driven into the top of the hub stake to locate the exact point.

- *Building layout or working control points* – These points are usually located with reference to the secondary control points. These are the points from which actual measurements for construction are taken. Building layout points are used to locate the corners of buildings and building lines. They are usually marked with a hub and a related marker stake (*Figure 3*). The marker stake is typically a ¾" × 1½" piece of wood that varies in length, with 24" to 36" being typical. In addition to serving as hub markers, these stakes are also used to mark line or grade and other information for center lines, offset lines, slope stakes, etc.

Hubs

Hubs are commonly made by sawing 2 × 4s in half. When necessary to drive wooden hubs into hard-packed ground, the job can be made easier by driving a tempered steel pin called a gad into the ground first to start a pilot hole.

Placement of Control Points

Good practice dictates that a control point should always be placed so that three other control points are visible from it at all times. This is done in case the control point should become covered up or destroyed for some reason. If this were to happen, two tapes can be stretched from the other points in order to relocate the control point.

Control points and other markers are identified by color-coding them—both to identify their purpose and so that they can be easily seen and recognized. Color-coding can be done by applying paint to monuments, hubs, or other field markers, applying ribbons on stakes, attaching flags on wire markers, etc. Note that color-coding of field markers is not standardized; however, many construction or field engineering organizations have established their own color-coding systems. When performing layout work at a site, you should ask your supervisor what color-coding scheme to use, and then follow it.

2.1.2 Leveling Instruments

A wide variety of leveling instruments can be used to perform leveling and other on-site layout tasks. The procedural data relating to differential leveling given later in this module emphasizes the use of conventional leveling instruments, such as the builder's level.

NOTE

The calibration of leveling instruments must be checked before use as specified in the manufacturers instructions.

- *Builder's level* – The builder's level (*Figure 4*) is an instrument used to check and establish grades and elevations and to set up level points over long distances. It consists of a telescope, a bubble spirit level (leveling vial) mounted parallel with the telescope, and a leveling head mounted on a circular base with a horizontal circle scale graduated in degrees. The telescope can be rotated 360 degrees for measuring

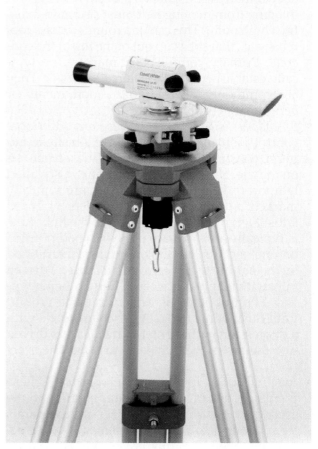

307F04.EPS

Figure 4 ◆ Typical builder's level.

approximate horizontal angles to an accuracy of 5 to 15 arc minutes. On at least one manufacturer's unit, the telescope can be tilted vertically about ±1 degree for initial sighting purposes. Builder's levels are mounted on a tripod when in use.

Figure 39 ◆ Footings placed without forms.

4.2.2 Grade Beams

Grade beams are heavily reinforced foundations that generally rest at grade level on pile caps, large caissons, or spread footings. They are used to distribute the large wall loads of a building equally along the pile caps, caissons, or spread footings when the soil underneath is of low loadbearing capacity. In cases where the soil has high clay content, grade beams supported by pile caps or caissons are cast with a **void** or crushable fiber filler underneath to prevent upheaval when the clay expands due to water absorption. In soils with high loadbearing capacity, the beams can be placed without additional support. *Figure 40* shows completed job-built forms and reinforcement for a grade beam terminating in the reinforcement for a pile cap at the end of a loadbearing wall. Note the storm sewer sleeve through the grade beam. Also, note the **cross braces** with the form hold-down stakes used at the top of the pile cap and grade beam forms. The cross braces for the pile cap form serve as part of the templating used to position and support the anchor bolts for a column. Because of the concrete volume to be placed, the hold-down stakes will help to keep the form from being lifted up by the concrete. A closeup view of a job-built intermediate pile cap form with grade beam reinforcement passing through and integrated with the pile cap reinforcement is shown in *Figure 41*. Again, note the cross braces with the form hold-down stakes and the column rebar dowel templating.

Figure 42 shows partially completed reinforcement between manufactured steel forms for a grade beam. Note the two integrated parallel grade beams at the back of the partial completed form. The completed double beams are supported over water by the pilings visible underneath.

Figure 40 ◆ A grade beam terminated into a pile cap.

Figure 41 ◆ An intermediate pile cap integrated with grade beams on both sides.

Figure 42 ◆ Partially completed grade beam reinforcement between manufactured steel forms.

4.2.3 Cast-In-Place Walls

Foundation walls can be cast in place using forms. *Figure 43* shows a partially constructed job-built wood form with reinforcement for a cast-in-place concrete wall over a strip footing.

4.2.4 Masonry Walls

The most common CMUs used for foundation walls are concrete blocks. They are available in a myriad of sizes and shapes. Concrete blocks are produced in four classes:

- Solid loadbearing
- Hollow loadbearing
- Solid nonbearing
- Hollow nonbearing

Figure 43 ◆ Partially constructed job-built wood wall form.

Because foundation walls are loadbearing, only the first two classes are used. The remaining two classes are used for curtain walls. Standard concrete blocks are specified in nominal 4" multiples. The specified nominal versus the actual dimensions (which allows for a ⅜" mortar joint) of common concrete blocks are as follows:

- Standard block nominal size is 8" × 8" × 16" with an actual size of 7⅝" × 7⅝" × 15⅝".
- Standard pilaster block nominal size is 8" × 16" × 16" with an actual size of 7⅝" × 15⅝" × 15⅝".

Several common types of standard concrete blocks with an identification of their parts are shown in *Figures 44* and *45*.

Pilaster blocks are also available in actual widths and lengths of 16-⅝" × 16-⅝" and 15-⅝" × 18-⅝". Pilasters are used as stabilizing columns in long concrete block walls and as beam supports. The thickness of loadbearing walls may be specified as single wythe (one block) or multiwythe (two or more blocks). Multiwythe walls can be built as solid walls or walls with a cavity for insulation. Long, loadbearing concrete walls must be built with horizontal or vertical supports at right angles to the face of the wall. The vertical support may be provided by cross walls, pilasters, or buttresses. Embedding wire reinforcement in the horizontal joints between each course or every other course provides horizontal support. Wire reinforcement is available in various styles, two of which are shown in *Figure 46*. To provide additional vertical and horizontal support, vertical rebar may be specified. In this case, rebar is placed

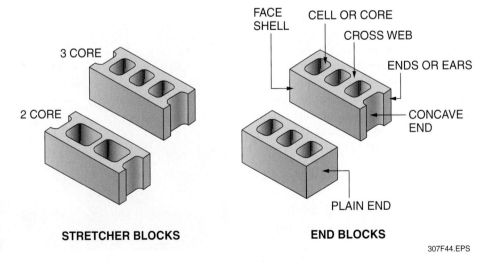

Figure 44 ◆ Identification of the parts of some common types of blocks.

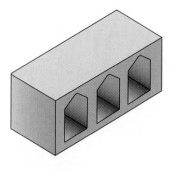

**THREE-CORE TERMITE
DOUBLE CORNER BLOCK**

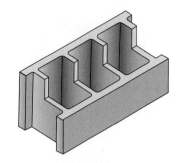

**FULL CUT OUT
HEADER BLOCK**

307F45.EPS

Figure 45 ◆ Corner and header blocks.

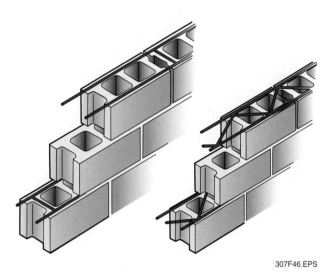

307F46.EPS

Figure 46 ◆ Two types of horizontal joint reinforcement wire.

and grouted inside the cores of hollow blocks at various intervals. The grout is normally forced into the cores through a hose from a pump. Like concrete-slab construction joints, control joints are used in masonry to prevent cracking of walls due to expansion and contraction. *Figure 47* shows a vertical control joint made with flexible sealant and plastic backer rods.

Concrete blocks must be kept dry at all times, particularly during job site storage and laying operations. All stored blocks and freshly laid walls must be covered with tarps to prevent rain penetration of the blocks and/or damage to uncured mortar joints. Long, freshly laid short-height foundation walls at or below grade are generally not affected by high winds during storms; however, it may be necessary to brace them if they are deep walls and the area within them is totally excavated or the walls project above grade a significant amount. Temporary vertical wood bracing can be erected at intervals on both sides of the walls to secure them until the mortar has cured.

The techniques of laying concrete block or other masonry are beyond the scope of this curriculum because the majority of commercial work is done by qualified masons or by masonry contractors. However, from a building standpoint, one of the most important aspects of masonry is that masonry walls must be constantly checked for levelness and height as the work progresses.

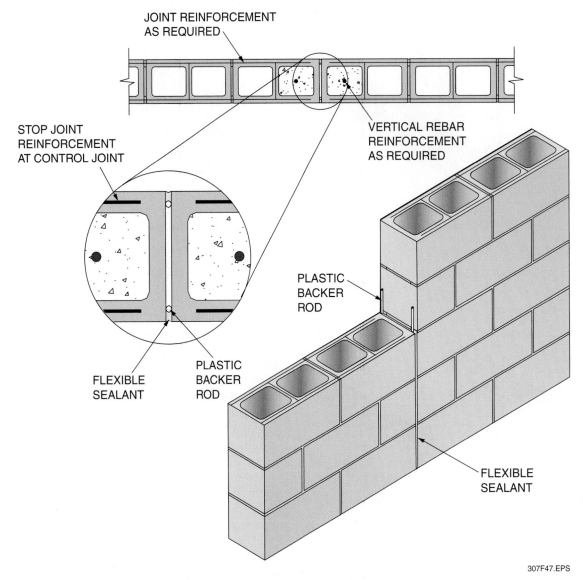

JOINT REINFORCEMENT
AS REQUIRED

STOP JOINT
REINFORCEMENT
AT CONTROL JOINT

VERTICAL REBAR
REINFORCEMENT
AS REQUIRED

PLASTIC
BACKER
ROD

FLEXIBLE
SEALANT

PLASTIC
BACKER
ROD

FLEXIBLE
SEALANT

307F47.EPS

Figure 47 ◆ Vertical control joint made with flexible sealant and plastic backer rod.

5.0.0 ◆ SLABS-ON-GRADE

Slabs-on-grade, also called slabs-on-ground, are totally supported by the ground beneath them. There are nine classes of slabs as defined by American Concrete Institute (ACI) *302.1R-04, Guide for Concrete Floor and Slab Construction* that are used for elevated slabs and slabs-on-grade. These slab classifications are shown in *Table 1*. A brief description of the various classes of slabs follows:

- *Single-course monolithic slabs (Classes 1, 2, 4, 5, and 6)* – Five classes of slabs are constructed with monolithic concrete, and each varies in strength and final finishing methods. If abrasion is anticipated, these slabs may require a special mineral or metallic aggregate monolithic surface treatment or higher strength concrete.

- *Two-course slabs (Classes 3, 7, and 8)* – The base courses of Class 3 (unbonded topping) and Class 8 slabs can be slab-on-grade or elevated slabs. For Class 3 slabs the topping material is similar to the base slab concrete. The top courses for Class 8 slabs require a hard-steel troweling and normally have higher compressive strength than the base course. Unbonded toppings are used so that the two courses can move independently or so that the top course can be easily replaced at a later time. Plastic sheeting, roofing felt, or a bond-breaking compound is used to prevent the top course from bonding with the base course. Unbonded toppings should have a minimum thickness of 3". Joint spacing should be coordinated with the base slab joints. Additional joints are required if

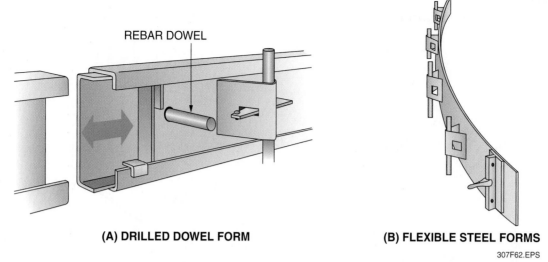

REBAR DOWEL

(A) DRILLED DOWEL FORM

(B) FLEXIBLE STEEL FORMS

307F62.EPS

Figure 62 ◆ Specialty edge forms.

or between slabs and footings. This form is equipped with a sliding end connection to allow stripping over the dowels. A reinforced right-angle form is available with a heavy top rail and wide base with gusset braces along the form designed to support screed equipment when very level, super-flat slabs must be placed. Steel key-way forms that can be attached to standard forms are also available to allow slab connection to footings or adjacent slabs. Flexible steel forms (*Figure 62B*) can be obtained in various heights for all types of curve and radius work.

The same manufacturer also has a line of rigid and flexible durable plastic edge forms (*Figure 63*). They are very light and are available in stackable 4" and 6" sizes that are 12' long. The forms can be easily cut to shorter lengths as desired. Three different steel stake pockets with wedges are used; a twist pocket, a sliding pocket, and an optional stacking pocket. The twist pocket can be located any place along the form and also provides a multiple stacking option. They can be attached before or after the forms are set to grade. The slide pocket, which can also be used when stacking forms, is inserted at one end of the form and is slid over the joint between the adjacent forms before staking. The optional stacking pocket, which provides a more rigid connection, is similar to the sliding pocket and is available in three different configurations for stacking two 4" forms, two 6" forms, and a 4" with a 6" form. The rigid versions of the form have square aluminum tubing through them that is offset several inches to provide a rigid alignment with an adjacent form. The flexible versions of the forms omit the tubing and can be bent into radiuses as little as 3'.

TWIST-POCKET   FLEXIBLE FORM

307F63.EPS

Figure 63 ◆ Plastic edge forms.

6.2.3 Footing Form Systems

At least one manufacturer is making an aluminum forming system for use in the construction of continuous strip/spread footings or for piers. *Figure 64* shows the components of the system and describes their functions. Little if any external bracing is required because of form ties that are also used to support reinforcement. The ties are available in widths of 16", 18", 20", and 24". The forms come in standard heights of 8", 10", and 12" and are stackable. They are available in lengths from 6" to 12'. Step footings are easily accommodated with the step form component of the system. *Figure 65* shows a strip footing partially concreted to grade markers on the inside of the forms. *Figure 66* shows a concreted step footing with the forms still in place. *Figure 67* shows part of a completed footing with the forms stripped and rebar dowels for a cast-in-place wall.

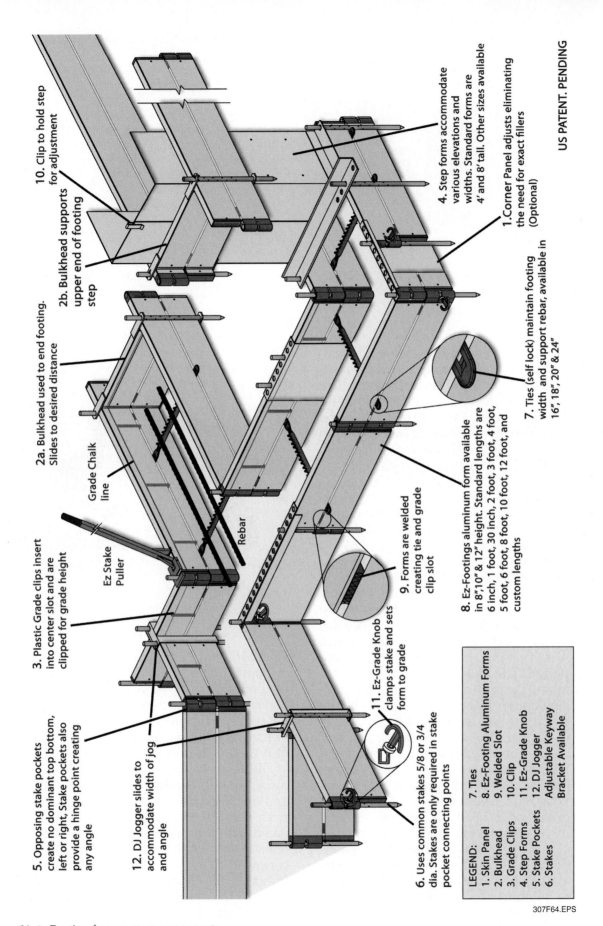

10. Clip to hold step for adjustment

2b. Bulkhead supports upper end of footing step

4. Step forms accommodate various elevations and widths. Standard forms are 4' and 8' tall. Other sizes available

1. Corner Panel adjusts eliminating the need for exact fillers (Optional)

US PATENT. PENDING

2a. Bulkhead used to end footing. Slides to desired distance

Grade Chalk line

Rebar

Ez Stake Puller

3. Plastic Grade clips insert into center slot and are clipped for grade height

7. Ties (self lock) maintain footing width and support rebar, available in 16", 18", 20" & 24"

8. Ez-Footings aluminum form available in 8',10" & 12" height. Standard lengths are 6 inch, 1 foot, 30 inch, 2 foot, 3 foot, 4 foot, 5 foot, 6 foot, 8 foot, 10 foot, 12 foot, and custom lengths

9. Forms are welded creating tie and grade clip slot

11. Ez-Grade Knob clamps stake and sets form to grade

5. Opposing stake pockets create no dominant top bottom, left or right, Stake pockets also provide a hinge point creating any angle

12. DJ Jogger slides to accommodate width of jog and angle

6. Uses common stakes 5/8 or 3/4 dia. Stakes are only required in stake pocket connecting points

LEGEND:
1. Skin Panel
2. Bulkhead
3. Grade Clips
4. Step Forms
5. Stake Pockets
6. Stakes

7. Ties
8. Ez-Footing Aluminum Forms
9. Welded Slot
10. Clip
11. Ez-Grade Knob
12. DJ Jogger
Adjustable Keyway
Bracket Available

307F64.EPS

Figure 64 ◆ Footing form system components.

This module is intended to be a thorough resource for task training. The following reference works are suggested for further study. These are optional materials for continued education rather than for task training.

American Concrete Institute, www.aci–int.org.

Principles and Practices of Commercial Construction, Prentice Hall, Upper Saddle River, NJ.

The Concrete Network, www.concretenetwork.com.

NCCER makes every effort to keep these textbooks up-to-date and free of technical errors. We appreciate your help in this process. If you have an idea for improving this textbook, or if you find an error, a typographical mistake, or an inaccuracy in NCCER's Contren® textbooks, please write us, using this form or a photocopy. Be sure to include the exact module number, page number, a detailed description, and the correction, if applicable. Your input will be brought to the attention of the Technical Review Committee. Thank you for your assistance.

Instructors – If you found that additional materials were necessary in order to teach this module effectively, please let us know so that we may include them in the Equipment/Materials list in the Annotated Instructor's Guide.

Write:	Product Development and Revision
	National Center for Construction Education and Research
	3600 NW 43rd St., Bldg. G, Gainesville, FL 32606
Fax:	352-334-0932
E-mail:	curriculum@nccer.org

Craft

Module Name

Copyright Date

Module Number

Page Number(s)

Description

(Optional) Correction

(Optional) Your Name and Address

27308-07
Vertical Formwork

Topics to be presented in this module include:

Overview

The ability to work with concrete forms is essential in commercial and industrial carpentry work. A residential carpenter may work with forms, but for the commercial and industrial carpenter, working with forms is a way of life. The carpenter is involved in erecting and bracing the forms, and in stripping, cleaning, and storing the forms after the concrete has hardened.

Forms are used in the construction of everything from retaining walls to bridges to high-rise buildings. Vertical forms are used in building walls, columns, and stairs. Slipforms and climbing forms are used in building piers, silos, elevator and stair cores for buildings, and even entire building structures.

The majority of the forms you work with will be manufactured form systems that include the form panels, horizontal and vertical supports, attaching hardware, and braces. Each manufacturer of a forming system has its own unique equipment and assembly requirements, so you may have to receive special training on the form system used by your employer.

Objectives

When you have completed this module, you will be able to do the following:

1. Explain the safety procedures associated with using concrete wall forms.
2. Identify the various types of concrete wall forms.
3. Identify the components of each type of vertical forming system.
4. Erect, plumb, and brace a selected wall.
5. Recognize various types of manufactured forms.
6. State the differences in construction and use among different types of forms.
7. Erect, plumb, and brace a column form.
8. Erect, plumb, and brace a stair form.
9. Locate and install bulkheads and embedded forms.

Trade Terms

Architectural concrete	Rustication line
Batten	Sheathing
Brace	Shiplap
Buck	Slipform
Climbing form	Spreader
Gang form	Strongback
Plastic concrete	Studs

Required Trainee Materials

1. Pencil and paper
2. Appropriate personal protective equipment

Prerequisites

Before you begin this module, it is recommended that you successfully complete *Core Curriculum*; *Carpentry Level One*; *Carpentry Level Two*; and *Carpentry Level Three*, Modules 27301-07 through 27307-07.

This course map shows all of the modules in the third level of the *Carpentry* curriculum. The suggested training order begins at the bottom and proceeds up. Skill levels increase as you advance on the course map. The local Training Program Sponsor may adjust the training order.

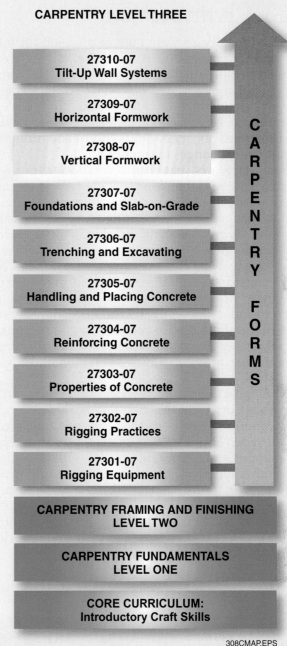

CARPENTRY LEVEL THREE

27310-07
Tilt-Up Wall Systems

27309-07
Horizontal Formwork

27308-07
Vertical Formwork

27307-07
Foundations and Slab-on-Grade

27306-07
Trenching and Excavating

27305-07
Handling and Placing Concrete

27304-07
Reinforcing Concrete

27303-07
Properties of Concrete

27302-07
Rigging Practices

27301-07
Rigging Equipment

CARPENTRY FORMS

CARPENTRY FRAMING AND FINISHING
LEVEL TWO

CARPENTRY FUNDAMENTALS
LEVEL ONE

CORE CURRICULUM:
Introductory Craft Skills

308CMAP.EPS

1.0.0 ◆ INTRODUCTION

At one time, forms were built in place on the job site and torn down after a single use. Salvage was limited to individual boards or timbers. This practice is still common in residential and light commercial construction. However, in heavy commercial construction, increasing labor costs and the need for mass production have brought about many changes in formwork.

Manufacturers' patented forms, prefabricated forms, and reusable form panels have become standard items of construction equipment. Panels can be ganged into large units for efficient wall forming. Tying, fastening, bracing, and supporting accessories continue to increase in number and variety. New materials have been applied to form construction by the patented form industry, and new uses for conventional materials have been found. Plastics, fiberglass, steel, aluminum, and rubber, both as raw materials and in patented prefabricated shapes, have simplified the forming of concrete to meet contemporary architectural demands.

The most common vertical forms you will encounter on a construction site are wall forms and column forms. In this module, we will focus on the much larger forming systems you are likely to encounter on large projects. We will also discuss other types of vertical forms, including slip-forms, stair forms, and polystyrene forms. And we will cover the architectural forms used to achieve a decorative surface appearance in concrete. *Figure 1* shows examples of forms used in commercial construction work.

2.0.0 ◆ FORMWORK PLANNING

Formwork represents one-third to one-half of the total installed cost of concrete. Therefore, contractors consider the following factors:

- The most cost-efficient forming materials that will safely handle the load
- Reusability of the forms
- Effective planning for use of forms
- Crew makeup
- Amount of labor needed to assemble, strip, and clean the forms

Other factors that enter into the planning process are the availability and capacity of cranes, the space available to assemble and move formwork, and the numbers and types of penetrations for pipe, conduit, and openings.

Contractors will generally select the most economical formwork for a particular job. However, if a contractor expects to use the same kinds of forms on other projects, or several times on the same project, it is often more economical to purchase more durable forms. The more times a form can be reused, the lower the cost per project.

Contractors try to plan so that crews are available to place forms, pour concrete, and strip forms in the shortest amount of time possible. A contractor loses money every time a job has to stop because equipment is not on hand and workers have to stand around and wait. Delays can be especially costly when the forms are rented or when the forms are needed for another project.

It's not just a matter of finding the least expensive form. The formwork must be used efficiently.

308F01.EPS

Figure 1 ◆ Examples of concrete forms used in commercial construction work.

For example, if formwork is rented for $10,000 a month and is used once during the month, the cost per concrete structure is $10,000. If the formwork is used ten times during the month, the cost per structure is only $1,000.

The amount of formwork needed can be determined by the amount of wall to be formed, the time available in the schedule, and the time required to cure the concrete before the formwork can be moved.

As you will see, every form system is different. It takes time and training for work crews to get to know a particular form system well enough to set it up, strip it, and tear it down efficiently. For that reason, a contractor is likely to develop expertise with one particular system and to use it whenever possible.

Another aspect of planning is allocation of work areas at the site. Space is needed to assemble, clean, and store the forms. Most large projects will have a shop area where the forms can be assembled. Moving the forms requires special planning. If the forms are to be moved with a crane, there has to be a clear area in which to operate. This is a major concern. It would be costly to have to dismantle the crane in order to move the forms from one part of the site to another.

3.0.0 ◆ WALL FORMS

A wall form is a retainer or mold that is built in such a way as to give the desired shape, support, and finish to a concrete wall. Wall forms, or any of the types of forms discussed in this module, all have one thing in common: Manufacturers design formwork to produce the lightest form that will support the weight of concrete, along with any workers (such as carpenters and rebar installers) who might need to work on the form.

There are a variety of wall form systems. Simple job-built wall forms can be made of lumber and plywood secured with duplex nails and separated by wall ties. Other systems use manufactured form panels and attaching hardware, with walers and **strongbacks** made of lumber or metal. Some manufacturers offer proprietary systems in which all the form components come from the same source. In many instances, horizontal and vertical supports are built into the form panels, so separate walers and strongbacks are unnecessary.

Formwork is designed for simplicity in construction and for the support it provides. Formwork can be assembled with metal clamps or special wedge pin connections that are secure, yet make the form easy to assemble and disassemble (*Figure 2*). Handles, or a wood strip that has been nailed or screwed to the form, give the worker a means of grabbing the form side so that it can be pulled away from the concrete. This minimizes or eliminates the use of pry bars or hammers in prying the form loose. It also reduces damage. Some systems provide lifting eyes and other hardware that make it easy to move the form sections.

The weight of **plastic concrete** puts enormous pressure on formwork. To avoid formwork failure or stretching, it is important to use forms that are designed and built correctly and have the proper bracing for the job at hand.

Safety should always be first in your mind. *OSHA Standard 1926:700-701* covers the safety regulations related to formwork. To ensure safety, wall forms must be constructed exactly as designed, following a safe erection procedure. Forms must be checked before each use. If they are damaged in any way, they must be repaired. Parts that are missing must be replaced. If damaged formwork is used, it could lead to weakness in the system and cause form failure. For safety purposes, it is also important to know the required rate of pour, the height of the pour, and the spacing between pours. Above all, contractors should be concerned with the safety of their crews.

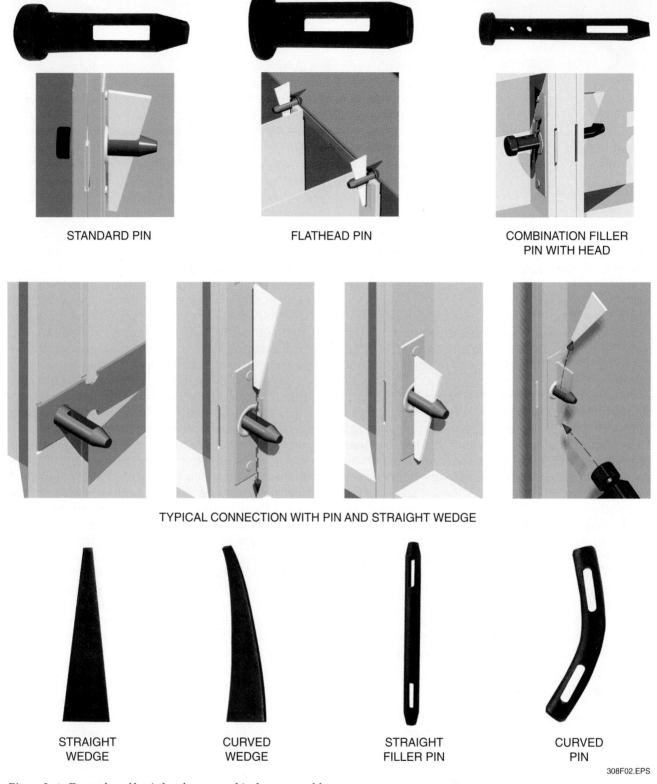

STANDARD PIN

FLATHEAD PIN

COMBINATION FILLER
PIN WITH HEAD

TYPICAL CONNECTION WITH PIN AND STRAIGHT WEDGE

STRAIGHT
WEDGE

CURVED
WEDGE

STRAIGHT
FILLER PIN

CURVED
PIN

308F02.EPS

Figure 2 ◆ Examples of basic hardware used in form assembly.

3.1.0 Parts and Accessories

The following section describes various wall form parts and accessories.

- *Walers* – Horizontal components used in form construction to keep the forms in line and through which the ties are fastened. Walers can either run vertically or horizontally, depending on the design of the formwork. They are also sometimes called ribs, stringers, or rangers. See *Figure 3*. Walers are placed directly against the form.

- *Strongbacks* – Vertical supports used to align, straighten, support, and level the walers. Along with the ties, the strongbacks support and align the walers. Because they align, it is very important that only straight members be used. See *Figure 4*. Strongbacks are placed against the walers.

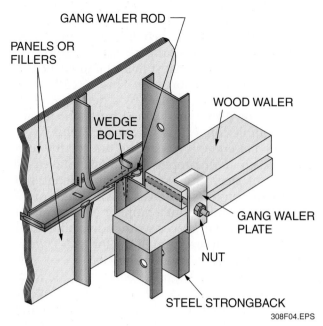

Figure 4 ◆ Strongbacks.

308F04.EPS

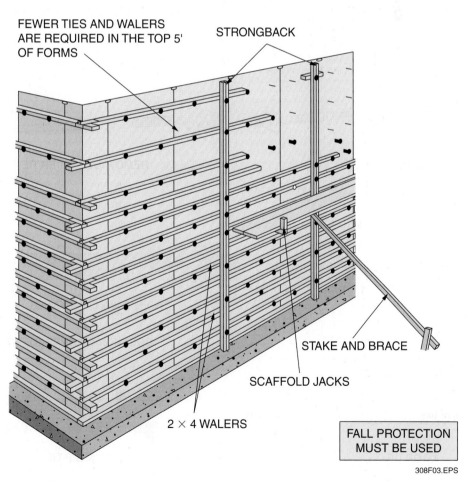

Figure 3 ◆ Gang form with walers.

308F03.EPS

- *Ties and spreaders* – A tie is a wire or rod used to keep the formwork tied together. **Spreaders** keep the form walls properly spaced before the concrete is placed. Most manufactured ties are equipped with a spreader. This spreader may be a washer held in place by a deformation on the tie, or it may be formed by a stiff tie and compatible connecting hardware (*Figure 5*).
- *Stakes and braces* – Needed to anchor the form and keep it in proper alignment. Stakes are made of steel or wood in various lengths to meet job conditions. **Braces** may be made of 2 × 4 or 2 × 6 lumber, but a number of form manufacturers make braces with adjustable turnbuckles to help in aligning the forms (*Figure 6*). Many contractors use pipe braces.
- *Plates* – Serve to align the bottom of the form. They also provide a means for fastening the form to the footing in order to maintain alignment at the bottom of the form. Using plates for alignment helps the job go faster. Plates are not used on all wall forms. In many cases, they are used on only one side of the wall form. Dowel pins made of rebar are used for **gang forms**. They are embedded in the footing.

3.2.0 Panel-Forming Systems

Patented manufactured panels are available for building all kinds of wall forms. Although these panel-forming systems vary widely in detail, there are basically five types of systems:

- *Unframed plywood panels* – Unframed plywood sheets are sometimes backed by steel braces. Locking and tying hardware are the essential parts of this forming system. The lock that holds the ties is frequently part of the waler support.
- *All-metal panels* – All-metal panels (*Figure 7A*) are made up of metal plates supported by a metal frame. These panels are available in steel as well as aluminum. All-aluminum forms consist of an aluminum framework and an aluminum face sheet, which is usually ⅛" thick. They generally come in 3' × 8' sections. They are lightweight and easy to handle. Because of the cost of aluminum, however, they are very expensive and more subject to theft. Aluminum can also react chemically with concrete, causing the concrete to adhere to the form and making it unsuitable for **architectural concrete**.

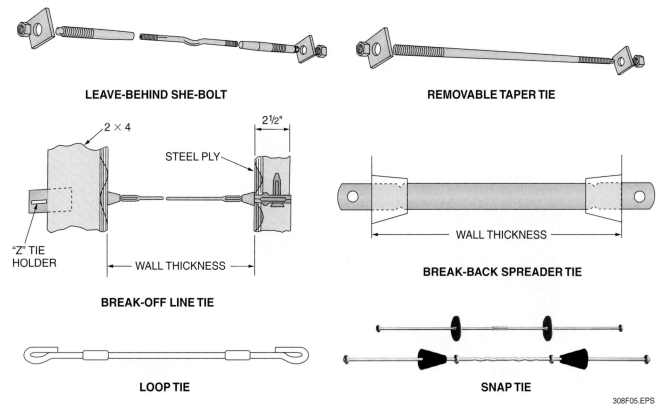

LEAVE-BEHIND SHE-BOLT

REMOVABLE TAPER TIE

2 × 4

STEEL PLY

2½"

"Z" TIE HOLDER

WALL THICKNESS

BREAK-OFF LINE TIE

WALL THICKNESS

BREAK-BACK SPREADER TIE

LOOP TIE

SNAP TIE

308F05.EPS

Figure 5 ◆ Wall ties.

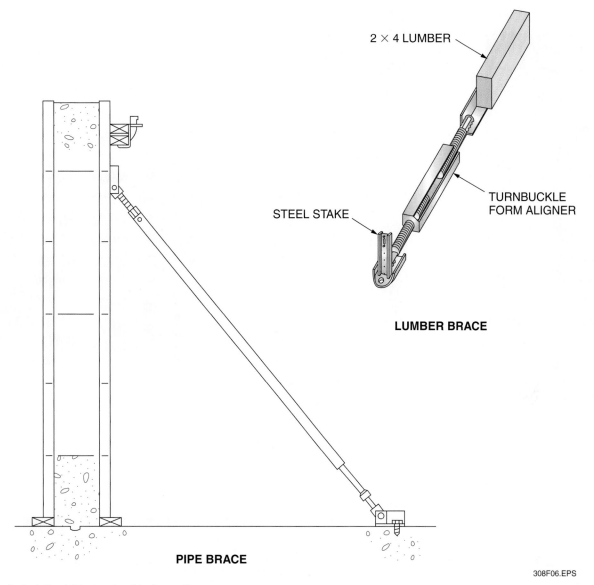

2 × 4 LUMBER

TURNBUCKLE
FORM ALIGNER

STEEL STAKE

LUMBER BRACE

PIPE BRACE

308F06.EPS

Figure 6 ◆ Adjustable turnbuckle form aligner.

Because they are heavier than aluminum forms, all-steel forms come in smaller modules, usually 2' × 4'. Although steel forms are less efficient than aluminum because of the smaller size, they are very durable and can be used over and over again if properly maintained and stored. Steel forms can be used for architectural concrete if a liner is applied to the form.

• *Plywood and metal frames* – These forms may be ganged or hand-set. They consist of ½" or ⅝" plywood sheets recessed into a steel or aluminum framework (*Figure 7B*). They may not require bracing and are used in all types of construction.

• *Heavy steel-framed panels* – These panels are made to handle the greater pressures of poured concrete (*Figure 7C*). They are built with lumber, plywood, or synthetic sheathing. Because they are designed for heavy loads, they have hardware built into the panels for crane handling and are often ganged together for longer runs.

• *Plastic panels* – Some manufacturers are now making form panels of heavy-gauge plastic. These panels are light and easy to handle. The horizontal and vertical support members are built into the panel as it is formed.

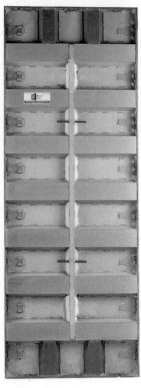

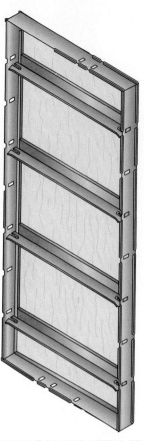

PERI GmbH

(A) ALL-METAL PANEL   (B) PLYWOOD AND METAL FRAME   (C) HEAVY-DUTY PANEL

308F07.EPS

Figure 7 ◆ Examples of form panels.

Wall Form Construction in Process

INSIDE TRACK

This is an example of a hand-set wall form using plywood panels installed in manufactured frames, along with wooden walers, strongbacks, and braces. The braces are secured to temporary concrete blocks called deadmen, which were poured for that purpose. On the other side of the form, you can see that the plywood panels have been sprayed with form release agent. The rebar mat has been placed in preparation for construction of the other half of the form on the footing.

308SA01.EPS

3.3.0 Gang Forms

Steel and plywood panels and all-steel panels are designed so they can be connected into large panels called gang forms or gangs (*Figure 8*).

Using the special ties and connecting hardware supplied by the manufacturer, large panels can be built on the ground where it is easier to work. The final gang form may be 40' to 50' wide. These gang panel forms are raised by the use of cranes and other mechanical movers.

Gang forms are commonly used to build retaining walls, sound barriers, and bridge abutments, in addition to walls and columns. Gang forms are designed with extra strength to withstand the stresses of being lifted and moved. They are considered to be easier to strip than so-called handset forms because the form is heavier and the crane applies a lifting force to the form.

308F08.EPS

Figure 8 ◆ Gang forms.

 WARNING!

The crane should never be used to break a gang form free from the concrete because it could endanger workers. The form should be pried loose from the top while the crane is supporting it.

 *INSIDE TRACK*

Gang Forms

The heavier the form material, the larger the crane required to move it. Some contractors use aluminum forming systems that can be moved with a small crane. This can save considerable expense. Steel frames are much heavier, but are also able to withstand greater lateral pressure. Some guidelines to ensure the safe lifting of gang wall forms are:

- Attach the crane rigging only to lifting brackets made for use with the form system.
- Make sure that the rigging does not overload any one lifting bracket.
- Use a lifting (spreader) beam for all lifts, especially those involving gang forms that have several lifting brackets.
- When the gang form is being lifted, make sure it hangs plumb and straight.
- Use a minimum of two tag lines to safely control the movement of the gang form while it is being lifted.
- Make sure that the gang form is adequately braced and securely fastened in position before releasing the lifting mechanism.
- Be sure to insert a tie-off connector in the concrete for the last form section in a gang. Never tie off to the form itself when breaking the form loose.

A large portion of the cost of concrete-in-place is the concrete formwork. Any system that works satisfactorily in achieving the end results in a safe and economical way is advantageous. The advantages of gang panel forms are:

- *Less time in erecting the form* – Gang forms can be built on the ground (*Figure 9*), then raised by crane to their position.
- *Less time in stripping* – Stripping is quicker because the large forms are stripped as a unit.
- *Reuse* – If the forms are assembled and used correctly, then stripped and cleaned with reasonable care, most systems can be reused. Some form panels can be used hundreds of times before they need to be replaced.

WALER   STRONGBACK   FORM PANEL

308F09.EPS

Figure 9 ◆ Gang form assembly.

4.0.0 ◆ PATENTED WALL-FORMING SYSTEMS

This section provides examples of manufactured wall-forming systems. These systems are all designed to perform the same basic function, but each of them has different framework designs, attaching hardware, and accessories. Keep in mind that these examples are a small sampling of the many types of wall forms available. There are many manufacturers of wall forms, and each of the manufacturers may have several product lines within the broad category of wall forms.

The purpose of this material is to familiarize you with some of the different designs. It is your responsibility to obtain and read the manufacturer's instructions for assembly, stripping, and storage of the particular forms used at the job site.

The examples in *Figures 10* and *11* are light-weight panel systems designed to be hand-set. They require no crane. Other systems, such as the EFCO® gang form shown in *Figure 12*, are designed to be assembled at the site assembly area, then moved to the pour site by a crane. Such forms are larger and much heavier than the assemble-in-place type. They are made of ⅛" steel plate with heavy-duty support members. One form panel can weigh up to 500 pounds, in comparison to the system shown in *Figure 10*, where the largest panel weighs about 50 pounds.

In contrast to the previously described systems, EFCO's heaviest-duty form system can weigh over 2,100 pounds per panel, with panels as large as 96 square feet (12' × 8').

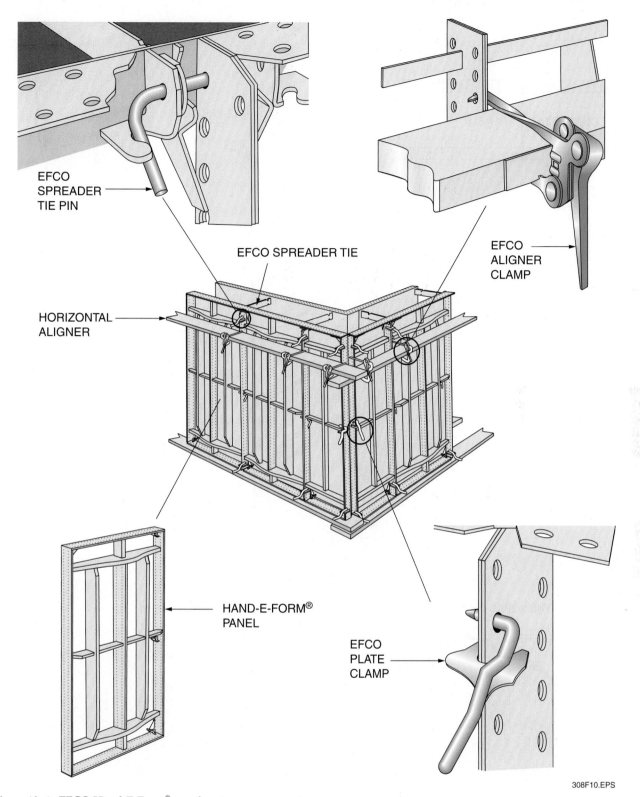

EFCO SPREADER TIE PIN

EFCO SPREADER TIE

EFCO ALIGNER CLAMP

HORIZONTAL ALIGNER

HAND-E-FORM® PANEL

EFCO PLATE CLAMP

308F10.EPS

Figure 10 ◆ EFCO Hand-E-Form® panel system components.

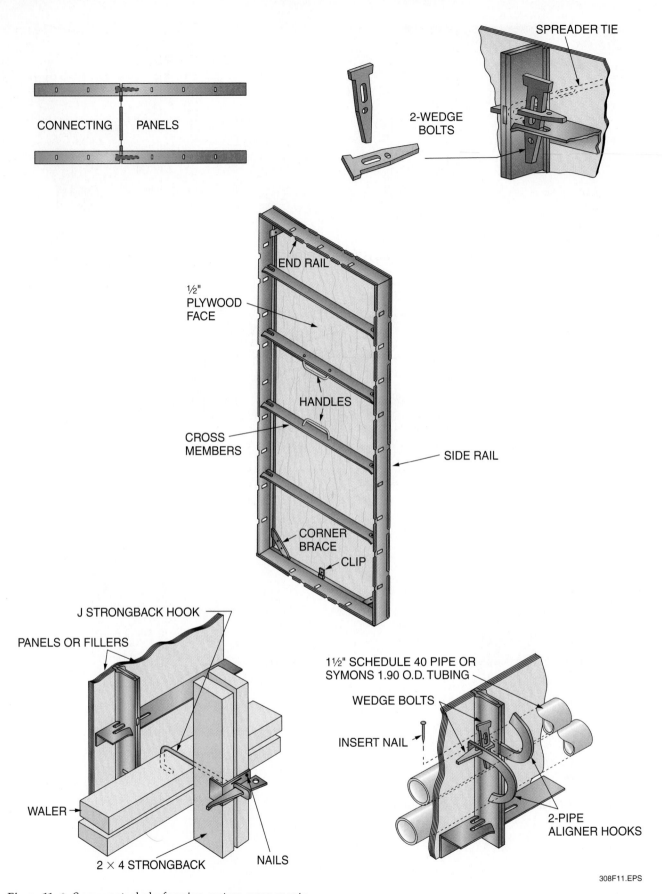

Figure 11 ◆ Symons steel ply-forming system components.

308F11.EPS

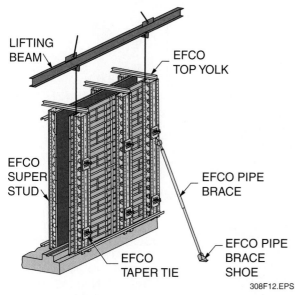

LIFTING BEAM

EFCO TOP YOLK

EFCO SUPER STUD

EFCO PIPE BRACE

EFCO PIPE BRACE SHOE

EFCO TAPER TIE

308F12.EPS

Figure 12 ◆ Example of gang wall form made of EFCO "Lite" panels.

Figure 13 shows a heavy-duty wall-forming system manufactured by Symons Corporation. Note that it is has larger frame members and is assembled with bolts and nuts rather than the quick-connect hardware used with the light-duty Symons form shown in *Figure 11*.

Figures 14, 15, and *16* show three different levels of the form system manufactured by Gates & Sons. Unlike the wall systems shown previously, the Gates system does not include panels. It is a system of hardware components designed to be used with plywood and lumber or with panels produced by other manufacturers.

NOTE

Gang forms are never pinned. They are either bolted or connected with proprietary locking devices.

Pouring and Inspection Windows in Forms

The design of most manufactured straight and curved forming systems allows an individual form panel to be removed and replaced at any time from an installed formwork without disturbing the other form panels. This provides a temporary window in the formwork that can be used to clean, inspect, or place concrete in the form.

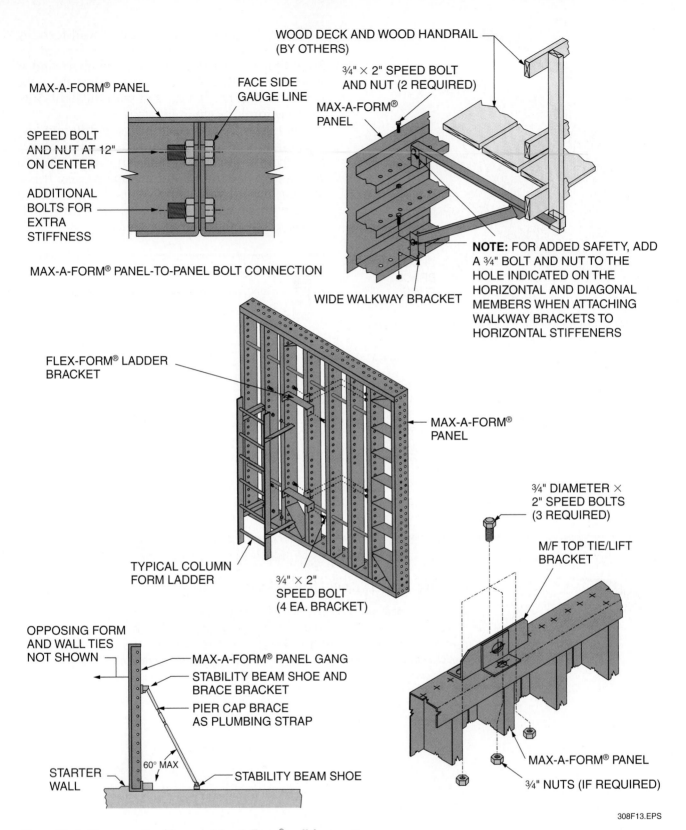

MAX-A-FORM® PANEL

FACE SIDE GAUGE LINE

SPEED BOLT AND NUT AT 12" ON CENTER

ADDITIONAL BOLTS FOR EXTRA STIFFNESS

MAX-A-FORM® PANEL-TO-PANEL BOLT CONNECTION

WOOD DECK AND WOOD HANDRAIL (BY OTHERS)

¾" × 2" SPEED BOLT AND NUT (2 REQUIRED)

MAX-A-FORM® PANEL

WIDE WALKWAY BRACKET

NOTE: FOR ADDED SAFETY, ADD A ¾" BOLT AND NUT TO THE HOLE INDICATED ON THE HORIZONTAL AND DIAGONAL MEMBERS WHEN ATTACHING WALKWAY BRACKETS TO HORIZONTAL STIFFENERS

FLEX-FORM® LADDER BRACKET

MAX-A-FORM® PANEL

TYPICAL COLUMN FORM LADDER

¾" × 2" SPEED BOLT (4 EA. BRACKET)

¾" DIAMETER × 2" SPEED BOLTS (3 REQUIRED)

M/F TOP TIE/LIFT BRACKET

OPPOSING FORM AND WALL TIES NOT SHOWN

MAX-A-FORM® PANEL GANG

STABILITY BEAM SHOE AND BRACE BRACKET

PIER CAP BRACE AS PLUMBING STRAP

STARTER WALL

60° MAX

STABILITY BEAM SHOE

MAX-A-FORM® PANEL

¾" NUTS (IF REQUIRED)

308F13.EPS

Figure 13 ◆ Components of Symons Max-A-Form® wall form system.

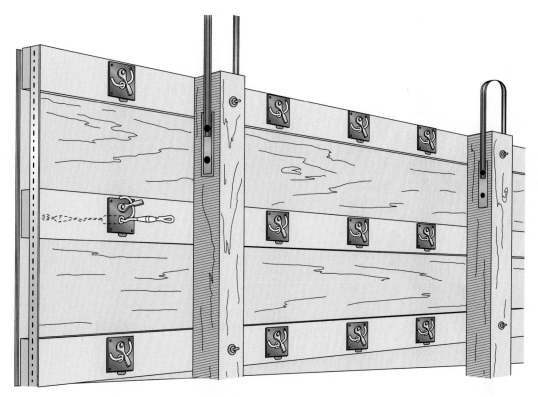

308F14.EPS

Figure 14 ◆ Gates Anchor-Lock® forming system—regular duty.

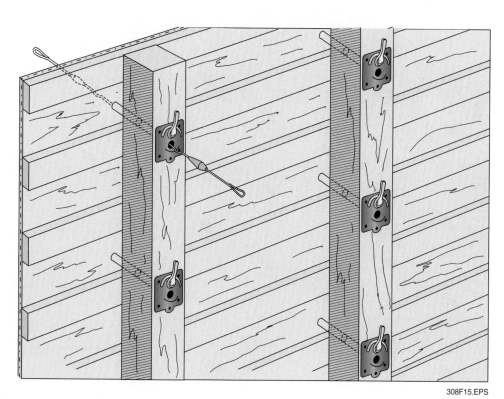

308F15.EPS

Figure 15 ◆ Gates Anchor-Lock® forming system—medium duty.

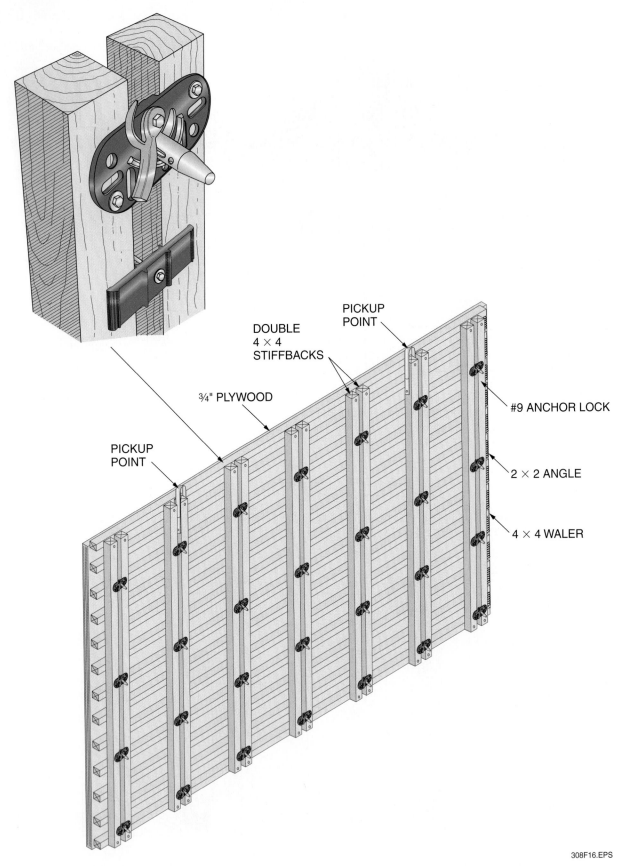

PICKUP
POINT

DOUBLE
4 × 4
STIFFBACKS

¾" PLYWOOD

PICKUP
POINT

#9 ANCHOR LOCK

2 × 2 ANGLE

4 × 4 WALER

308F16.EPS

Figure 16 ◆ Gates Anchor-Lock® forming system—heavy duty.

4.1.0 Curved Forms

Several manufacturers offer flexible wall forms that can be used to form tanks, retaining walls, and a variety of other curved surfaces (*Figure 17*). Several different styles of these forms are available. Some are made of flexible steel or aluminum panels shaped by curved ribs (*Figure 18*). Others use curved walers combined with strongbacks of metal or wood such as the Gates systems shown in *Figure 19*.

Still other radius form systems use panels with flexible joints. These panels are placed into special templates, and their tension bolts are adjusted to form the panel to the curvature of the template (*Figure 20*).

Although patented forms for curved walls are readily available, curved forms can also be made from wood. In a curved wood frame, the top and bottom plates of the form panel, as well as the panel itself, are made of plywood or plyform (*Figure 21*). In cases where the weight of the concrete demands heavier-gauge plates and plywood, sections can be cut out and laminated to obtain the necessary thickness. Radius walers are cut the same way.

In order to bend sheathing into short-radius curves, it may be necessary to cut notches (kerfs) in the plywood with a circular saw (*Figure 22*). It is generally better to use two sheets of thinner sheathing than to kerf a thick sheet, because scoring the sheathing may reduce its strength.

It makes a difference how the bend is made in relation to the face grain of the plywood. A bend made with the face grain can achieve a tighter radius than one made against the face grain.

308F17.EPS

Figure 17 ◆ Example of curved form use.

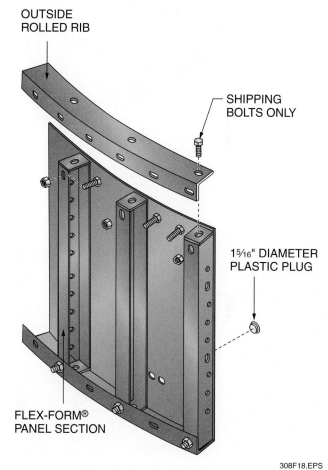

OUTSIDE ROLLED RIB

SHIPPING BOLTS ONLY

1⁵⁄₁₆" DIAMETER PLASTIC PLUG

FLEX-FORM® PANEL SECTION

308F18.EPS

Figure 18 ◆ Symons Flex-Form® system.

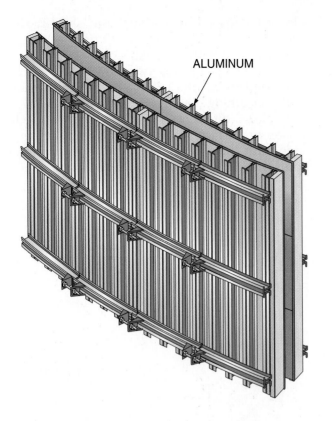
ALUMINUM

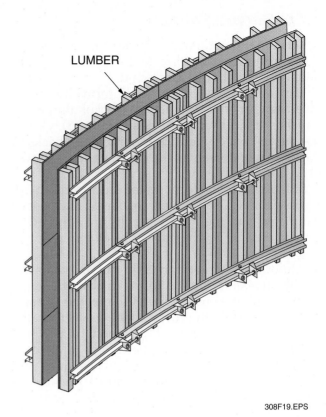
LUMBER

308F19.EPS

Figure 19 ◆ Gates and Sons radius waler system.

PERI GmbH

308F20.EPS

Figure 20 ◆ Radius form template.

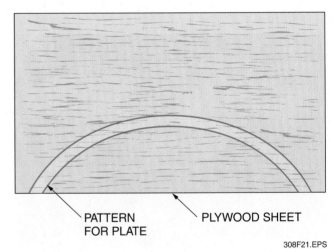
PATTERN
FOR PLATE

PLYWOOD SHEET

308F21.EPS

Figure 21 ◆ Cutting a curved form plate from a sheet of plywood.

Safety

Any formwork 5' and higher requires the use of scaffolding equipped with guardrails, midrails, and toe boards along all open sides and ends. When working on this scaffolding, fall protection equipment must also be worn. These requirements are covered in *OSHA 29 CFR, Part 1926, Subsection 500*. Some form panels contain bars that can be used to secure a safety line. This allows workers to work safely with both hands while building or stripping forms.

308SA02.EPS

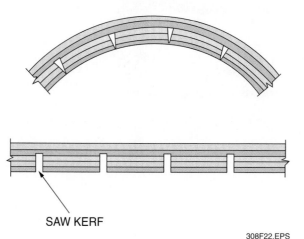

SAW KERF

308F22.EPS

Figure 22 ◆ Using saw kerfs to bend sheathing.

Form Faces

The steel frame and plywood on some forming systems will leave marks on the concrete, so these forms cannot be used for architectural finishes. For example, when a plywood panel has defects in it, those defects will be transferred to the concrete finish. Some newer systems have a plastic-coated form face. If it gets damaged, the defect can be covered by applying a plastic filler and sanding it smooth.

4.2.0 Framing Wall Openings

Openings for windows and doors can be formed using **bucks**, which are wood or steel frames installed between the inner and outer wall forms. A typical buck consists of a plywood or lumber frame supported by braces (*Figure 23*). In some cases, the metal window or door frame itself can be set into the form and used as a buck. In such cases, the frame must be plumbed, aligned, and properly braced to ensure that proper placement is maintained through the pour.

If small openings are needed for ducts, vents, and large pipes, small wood box frames, rigid foam plastic blocks, or frames made of sheet metal or fiber can be used. Vibrator holes are needed in the window bucks to make sure the concrete fills the space beneath the window opening. The plugs are put back in place after the concrete is vibrated.

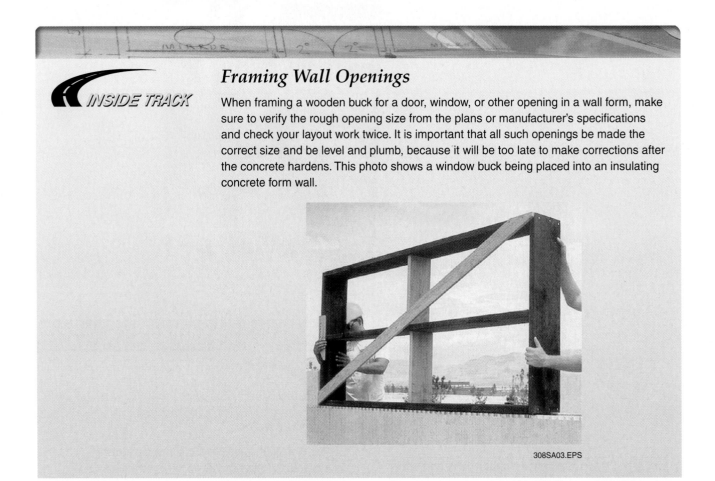

INSIDE TRACK

Framing Wall Openings

When framing a wooden buck for a door, window, or other opening in a wall form, make sure to verify the rough opening size from the plans or manufacturer's specifications and check your layout work twice. It is important that all such openings be made the correct size and be level and plumb, because it will be too late to make corrections after the concrete hardens. This photo shows a window buck being placed into an insulating concrete form wall.

308SA03.EPS

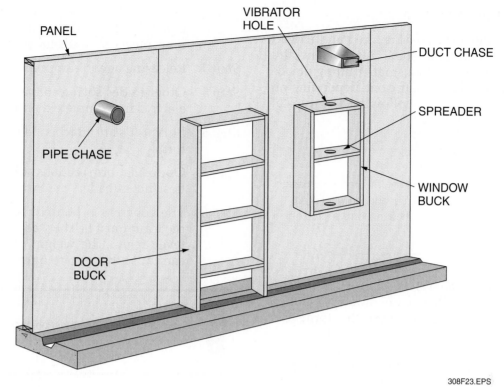

Figure 23 ◆ Wall form openings.

308F23.EPS

5.0.0 ◆ FORM CONSTRUCTION

When erecting forms, it is critical to have the right materials and equipment in the right place at the right time. Any delays can cause a heavy cost burden in wasted manpower, as well as the rental cost for equipment and materials. For starters, formwork needs to be properly staged in preparation for construction.

5.1.0 Preparation

- Formwork must be received from the storage yard or from the formwork leasing company.
- As the formwork components and attaching hardware are offloaded, they must be checked against the order to make sure everything is present.
- Tools needed to construct the forms must be gathered. This includes spud wrenches, impact wrenches, pry bars, and any proprietary tools.
- The wall must be laid out on the foundation and the sill prepared to receive the form.
- Someone must shoot the grades and place shims to level the form.

5.2.0 Assembling the Form

Gang forms are usually assembled on the ground, then moved by crane or other lifting device to the erection location.

- The formwork is first laid out in accordance with the supplier's shop drawings.
- The form sections are then assembled per the manufacturer's instructions. During the assembly, the forms must be checked to ensure that they are true and straight.
- Lifting eyes must be placed in accordance with the drawings and must be installed correctly.

 WARNING!
It is very important to determine the weight of the finished form and to make sure the lifting eyes will support that weight.

- Once the form section is assembled, it must be flipped over. Make sure the braces are installed before that is done.
- Once the form section is flipped over, the form liners, reveals, and other materials are placed.
- Before lifting the form, make sure the hardware is lubricated.

5.3.0 Setting the Form

At this point, the form panel is lifted and moved into place on the foundation. A crane is generally used for this purpose, but a smaller lifting device such as a forklift may be sufficient, depending on the size of the form. The following is a typical sequence.

WARNING!
This is a critical time in the form erection process. Make sure tag lines are set and the wind is not going to be a problem once the form is lifted off the ground.

Step 1 The form panel is flown in, set into place, and braced. Pins made of rebar are often set into the foundation so that forms can be pushed up against them to ensure proper placement as shown in *Figure 24*. Note the rebar mat already in place. There are other methods of positioning the form, including the use of a fiberglass product or placing the form on a wood sill.

Step 2 The form must be checked for level and plumb, and the braces adjusted as necessary.

Step 3 Once the form is braced-off, the form panel is unhooked from the crane. At that time, blockouts and embeds are installed.

Step 4 Releasing agent is applied to the form.

Step 5 Other trades such as rebar installers and electricians complete their work.

Step 6 Bulkheads are attached to the ends of the form.

Step 7 Opposing form sections are placed. Form ties and spreaders are installed.

Step 8 The concrete is poured. After the pour, the form must be checked for plumb and level again. The weight of the concrete can cause the form to move.

NOTE
Project specifications must be checked to determine when the form can be stripped.

Step 9 When it is time to strip the form, ties, braces, and spreaders are removed, but one tie is left in place.

Step 10 The crane is hooked up to the form.

NOTE
At this point, it is important to have an experienced crane operator and signal person to ensure that the right amount of tension is applied to the form.

Step 11 The final tie is removed and the form is pried loose from the concrete using wedges.

Step 12 The form is flown out, then cleaned, lubricated, and reset for the next pour.

Step 13 Tie holes in the finished concrete are filled, and other necessary patching is done.

When the formwork is no longer needed, it is returned to the staging area. All the materials must be cleaned and lubricated at that time.

An inventory of all materials must be performed and verified against the received inventory. If the formwork is rented, the rental company will have a detailed inventory. If any material is not returned, they will charge your company for it. This can become very expensive.

308F24.EPS

Figure 24 ◆ Pins for positioning new gang form sections.

6.0.0 ◆ COLUMN FORMS

Column forms are made from a variety of materials. They may be round, oval, square, or rectangular (*Figure 25*). Column forms require tight joints and strong tie supports.

Multi-purpose metal forms can also be used as column forms. *Figure 26* is an example of a square form constructed from the same panels and hardware used for build-in-place wall forms.

Round forms are made of fiber, fiberglass, fiberglass-reinforced plastic, or steel. Although it is possible to build round forms entirely from lumber, that method is very labor intensive and is therefore not commonly used.

Figure 27 shows a one-piece form made of reinforced fiberglass manufactured by MFG. The bracing collar is attached near the top, then the

MOLDED FIBERGLASS

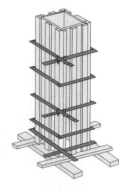

PLYWOOD

STEEL

FIBER (PAPER)

308F25.EPS

Figure 25 ◆ Materials commonly used for column forms.

unit is aligned with a plumb bob and braces are installed to keep it in position. When the concrete is dry, the bolts are taken off and the form is spread apart at the flange and removed. It can also be lifted off the column by a crane.

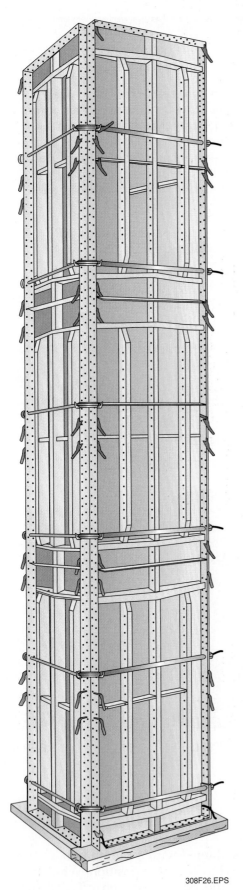

Figure 26 ◆ Square column constructed with EFCO Hand-E-Form® system.

308F26.EPS

6.1.0 Fiber Column Forms

Fiber forms (*Figure 28*) are manufactured by wrapping layers of fiber in a spiral to produce tubes of the desired diameter. They are easily sawed to any length and can be erected quickly.

Most fiber forms are made to be used once. If there is a delay in placing concrete after a fiber form has been set in position, the form must be protected against rain and snow by covering the top with a waterproof sheathing and by keeping snow and rain from accumulating around the base.

6.2.0 Steel Column Forms

Steel forms consisting of sheet metal attached to prefabricated steel shapes are frequently used for round columns when the number of reuses justifies the initial cost or where special conditions require their use. Full circles are assembled by joining two half-circles with steel bolts. Sections may be stacked on top of each other and bolted together to provide forms of any desired height.

Figure 29 shows an all-steel form manufactured by EFCO. These forms are available in diameters from 12" to 48" and are furnished in 180-degree sections.

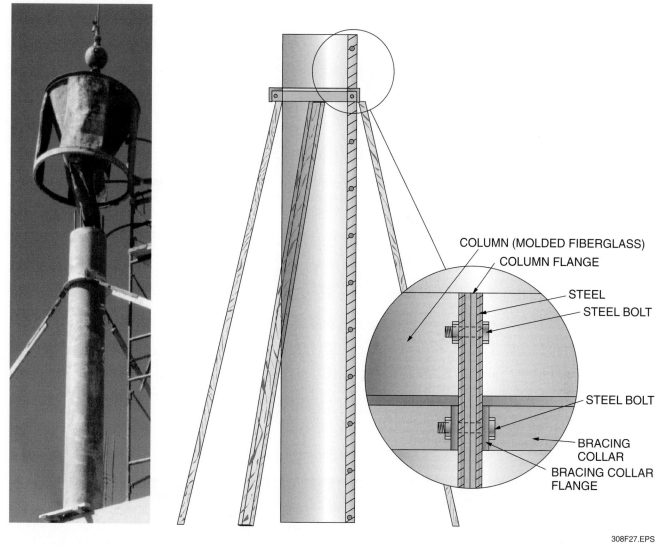

COLUMN (MOLDED FIBERGLASS)
COLUMN FLANGE
STEEL
STEEL BOLT
STEEL BOLT
BRACING COLLAR
BRACING COLLAR FLANGE

308F27.EPS

Figure 27 ◆ MFG round column form.

308F28.EPS

Figure 28 ◆ Fiber column forms.

Forms of larger diameters (up to 120") are furnished in either 90-degree or 60-degree sections. These standard forms are available in 1', 2', 4', and 12' lengths, or by special order in 6', 8', and 10' lengths. The column form sections are assembled at horizontal and vertical joints by bolts made for use with this system. Specially designed split washers permit stripping with a crane without disassembly of the forms.

Form sections of the same diameter are interchangeable, and various lengths may be stacked to reach the desired height. Round column form sections have lifting eyes at the top of each section for easy lifting with a crane. A combination of round and flat form sections can be used to build the form for an oval (bullnose) pier (*Figure 30*). The same types of components can be used to build the girders that sit on top of piers.

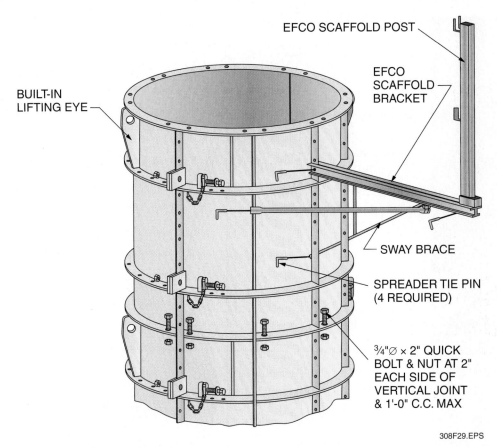

BUILT-IN
LIFTING EYE

EFCO SCAFFOLD POST

EFCO
SCAFFOLD
BRACKET

SWAY BRACE

SPREADER TIE PIN
(4 REQUIRED)

¾"∅ × 2" QUICK
BOLT & NUT AT 2"
EACH SIDE OF
VERTICAL JOINT
& 1'-0" C.C. MAX

308F29.EPS

Figure 29 ◆ All-steel round column form.

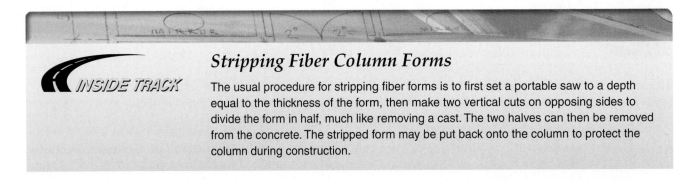

Stripping Fiber Column Forms

The usual procedure for stripping fiber forms is to first set a portable saw to a depth equal to the thickness of the form, then make two vertical cuts on opposing sides to divide the form in half, much like removing a cast. The two halves can then be removed from the concrete. The stripped form may be put back onto the column to protect the column during construction.

6.3.0 Job-Built Column Forms

Although any type of column form, including round forms, can be made from lumber and sheathing, usually only square and rectangular forms are assembled in this manner. Round and oval columns are more likely to be made from pre-fabricated (manufactured) forms.

Square and rectangular column forms are made of sheathing and **battens**, which are 2 × 4 lumber placed flat against the sheathing to act as **studs** (*Figure 31*). Braces are used to support and align the forms. The use of battens helps reduce the number of column clamps that would otherwise be needed to prevent the sheathing from bulging.

Note that the clamps are spaced closer together at the bottom of the form because that is the area that is subjected to the greatest pressure from plastic concrete. *Figure 31* shows manufactured clamps, but 2 × 4 walers are also used.

Figure 32 shows the typical clamp spacing for 20' and 10' round forms. If the form is more than 36" square, or if there is a rapid pour rate, additional clamps may be needed. If manufactured clamps are used, the manufacturer will specify the spacing.

Figure 33 shows examples of the kinds of clamps used to hold column forms together. The clamps are used in place of walers.

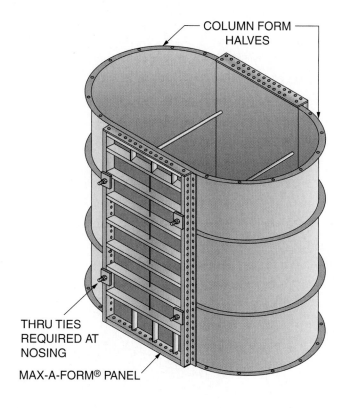

COLUMN FORM HALVES

THRU TIES REQUIRED AT NOSING

MAX-A-FORM® PANEL

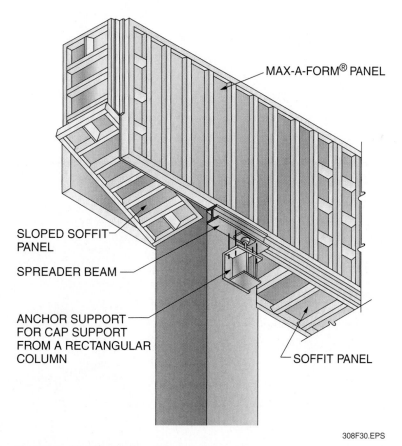

MAX-A-FORM® PANEL

SLOPED SOFFIT PANEL

SPREADER BEAM

ANCHOR SUPPORT FOR CAP SUPPORT FROM A RECTANGULAR COLUMN

SOFFIT PANEL

308F30.EPS

Figure 30 ◆ Bullnose pier constructed by heavy-duty form components.

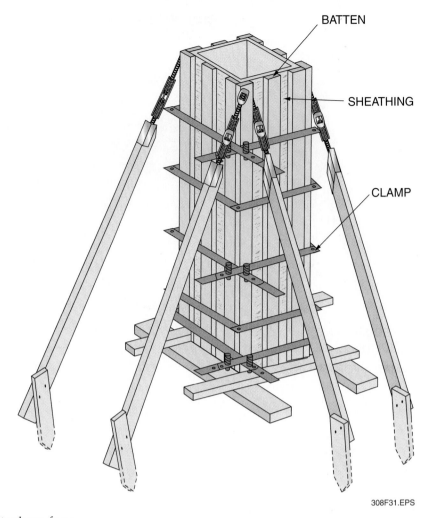

BATTEN

SHEATHING

CLAMP

308F31.EPS

Figure 31 ◆ Job-built column form.

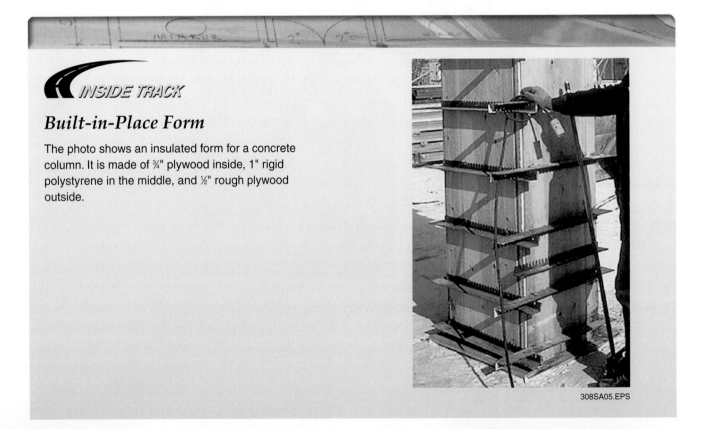

Built-in-Place Form

The photo shows an insulated form for a concrete column. It is made of ¾" plywood inside, 1" rigid polystyrene in the middle, and ½" rough plywood outside.

308SA05.EPS

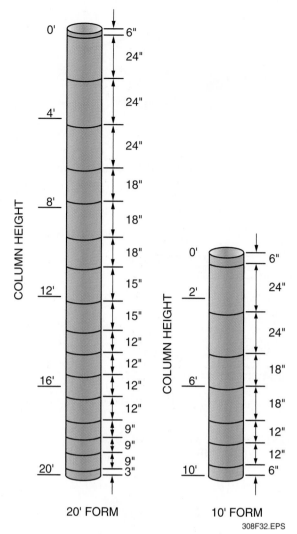

Figure 32 ◆ Typical spacing of column form clamps.

20' FORM

COLUMN HEIGHT

0' — 6"
24"
24"
4' — 24"
18"
8' — 18"
18"
15"
12' — 15"
12"
12"
16' — 12"
12"
9"
9"
9"
20' — 3"

10' FORM

COLUMN HEIGHT

0' — 6"
24"
2' — 24"
18"
6' — 18"
12"
12"
10' — 6"

308F32.EPS

INSIDE TRACK

Common Causes of Form Failure

The most common points of form failure are joints and corners. Some common causes of form failure include:

- Exceeding the form design working pressure as a result of:
  - Excessive rate of concrete placement
  - Concrete mix design not taken into account
  - Improper vibration of the concrete
  - Temperature not taken into account
- Form ties incorrectly placed or improperly fastened
- Improper form construction, especially when layout plans are not provided
- Form fillers, corners, and bulkheads not adequately designed and/or constructed
- Lack of or improper bracing of the form
- Connecting hardware not installed
- Not inspected by authorized qualified personnel to see if the form layout has been interpreted correctly

HINGED, DOUBLE-BAR CLAMP

SINGLE-BAR CLAMP

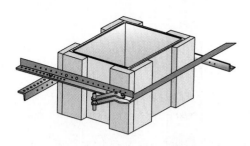

GATES LOK-FAST COLUMN CLAMP

SINGLE BAR CLAMP

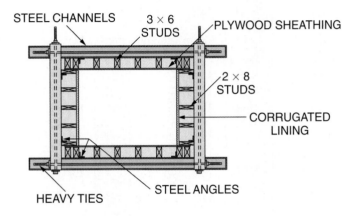

STEEL CHANNELS — 3 × 6 STUDS — PLYWOOD SHEATHING — 2 × 8 STUDS — CORRUGATED LINING — STEEL ANGLES — HEAVY TIES

STEEL CHANNEL AND TIE BOLTS (ALL THREAD)

SCISSORS CLAMP

LIGHT-DUTY CLAMP

308F33.EPS

Figure 33 ◆ Column form clamps.

Trade Terms
Introduced in This Module

Architectural concrete: Concrete that serves as the architectural finish material.

Batten: A thin, narrow strip of lumber used to cover the joint between wider boards. In forms, a batten is a strip of lumber laid flat against the sheathing to provide reinforcement.

Brace: A diagonal supporting member used to reinforce a form against the weight of the concrete.

Buck: A frame placed inside a concrete form to provide an opening for a window or door.

Climbing form: A form used to construct vertical walls in successive pours. It is raised to a new level for each pour.

Gang form: A form in which prefabricated panels are connected to create a larger unit.

Plastic concrete: Concrete in a liquid or a semiliquid workable state.

Rustication line: An indentation made in a concrete panel by attaching a thin (¾", for example) strip of tapered wood or plastic to the form.

Sheathing: Plywood, planks, or sheet metal that make up the surface of a form.

Shiplap: Boards that have been rabbeted on both edges so that they overlap when they are placed together.

Slipform: A form that moves continuously while the concrete is being placed.

Spreader: A wood or metal device used to hold the sides of a form apart.

Strongback: An upright supporting member attached to the back of a form to stiffen or reinforce it, especially around door and window openings.

Studs: Vertical members of a form panel used to support sheathing.

This module is intended to be a thorough resource for task training. The following reference works are suggested for further study. These are optional materials for continued education rather than for task training.

Principles and Practices of Commercial Construction, Prentice Hall, Upper Saddle River, NJ.

Scaffold, Shoring, and Forming Institute. www.ssfi.org.

NCCER makes every effort to keep these textbooks up-to-date and free of technical errors. We appreciate your help in this process. If you have an idea for improving this textbook, or if you find an error, a typographical mistake, or an inaccuracy in NCCER's Contren® textbooks, please write us, using this form or a photocopy. Be sure to include the exact module number, page number, a detailed description, and the correction, if applicable. Your input will be brought to the attention of the Technical Review Committee. Thank you for your assistance.

Instructors – If you found that additional materials were necessary in order to teach this module effectively, please let us know so that we may include them in the Equipment/Materials list in the Annotated Instructor's Guide.

Write: Product Development and Revision
National Center for Construction Education and Research
3600 NW 43rd St., Bldg. G, Gainesville, FL 32606

Fax: 352-334-0932

E-mail: curriculum@nccer.org

Craft _____ Module Name _____

Copyright Date _____ Module Number _____ Page Number(s) _____

Description _____

_____

_____

_____

(Optional) Correction _____

_____

_____

(Optional) Your Name and Address _____

_____

_____

Horizontal Formwork
27309-07

27309-07
Horizontal Formwork

Topics to be presented in this module include:

Overview

Concrete forms are used in the construction of building floors, bridge decks, culverts, beams, girders, and other horizontal concrete structures. Most of the horizontal forms you encounter will be specialized forms manufactured for a specific purpose, such as forming a bridge deck or the floors of a high-rise building. When a deck is being formed and poured, it must be supported from underneath by shoring until the concrete hardens. Anyone doing heavy commercial or industrial carpentry work can expect to work with these special forming and shoring systems.

Objectives

When you have completed this module, you will be able to do the following:

1. Identify the safety hazards associated with elevated deck formwork and explain how to eliminate them.
2. Identify the different types of elevated decks.
3. Identify the different types of flying form systems.
4. Identify different types of handset form systems.
5. Erect, plumb, brace, and level different types of handset deck form systems.
6. Install edge forms, blockouts, embedments, and construction joints.
7. Identify typical bridge and culvert form systems.

Trade Terms

Capital
Corrugated
Dead load
Haunch

Live load
Phosphatized
Profile

Required Trainee Materials

1. Pencil and paper
2. Appropriate personal protective equipment

Prerequisites

Before you begin this module, it is recommended that you successfully complete *Core Curriculum*; *Carpentry Level One*; *Carpentry Level Two*; and *Carpentry Level Three*, Modules 27301-07 through 27308-07.

   This course map shows all of the modules in the third level of the *Carpentry* curriculum. The suggested training order begins at the bottom and proceeds up. Skill levels increase as you advance on the course map. The local Training Program Sponsor may adjust the training order.

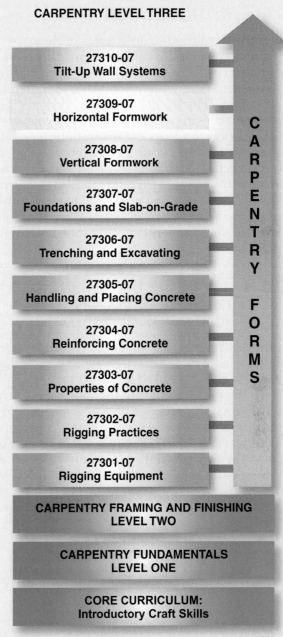

CARPENTRY LEVEL THREE

27310-07
Tilt-Up Wall Systems

27309-07
Horizontal Formwork

27308-07
Vertical Formwork

27307-07
Foundations and Slab-on-Grade

27306-07
Trenching and Excavating

27305-07
Handling and Placing Concrete

27304-07
Reinforcing Concrete

27303-07
Properties of Concrete

27302-07
Rigging Practices

27301-07
Rigging Equipment

CARPENTRY FRAMING AND FINISHING
LEVEL TWO

CARPENTRY FUNDAMENTALS
LEVEL ONE

CORE CURRICULUM:
Introductory Craft Skills

CARPENTRY FORMS

309CMAP.EPS

1.0.0 ◆ INTRODUCTION

This is the third module in a series of three modules about concrete forming systems. It provides information on various types of horizontal forming systems used widely in heavy commercial construction. Horizontal forming systems are used primarily in the construction of elevated structural floor and deck slabs in buildings and garages, in bridge decking construction, and in the construction of drainage and culvert systems. Also described in this module are the shoring methods used in conjunction with horizontal forming systems and the safety considerations related to working with shoring and horizontal forming systems.

2.0.0 ◆ TYPES OF STRUCTURAL-CONCRETE FLOOR AND ROOF SLABS

A number of elevated structurally reinforced concrete floor and roof slabs are used for buildings (*Figure 1*). The type used depends on the loads that will be imposed on the slab, the span of the slab between supports, the type of frame used for the building, and the number of stories. Structural slabs differ from slabs-on-grade in that they must support their own weight (**dead load**) as well as any weight that will be placed on the slab (**live load**). Slabs-on-grade and the loads placed on them are supported by compacted material below the slab.

2.1.0 One-Way Solid Slabs

One-way solid slabs are also called one-way beam and slab floors or roofs. One-way solid slabs span across parallel lines of support formed by beams or walls. In most cases the concrete for beams and slabs is placed at the same time. Sometimes, the concrete for supporting columns is placed at the same time as the beams and slabs. The slab reinforcement is placed across the span to beams or walls. Shrinkage steel runs perpendicular to the span. These types of slabs can support relatively high loads over short spans and are generally used for spans of less than 20' because their mass becomes too expensive for wider applications. Slab thickness ranges from 4" to 10". Structural engineers must design the shoring supporting the formwork for the slabs as well as the beams because of the massive weight of the concrete being placed all at once.

Instead of standard beams with a depth of 2 or 3 times the width, beams that are wider than they are deep (slab bands) are sometimes used. The slab band is thinner than the outside beams. It also reduces the width of the slab, which, in turn, reduces the slab thickness and the amount of slab reinforcement.

2.2.0 Two-Way Flat Slabs

These slabs have reinforcement placed in both directions at 90-degrees to each other (two ways). Except at the perimeter, beams and walls are not normally required to support two-way flat slabs because building columns with thickened drop

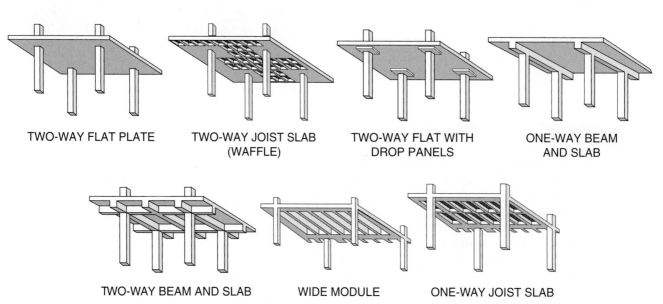

TWO-WAY FLAT PLATE   TWO-WAY JOIST SLAB (WAFFLE)   TWO-WAY FLAT WITH DROP PANELS   ONE-WAY BEAM AND SLAB

TWO-WAY BEAM AND SLAB   WIDE MODULE   ONE-WAY JOIST SLAB

309F01.EPS

Figure 1 ◆ Types of structural-concrete floor and roof slabs.

panels (heads) centered above each column support the slab. These floors are normally used for storage buildings and parking garages. For very heavily loaded industrial floors, a two-way slab is sometimes placed over a grid of beams and girders supported by columns. These are called two-way beam and slab floors. Two-way flat slabs are cast on temporary plywood decks supported by shoring and temporary wood or metal beams and stringers. In many cases, removable (flying) decks covered with plywood are used to eliminate having to tear down and re-erect the decks for each floor. Shoring and decking, including flying decks, are covered later in this module.

Slab thicknesses range between 4" and 12" depending on the span width, which is usually below 34'. The minimum size of the drop panel is ⅓ of the span and its thickness is normally 1¼ times the slab thickness. At one time, decorative mushroom **capitals** at the top of the columns were used in addition to the drop panels; however, they are not used much anymore because they are expensive to construct.

2.3.0 Two-Way Flat Plate Slabs

Two-way flat plate slabs are lighter duty versions of two-way solid flat slabs without drop panels. They vary in thickness from 5" to 10" with spans up to 32'. Because they are easily formed, they are generally used in high-rise apartment and office buildings with light floor loads. Both two-way solid flat slabs and flat plate slabs are generally cantilevered beyond the last row of columns for a distance of about 30 percent of the interior span to take advantage of the slab's structural continuity. If the cantilever is not used, additional reinforcement is added to the slab edge to carry the higher stresses that will result. Like two-way flat slabs, flat plate slabs are cast using decks constructed with individual components or flying decks.

2.4.0 One-Way Joist Slabs

One-way joist slabs, also called ribbed slabs, are comprised of reinforced concrete ribs or joists that are monolithically cast with a thin slab on top (*Figure 2*). The joists (ribs) are formed into the supporting beams or joist bands as shown in the figure. The joist ends that are formed into supporting beams or joist bands are sometimes broadened. Because stirrups are usually not used in the joists due to space limitations, the broadened concrete at the ends provides sufficient resistance to diagonal tension forces. Joist bands, which are the same depth as the slab, are very wide beams placed over supporting columns and take the place of

309F02.EPS

Figure 2 ◆ A portion of a one-way joist slab.

structural beams that would be deeper and would complicate the formwork. Joist bands are cast using the same formwork supporting the slab. Sometimes, a distribution rib may be used at midspan to spread live floor loads across the joists.

There is very little non-working concrete in a one-way joist slab. This reduces the dead load and allows wider spans. Because the reinforcement steel is concentrated in the ribs, the slab can be much thinner and requires only shrinkage-temperature reinforcement. Slab thickness varies between 2½" and 4½". Joist spacing varies between 20" and 30" with depths of 6" to 20". The spans can be up to 45' wide. Overlapping manufactured steel or fiberglass-reinforced plastic (FRP) pan forms fastened to plywood decking can be used for casting these types of slabs. If required, a tapered pan is used to form the broadened joist ends. Site-built wooden pan forms using engineered wood joists and plywood can also be used.

2.5.0 Two-Way Joist Slabs

Two-way joist slabs, also called waffle slabs, are economically similar to one-way joist slabs. They are comprised of reinforced concrete ribs or joists that run at 90 degrees to each other (*Figure 3*). The waffle slabs can be formed using manufactured metal or FRP dome pans fastened to plywood decking. From an aesthetic viewpoint, the undersides of waffle slabs are more desirable than one-way joist slabs. In addition, they allow wider spans. In most cases, dome pans are not installed around the columns. This allows solid reinforced sections, called heads, that are the same thickness as the joists to be cast along with the slab. These heads accomplish the same function as drop panels in two-way flat slabs.

Wide-Module Joist Slabs

Another version of a one-way slab that is popular is the wide-module joist slab, also called a skip-joist slab. These slabs are formed with deep, wide metal or site-built pans that result in deeper joists with a wide spacing of 4' to 6'. These types of slabs are used when a slab thickness of 4½" or more is required for fireproofing. The thicker slab allows the use of wider joist spacing. The formwork for the slab in the figure is being assembled on a flat temporary plywood deck. Note the wide joist band in the foreground of the figure. The reinforcement for the joists and joist band has not yet been placed. Loads are higher in wide module joists than in normal one-way joists. This usually requires that stirrups be used near the end of each joist. Because joist space is constricted, U-stirrups must be installed at an angle or single-leg stirrups must be used. The figure shows site-built skip-joint pans.

309SA01.EPS

309F03.EPS

Figure 3 ◆ Underside of a two-way joist slab.

Although other sizes are available, standard size domes (30" × 30" or 19" × 19") result in 6"-wide joists on 3' centers or 5"-wide joists on 2' centers with depths from 8" to 20". Slab thickness usually ranges from 3" to 5" and spans can be 25' to 50'. If the slab is not cantilevered at an edge, then a reinforced perimeter beam is required at that edge.

2.6.0 Composite Slabs

Composite slabs combine the compressive strength of concrete and the tensile strength of steel to form a bonded combination that is stronger than either material by itself. **Corrugated** steel decking that is fastened to structural steel beams and joists of a building is used as the slab form. The concrete and the decking, which is left in place, form the composite slab. The decking bonds to the slab and acts as the slab reinforcement after the concrete cures.

Two methods of composite slab construction are used. One requires that the structural steel of the building be strong enough to support the decking and concrete without additional support while the concrete cures and bonds to the decking. The other method requires temporary support of lighter structural steel until the concrete cures and bonds to the decking.

Welded Stud Anchors

Besides composite slabs, welded studs are also used with other types of slabs that are placed in structural steel buildings. In these cases, the studs provide the only anchorage for the slabs.

In either case, the decking must be securely fastened to the structural steel by plug welding or spot welding. Welded stud anchors are also used to provide additional slab anchorage between the concrete and the structural steel. A wide variety of decking is available for use in floor or roof slabs in various gauges and rib heights with specific load-bearing capacities. Normally, the strength of the decking specified by the structural engineers is such that no deck support is required between structural steel spans when the deck concrete is placed and while the concrete cures.

2.7.0 Post-Tensioned Concrete Slabs

Post-tensioning tendons made of very high strength stranded-steel cable that is sheathed in plastic can be used in any of the previously described site cast slabs and any supporting beams, girders, or joists. It is used to reduce the size of these members, eliminate the need for temperature reinforcement, reduce the amount of standard reinforcement required, reduce slab cracking, and extend the span of a slab. Two-way flat plate slabs are commonly post-tensioned, and placement of post-tensioning tendons in these slabs is different from the placement of conventional reinforcement.

In a typical installation, tendons are placed closely together between columns in one direction across the slab. These closely spaced tendons are called banded tendons. Other tendons, called distributed tendons, are placed evenly in the other direction across the slab. However, the same number of tendons is used in both directions. Rebar can also be used at the column to provide additional shear resistance for the slab. The banded tendons are chaired high at the columns and low between the columns and at the edges of the slab unless a column is at the slab edge. The distributed tendons are chaired high over the banded tendons and low between the banded tendons and at the edges of the slab. After curing of the concrete and tensioning of the tendons, this draping causes upward pressure on the slab at the low points of the tendons and downward pressure at the high points. For slabs supported by structural steel

Post-Tensioned Slabs-on-Grade

Post-tensioning of slabs-on-grade is common in some areas of the country, especially the south and southwest, where soil required for support of the slab may be poor. In these applications, the post-tensioning tendons are equally spaced across the slab in both directions. This virtually eliminates slab cracking and the need for welded wire reinforcement.

beams, girders, and columns (such as noncomposite slabs on a metal deck or removable form slabs), the tendons are evenly distributed in both directions and are chaired high across the beams and girders and low between the beams and girders.

Structural engineers calculate the dead and live loads as well as short and long-term tensioning losses to determine the amount of tensioning required. The losses include elastic shortening of the concrete, friction of the tendons, initial movement (set) of the anchorages, steel relaxation, concrete shrinkage, and creep. Certified personnel must perform placement and tensioning of post-tensioning tendons.

3.0.0 ◆ TYPES OF FORM SYSTEMS

A variety of form systems are used to cast structural concrete slabs in heavy construction. These include systems for:

- Concrete slabs with concrete beams and girders
- Concrete slabs with no beams (flat slabs)
- Concrete slabs and joists using fiberglass-reinforced plastic (FRP) or metal pan forms
- Composite concrete slabs using corrugated steel decking forms

Elevated slab forms require shoring for support (*Figure 4*) during the casting and curing of the concrete. Shoring is a temporary structure designed

Figure 4 ◆ Scaffold-supported shoring in place for a floor under construction.

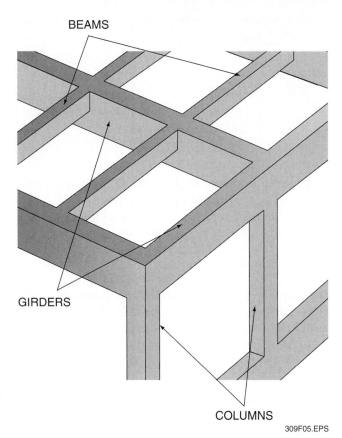

Figure 5 ◆ Beam/girder system.

to carry the weight of fresh concrete, reinforcing steel, and formwork, as well as any live loads (people, machines, etc.) that may be applied to the concrete during construction. The shoring is not removed until the concrete has reached a specified strength, typically 75 or 80 percent.

A concrete floor must be properly supported. Several methods are used for this purpose. For floors that will be required to bear heavy loads, a beam/girder system may be used (*Figure 5*). In this type of system, the beams and girders are tied to and rest on the columns. In some cases, the columns are poured first, then the beams and girders are formed. In other applications, the columns, beams, and girders are formed monolithically, which means that the concrete is poured for all three components at the same time to form one solid piece. The beams and girders are reinforced with steel bars that tie into the rebars of the columns above and below the floor.

Where lighter loads are involved, the slab receives its primary support from the columns. In some cases, a drop panel (*Figure 6*) is placed between the column and the slab. In the arrangement shown, a capital is added to the top of the column. The capital is an architectural rather than a structural feature.

3.1.0 Pan Forms

Commercial pan forms are mold-like steel or FRP forms that are used to construct concrete slab and beam joist systems. Two types are used: dome or square pans and long pans. Dome or square pans

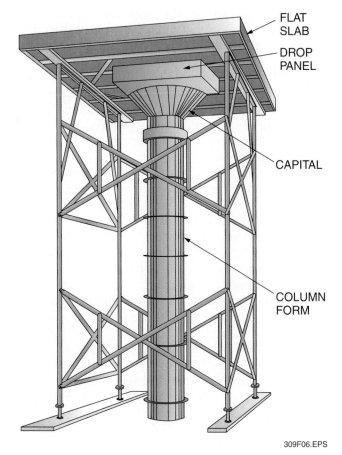

Figure 6 ◆ Drop-panel support system.

are used for two-way or waffle-type slab construction. Edge forms are retainers used to limit the horizontal spread of plastic concrete for slabs.

As mentioned in a previous section, manufactured standard dome or square pans are available in 19" × 19" and 30" × 30" sizes. Larger sizes with deeper depths are available to support spans up to 50' (*Figure 7*). The waffle slab shown in the figure was formed using large dome pans. In this application, beams were formed over the columns by spacing the pans farther apart at the beam locations.

In a typical installation, the edge flanges on the pans are butted up against each other to form the joists. Butting the pans produces a clean smooth surface on the bottom of the joist for appearance purposes. The pans are normally secured to the deck with nails along each edge, especially if the deck and pans will be stripped and used repeatedly for other floors on the same job. Where a beam or column head is to be formed, the edges of the pans facing them are nailed or screwed down more securely to resist the pressure of concrete that will be placed for the beam or head.

Once the slab has gained the specified strength, the temporary deck is lowered with all the pans securely attached. Sometimes, the pans are only minimally secured between each other and when the deck is lowered, the pans remain in the slab. Some dome pans are equipped with a valve (blowhole) on the underside to aid in stripping the pans.

Manufactured steel pans are also available to form one-way joist slabs. They are available in a number of lengths and widths. Standard length narrow and wide pan sections are shown in

Figures 8 and *9*. These pan sections, available in 2', 3', and 4' lengths, are overlapped end-to-end to form the slab and joists. Because the numerous overlaps are reflected in the undersurface of the slab, these forms are not suitable where appearance is important. Note the overlap indentations on the underside of the slab and the flange indentations on the bottom edges of the slab joists. When secured to a plywood deck, the flanges of these pans are not butted up to adjoining pans because the flanges are not wide enough to allow proper joist width. Overlapping end caps are used on the pans where they terminate for a beam, distribution rib, or column head.

Long versions (8', 12', and 16') of the narrow and wide pan forms are available to eliminate most of the lap joints and improve the appearance of the slab underside (*Figure 10*). As shown in the figure, separate support panels are installed on the deck before long wide pans are placed and secured. For the best underside appearance, at least one company will fabricate the pans to specified lengths and flange widths by butt-welding heavy gauge pans together. This eliminates any lap joint and flange indentations on the underside of the slab and joists.

Like dome pans, pan forms for one-way joist slabs must be fastened to the deck with nails or screws. End caps must be secured with additional nails or screws because of the higher pressure caused by concrete in these areas. Like other forms, steel pans and exposed deck sections should be coated with a form release agent (form oil) before the concrete is placed; however, reinforcement must not be coated. Although not used much anymore,

Figure 7 ◆ Large dome pans.

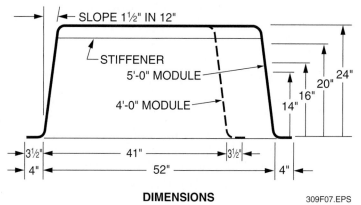

SLOPE 1½" IN 12"

STIFFENER

5'-0" MODULE

4'-0" MODULE

24"

20"

16"

14"

3½"   41"   3½"

4"   52"   4"

DIMENSIONS

309F07.EPS

**16" FOR 20"
STD. WIDTHS**

**TAPERED
ENDFORM**

3'-0"

SLOPE 1" IN 12"

STIFFENER

24"
20"
16"
14"

⁷⁄₈"   ⁷⁄₈"

30"

SLOPE 1" IN 12"

STIFFENER

20"
16"
14"

⁷⁄₈"   ⁷⁄₈"

20"/15"/10"
FILLER SIZES

DIMENSIONS

309F08.EPS

Figure 8 ◆ Standard length narrow pan forms.

FRP long pans are shown in *Figure 11*. In this figure, they are attached to a plywood surface of a flying deck that is being placed next to previously placed decks.

3.2.0 I-Joist Pan Forms

Long pans or wide module pans can be site-built using wood lattice joists or I-joists covered with plywood. *Figure 12* shows the partial construction of wide module pans with wood lattice joist supports secured to strips of plywood. The plywood strips, resting on shoring framework, are the bottom forms for the slab joists that will be poured along with the slab. *Figure 13* shows plywood sheeting secured to the top and sides of the wood lattice joists and the rebar being placed. Note the wide section at the left for a joist band that is the same depth as the slab joists. The band will be formed around the vertical column ties at the rear of the slab when the concrete for the slab and slab joists is placed. Also note the tapered sides of the pans along the slab joists to allow removal of the pans after the slab has gained sufficient strength for stripping. *Figure 14* shows a partially stripped slab with the slab joist bottom form strips removed and with the pans ready to be stripped.

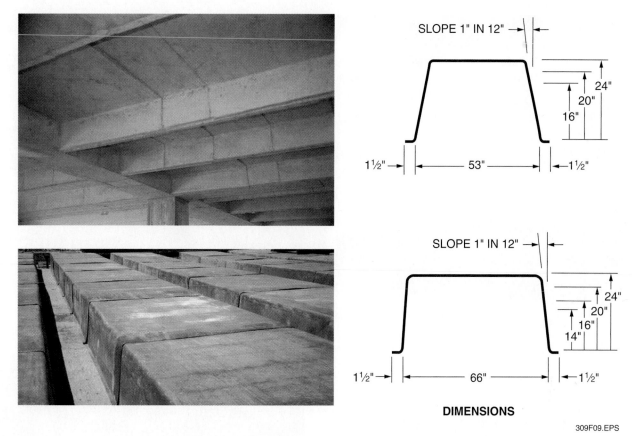

SLOPE 1" IN 12"

24"
20"
16"

1½" — 53" — 1½"

SLOPE 1" IN 12"

24"
20"
16"
14"

1½" — 66" — 1½"

DIMENSIONS

309F09.EPS

Figure 9 ◆ Standard length wide pan forms.

309F10.EPS

Figure 10 ◆ Long length pan forms.

Figure 11 ◆ FRP pans mounted on a flying deck.

Figure 12 ◆ Wood lattice joist supports.

Figure 13 ◆ Wood pan forms.

Figure 14 ◆ Partially stripped slab.

3.3.0 One- and Two-Way Beam and Slab Forms

Normally, beam and slab floors (*Figure 15*) are used only for special applications involving heavy live loads. This is because they are very expensive to construct. The beam, girder, and slab forms can be site-built or manufactured forms can be used.

3.3.1 Site-Built Beam and Slab Forms

Beams and girders are heavily reinforced with steel bars that tie into the rebars of the columns on which they rest. *Figure 16* shows four types of beams:

- Interior beam
- Cantilever beam
- Inverted or T beam
- Spandrel beam

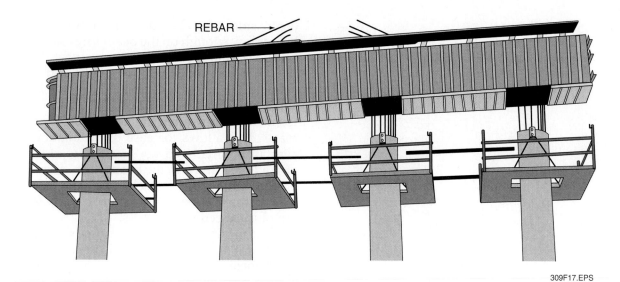

REBAR

309F17.EPS

Figure 17 ◆ Steel girder beam form without intermediate shoring.

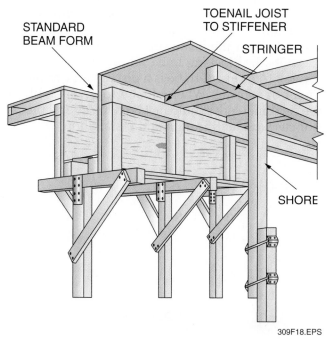

STANDARD BEAM FORM

TOENAIL JOIST TO STIFFENER

STRINGER

SHORE

309F18.EPS

Figure 18 ◆ Form for a small beam.

Beam and girder forms are often integral with the slab form, as in the spandrel beam shown in *Figure 21*. In this case, the slab and beam are poured together.

Beam and column forms may intersect, with the beam form resting on and supported by the column form, as shown in *Figure 22*.

Beam form bottoms are usually constructed of ¾" (minimum) form plywood and supporting members of 2 × 4 material. Beam sides are constructed of either stock lumber or form plywood, again ¾" minimum. If forms are constructed of stock lumber, 2 × 4 vertical cleats will be used. If form sides are constructed of form plywood, the vertical cleats will be eliminated and 2 × 4 vertical stiffeners will be used. Cleats for stock lumber form sides should be on 2' to 2½' centers. Vertical stiffeners will be placed according to plans and specifications.

The ledger is nailed to the beam form side at a certain point below the top to allow for the depth of joists that may have to be supported on the

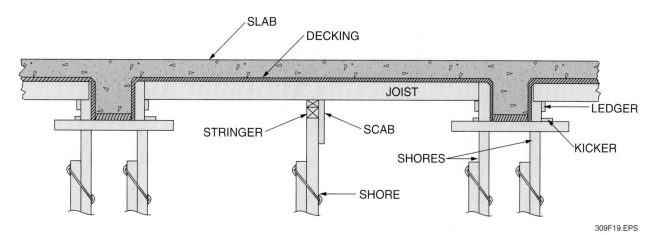

SLAB

DECKING

JOIST

LEDGER

KICKER

SHORES

STRINGER

SCAB

SHORE

309F19.EPS

Figure 19 ◆ Slab-and-beam forms supported by intermediate shores.

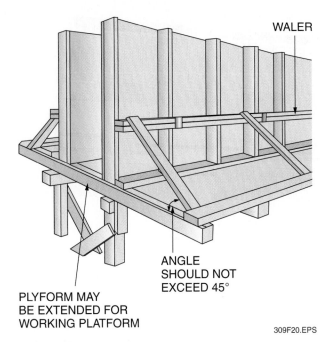

WALER

ANGLE
SHOULD NOT
EXCEED 45°

PLYFORM MAY
BE EXTENDED FOR
WORKING PLATFORM

309F20.EPS

Figure 20 ◆ Form for a large beam.

beam sides. Another design method places the ledger low enough on the beam form side to allow for the slab sheathing thickness.

The kicker is nailed flush with the bottom of the beam form side and later nailed to shore heads. In some cases, the kicker is not nailed to the beam form side until after the beam form side is in place. This allows for ease of installation. However, installing the kicker at the time of construction adds stiffness to the beam form side.

Both ledgers and kickers are normally cut shorter than the beam form side to allow for framing of intersecting members.

Vertical stiffeners are often nailed in place when the beam form side is fabricated. When deep beam form sides are constructed, it may be necessary to pre-drill for form ties. If vertical members act as transfer points to transfer slab loads to the shores, many contractors prefer to cut the required number of vertical pieces and attach them loosely to the beam form side. They are positioned when the beam form side is placed. This permits the blocking to be set directly over shore heads in the event there is a discrepancy in placement of shoring. When off-site form assembly is being done, care should be taken to code all pieces for ease in identification and installation.

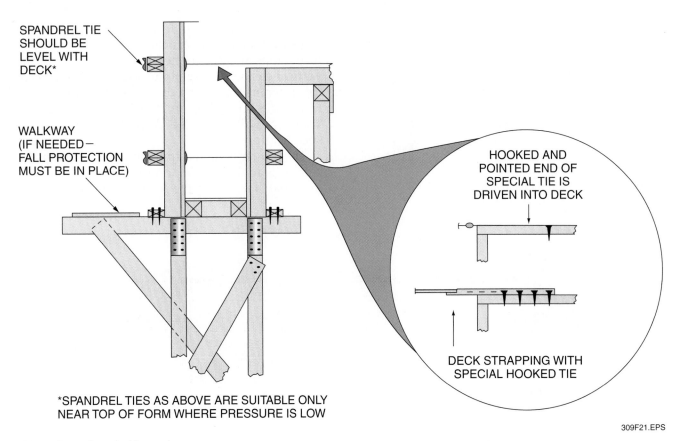

SPANDREL TIE
SHOULD BE
LEVEL WITH
DECK*

WALKWAY
(IF NEEDED –
FALL PROTECTION
MUST BE IN PLACE)

HOOKED AND
POINTED END OF
SPECIAL TIE IS
DRIVEN INTO DECK

DECK STRAPPING WITH
SPECIAL HOOKED TIE

*SPANDREL TIES AS ABOVE ARE SUITABLE ONLY
NEAR TOP OF FORM WHERE PRESSURE IS LOW

309F21.EPS

Figure 21 ◆ Spandrel beam form.

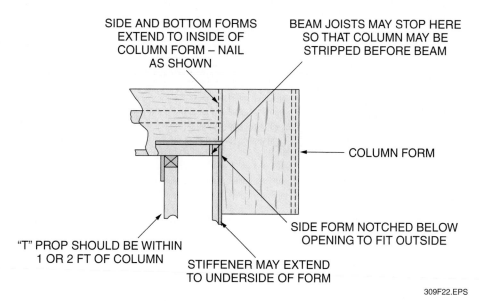

SIDE AND BOTTOM FORMS
EXTEND TO INSIDE OF
COLUMN FORM – NAIL
AS SHOWN

BEAM JOISTS MAY STOP HERE
SO THAT COLUMN MAY BE
STRIPPED BEFORE BEAM

COLUMN FORM

SIDE FORM NOTCHED BELOW
OPENING TO FIT OUTSIDE

"T" PROP SHOULD BE WITHIN
1 OR 2 FT OF COLUMN

STIFFENER MAY EXTEND
TO UNDERSIDE OF FORM

309F22.EPS

Figure 22 ◆ Intersection of beam and column forms.

The lengths of the beam form sides will depend on the framing methods used, the method of transportation, and the concrete placing technique employed at the job site. Forms may be constructed the same length as the clear span, minus the thickness of sheathing on the members the beam intersects, as well as a specific allowance for each end (1½", for example). The remaining gap is filled with a beveled 2 × 4 or other material suitable for a larger opening.

When framing beam pockets in girder sides, two methods are commonly used:

• The beam pocket may be constructed to the exact size of the final dimension of the beam, leaving a small allowance for give in the forms. The beam form is butted up against the opening in the girder form.

• In the second method, the beam form is made the size of the beam plus the thickness of the beam sides and bottom. The opening in the girder is made to accept the beam form, making sure that the beam form does not extend beyond the inside edge of the girder form.

3.3.2 Manufactured Beam and Slab Forms

These forms reduce the amount of time and workers required to construct beam and slab forms. One such application is long-span, post-tensioned, one-way beam and slab floors that are popular for minimum column parking structures (*Figure 23*). One version of a manufactured beam and slab forming system is shown in *Figure 24*. In this system, the only shoring used is directly under the beams. In this example, frame shoring

309F23.EPS

Figure 23 ◆ Typical long-span minimum-column parking structure.

was used, but flying truss tables can also be used. In either case, mechanical lifting is required to set and strip the beam and deck forms.

Steel beam form lengths of up to 60' with up to 31" of depth are available in a fixed 14" width or as 16"-wide split-bottom forms to accommodate wider beam requirements. To reduce project costs, beam depths are usually held constant and beam widths are varied to accommodate different loading within the project. For projects that cannot accommodate this manufacturer's steel forming system, the manufacturer also has engineered-wood form components available that are site-built for other beam and slab widths and depths (*Figure 25*).

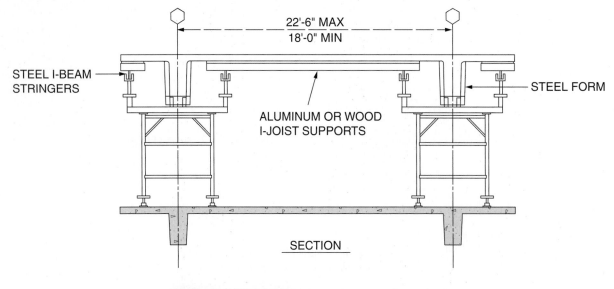

SECTION

Figure 24 ◆ A manufactured steel and aluminum beam and slab forming system.

309F24.EPS

309F25.EPS

Figure 25 ◆ Site-built beam and slab formwork using engineered wood form components.

3.4.0 Flat Slab or Flat Plate Forms

Flat slab or flat plate forms can be either erected (handset) forms that are usually surfaced with plywood and supported by post shoring with stringer and joist framing or some other type of decking system. Manufactured panelized forms with post shoring are also used. Flat slab formwork is more costly to build because of the drop panels required at each column. *Figure 26* shows the top of the formwork for a typical flat slab with drop panels. *Figure 27* shows the bottom of the drop panel formwork. Note the mixture of aluminum joists and stringers for the deck framing along with the wood stringers and formwork used for the drop panel. Also note the mixture of metal frame and wood post shoring used to support all of the formwork.

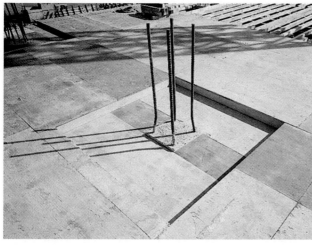

Figure 26 ♦ Typical flat slab form with drop panels.

Figure 27 ♦ Underside of flat slab form with drop panel.

3.5.0 Composite Slab Deck Forms

Steel deck form material, called composite floor decking or structural decking, is made from corrugated sheets of galvanized steel, **phosphatized/painted** steel, or stainless steel. Supported by steel joists, steel beams, or precast concrete joists, the decking material is installed as a floor deck over which concrete is placed to form a concrete floor (or roof) slab. The composite floor decking serves several purposes. It acts as a working platform, stabilizes the frame, and serves as a concrete form for the slab. It also reinforces the concrete slab to carry the design loads specified for the building floor.

Commonly used composite steel decking is made from 16-, 18-, 20-, and 22-gauge steel in 24" or 36" wide panels. Decking panels are made in various lengths ranging up to about 24' long. Deep-ribbed dimples, raised patterns, or rods crossing the corrugations are manufactured into the deck panels along with interlocking panel side laps to create a physical bond with the concrete, thus forming a strong floor slab. *Figure 28* shows a typical **profile** for composite floor decking and cellular composite floor decking panels. The raised portion of the decking panel profile is made in different heights, with 1½", 2", and 3" heights being typical. Generally, the higher the profile height used, the deeper and stronger the resulting concrete slab. Cellular panels have a flat bottom welded to the corrugated panel that provides utility conduits and presents a smooth ceiling to the floor below.

When using composite steel decking with a phosphatized/painted finish, the bare (phosphatized) top surface is the one that comes in contact with the concrete. The bottom side of the deck panel is coated with a primer. In comparison, galvanized steel decking has a zinc coating on both sides. Floor decking is installed in accordance with the manufacturer's guidelines and the job erection drawings. During installation, the deck panels should be overlapped and installed in the opposite direction of the concrete placement to prevent loss of concrete through the joints. It is important to maintain rib alignment across the structure in order to achieve continuous concrete ribs across abutting panel ends.

Floor deck panels should be fastened in place as soon as possible after their placement. Spot welding or electric arc plug welding is the best and most efficient method for fastening composite deck panels to structural supports. In many cases, studs are arc welded through the panels to the structural steel to anchor the concrete slab. The studs are welded using a special tool (*Figure 29*).

Once the decking is installed, edge forms are placed to contain the concrete for the slab. Where penetrations are needed, one forming method is to block out concrete from the floor locations. After the concrete is sufficiently cured, a cutting torch is used to cut the penetration area decking away. Concrete should be placed in the deck form from a low level in a uniform manner over the supporting structure and spread toward the center of the deck span. If necessary to store decking on site prior to its installation, it should be stored off the ground with one end elevated and protected with a tarpaulin or other weatherproof

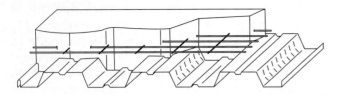

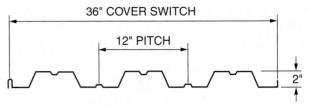

COMPOSITE FLOOR DECKING

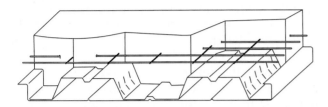

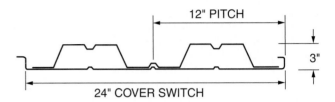

CELLULAR COMPOSITE FLOOR DECKING

309F28.EPS

Figure 28 ◆ Typical composite floor decking profile.

309F29.EPS

Figure 29 ◆ Arc welding anchor studs through a panel.

covering. It also should be ventilated to prevent condensation.

Some specific safety considerations when working with composite decking include:

- Unfastened composite decking should not be used as a work or storage platform.
- Caution must be used with construction loading so that deck capacity is not exceeded and the deck is not damaged.
- When placing concrete in the deck form, care must be taken so that the deck is not subjected to impact that exceeds the design capacity of the deck.

CAUTION

Concrete containing chloride admixtures or admixtures containing chloride salts should not be used with composite steel decking. This is because such admixtures can deteriorate the steel.

INSIDE TRACK

Metal Decking Panels

Corrugated steel metal decking panels without deep-ribbed profiles or embossments are sometimes used to construct noncomposite type floor slabs. When such metal decking is used solely as a form, slab reinforcement and concrete must be designed to carry the total slab load.

4.0.0 ◆ TYPES OF SHORING

Shoring and reshoring are the most important aspects of elevated slab construction. Shoring refers to the temporary support system constructed to carry the dead load of fresh cast-in-place concrete for horizontal decks and slabs, including the dead load of the reinforcing steel and forms as well as the live loads that occur during construction. Reshoring is the operation done in multi-story building construction when shoring equipment is removed from a partially cured slab. The reshoring is installed as the shoring equipment is removed. As the construction of multi-story concrete buildings moves up, shoring for the lowest shored slab is stripped and placed on top of the highest shored slab in order to cast the next floor slab (*Figure 30*). The stripped lower slabs, normally at least two floor slabs below, must remain reshored to support the partially cured concrete and construction loads.

Unless specified otherwise, reshoring is normally accomplished on a leg-for-leg basis as a safety precaution. This means that the vertical supports for each reshored floor are placed directly under each of the supports for the floor above. Reshoring for these slabs must be released and reset after placement of concrete on the floor being cast. Sometimes, preshoring, also called backshoring, is used when formwork must be stripped from a floor that has been cast, but has not yet achieved sufficient strength to support itself. Vertical supports are installed through the formwork while the formwork is carefully removed. Some manufactured formwork systems allow the formwork to be removed without disturbing the existing shoring (*Figure 31*). Backshoring must not be confused with reshoring.

Reshoring is used to transfer loads from shoring or backshoring to the floors below.

If a slab-on-grade has not yet been placed and cured, mudsills (*Figure 32*) must be placed on the soil under the shoring or reshoring for the first floor. Mudsills are normally made of hardwood and can be planks or square pads depending on the soil. They are used to prevent shoring or reshoring from sinking into the soil and causing floor collapse when the concrete for the first and any succeeding floors is placed.

Both safety and cost must be taken into consideration in order to determine the appropriate shoring/reshoring method. The factors that must be considered include: the time duration between the concrete placement of consecutive concrete slabs, the strength of the concrete, the configuration of the building, and the dimensions of the

309F31.EPS

Figure 31 ◆ Formwork removed from existing shoring.

309F30.EPS

Figure 30 ◆ Reshoring in a multi-story building.

309F32.EPS

Figure 32 ◆ Pad type mudsills.

building and shoring structural members. Inadequate or improperly installed decking, deck framing, shoring, and reshoring can result in catastrophic collapse of one or more floors of a building when concrete is being placed on the floor under construction.

It is essential that all shoring and reshoring be installed by qualified individuals in accordance with the building plans and the shoring manufacturer's instructions. Except in certain applications involving edge support of cantilever slabs and work decks, all shoring and reshoring members must be vertically plumbed when installed to prevent lateral loads on the shoring member and any decking member above the shoring. Lateral loading can significantly reduce the vertical load-bearing capacity of the shoring member as well as any deck framing member above it.

When concrete is being placed for a floor, qualified individuals must constantly check the underside of the decking, deck framing, shoring, and the reshoring below for any signs of cracking, sagging, or bending that could signal impending failure. If any such signs are observed, immediate communications must occur so that concrete placement stops and workers leave the area. Structural engineers or other qualified individuals must then evaluate the decking, deck framing, shoring, and reshoring to determine the proper course of action. For this reason, both shoring and reshoring for a building must be designed and planned in advance by a qualified structural engineer, approved by the project architect/engineer, and installed and monitored by qualified individuals.

Vertical shores can be constructed from wood using patented manufactured metal components. Other types of patented manufactured steel and aluminum shores are also used.

4.1.0 Adjustable Wood Shoring

One adjustable post-type wood shore widely used is made from two 4 × 4 (nominal) wooden posts and two patented 4 × 4 shore clamps (Ellis™ shore clamps). This type of shore can also be made using 4 × 6 or 6 × 6 wood posts (nominal) with the appropriate size shore clamps. The typical length of the lower shore post is 5'-6" or 6', with the upper shore post long enough to reach the desired height plus provide for a 24" overlap of the two wood posts.

The two shore clamps are attached to the lower shore post 12" apart on center with the top clamp placed 2" below the post top. The shore clamps are then nailed through the holes in the clamp castings. Following this, the upper shore post is placed alongside the lower shore post and slid through the clamps until it is at the desired height. Final height adjustment is then made using a removable jack wrench especially designed for use with the shore clamps. The jack grips the wood of the lower shore post, and the upper shore post can be raised about 1" per stroke by a cam on the wrench lever. After the final height is obtained, the clamps on the upper shore post are tapped down to seat them, and a safety nail is driven into the upper shore post above each of the two clamp castings to prevent the clamps from vibrating loose. Loosening and removal of this shore is done by removing the safety nails from the upper shore post only, then loosening each clamp casting by tapping them up with a hammer one at a time.

A 4 × 4 Ellis™ shore can support 3,000- to 6,000-lb loads depending on height. The 4 × 6 and 6 × 6 shores can support 3,200 to 9,600 lbs and 7,200 to 16,000 lbs, respectively, depending on height. The advantages of these shores are that they are not expensive and they can be fabricated on the job site as necessary. However, in comparison to steel or aluminum post shores, they are heavy to handle and more of them are required because of their lower weight capacity.

When used as reshoring, this pole-type wood shore can be equipped with a reshoring spring that is nailed to the top of the upper post. The spring holds the shore snugly in place against a slab during the initial setting operation and any subsequent release/resetting operations.

When the shore is in place, the reshoring spring is compressed flat between the upper shore pole and slab when 200 lbs or more of force is applied. When removed from compression, it returns to its original shape and can be used over and over again. Other shoring accessories, including screw timber jacks, pivoting or fixed shore cups, and wireheads are also made for use with wood post-type shores.

4.2.0 Manufactured Shoring

Today, vertical shoring used for most large commercial jobs is constructed using patented manufactured metal components and systems. There are many configurations, depending on the manufacturer and application. These typically involve steel frame or single-post shoring used with wood, laminated, and/or aluminum joists and stringers.

4.2.1 Frame Shoring

Typical frame shoring is shown in *Figure 33*. Note the cross bracing used between the frames to support and maintain the frame positions. Also note

Adjustable Horizontal Shores

These types of shores normally do not require intermediate support and are used to support deck framing without the use of post shoring. They are available in a number of lengths to cover spans from 4½" to 20'. Constructed of double lattice steel sections that telescope, they can be templated at floor level to the prescribed length, locked, and then installed on stringers or on structural steel building beams using a hanger at each end. Most have a predetermined camber to accommodate loading sag. Wedge-type locks on the shore maintain the shore length and any camber.

309SA03.EPS

5.0.0 ◆ TYPES OF DECKS

Many decks are erected (handset) in a labor-intensive multi-component fashion using post or frame shoring with separate stringer and joist framing members and separate sheets of plywood for the deck form. Other decks are constructed using handset panelized systems that are comprised of shoring and panelized deck forms with integral framing and plywood deck surfaces or, in some cases, plastic surfaces. These types of decks are less labor intensive to put in place. In many high-rise projects, truss tables or column-mounted tables are used as decks. The tables are assembled once at a job site and then flown from floor-to-floor by a crane as construction progresses. Often called flying decks or flying forms, the tables are the least labor-intensive type of deck. They only require handset filler panels with appropriate shoring around columns and across adjacent decks. All deck framing and deck tables must be carefully placed so that they are properly positioned for the edges of the slab and aligned with the supporting columns or walls. Once set, handset deck framing or panelized decking as well as tables must be graded (leveled) as described later in this module.

5.1.0 Decking Surfaces

The form surfaces most commonly used for all types of decks are exterior (waterproof) grades of plywood. Any exterior grade plywood can be used, but the plywood industry makes a special proprietary product called Plyform® that is recommended for formwork. Plyform® is limited to certain wood species and veneer (outer face surfaces) grades for high performance. Plyform® products bearing the trademark *APA-The Engineered Wood Association* are available in three basic grades that are marked on the plywood. All three grades of Plyform® are available with or without medium density overlay (MDO) or high density overlay (HDO) thermoset resins:

- *Structural I* – This grade has high-strength plies throughout and is the strongest of the grades. It is recommended if the face grain must be used parallel with the support framing.
- *Class I* – This grade has high-strength veneer faces for high strength and stiffness.
- *Class II* – This grade has lower strength veneer faces, but still provides adequate strength for formwork.

MDO and HDO surfaces are bonded to plywood faces under high heat and pressure. These overlays add stability, reduce adherence of concrete to the surface, and provide a smooth and durable forming surface. Regular MDO is intended for painted surfaces and should not be used for concrete forming. Special MDO plywood must be used for concrete forming. The MDO is usually applied to one surface only. HDO is a tougher, more abrasion resistant surface that is usually applied to both faces of the plywood. This type of overlay can produce a nearly polished concrete surface on the underside of the slab. However, scratches and dents on the back side of the panel, caused by fastening the panels to framing members, may make the use of the back side impractical for a polished concrete appearance. If reasonable care is used, an HDO surface will normally produce 20 to 50 reuses or more. In some cases, 200 or more reuses have been achieved.

Another type of Plyform® product that is not overlaid is B-B Plyform®. It is made with different veneer faces that are sanded on both sides and treated with a release agent at the mill (mill oiled). It is available as Structural I, Class I, and Class II and can be reused five to ten times. With Plyform® products, an edge sealer must be applied before first usage (if not applied at the mill). Form release agent must be applied to the slab side surface before concrete placement to allow easy stripping. Release agent must also be applied after stripping and cleaning to preserve the surface.

For most slab formwork, ¾" or thicker 4 × 8 plywood sheets are used. Normally, the grain of the face veneer is parallel with the long sides of the sheet. For maximum strength, the face grain (long side of the sheet) should be placed so that it crosses over the supporting framing members directly under the sheet. An exception is the Structural I plywood where the face grain can be parallel with the framing members. To prevent skewing of plywood panels and resultant fit-up problems across an entire deck, a row of panels should be laid first along the longest edge of the slab and checked to ensure that they are square with the support framing.

5.2.0 Handset Multi-Component Decks

These types of decks can be cost effective for small or medium size projects. Stringers are normally placed atop the shoring and the joists span across the top of the stringers. Cross-sections of typical aluminum stringers, also called beams, and joists are shown in *Figure 43*. They have a wood or plastic insert at the top and some have holes in the base flange for nailing purposes. Others have attachment clamps available to secure stringers to post or frame shoring. In other cases, as shown in *Figure 44*, engineered wood I-joists are used as stringers and joists. The ones shown in the figure

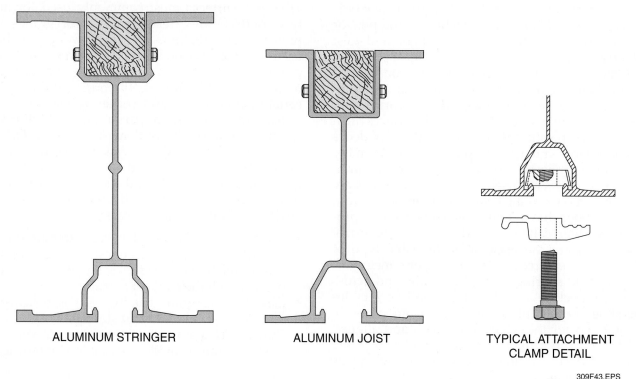

ALUMINUM STRINGER   ALUMINUM JOIST   TYPICAL ATTACHMENT CLAMP DETAIL

309F43.EPS

Figure 43 ◆ Cross-sections of typical aluminum stringers and joists.

PERI GmbH

Figure 44 ◆ Engineered wood I-joist framing members.

309F44.EPS

are specially designed for formwork framing and are available in various lengths. In many cases, standard engineered wood I-joists used in construction are substituted for the specially designed I-joists. In the figure, note the use of tripods to support some of the post shoring while the framing is being installed.

Deck framing that uses a proprietary multi-component aluminum system is shown in *Figure 45*. This type of framing is more expensive than individual aluminum framing stringers and joists. The particular manufacturer of this system refers to the stringers as main beams and the joists as secondary beams. The main and secondary beams are supplied in only two standard lengths, 5'-7" and 3'-9". This makes the framing very modular and uniform when installed. The secondary beams interlock with a lip at the bottom of the main beams at any point and the main beams can interlock with each other and with proprietary drop-heads used on post shoring as shown in *Figure 46*. In the figure, note the drop panel framing using short (filler) main beams and supported by hangers from the lip of short main beams used under the slab decking. *Figure 47* shows typical two-man installation of this type of deck framing

309F45.EPS

Figure 45 ◆ Proprietary multi-component aluminum deck framing.

supported by drop-head post shoring. Note the tripods used for post shoring support as the installation advances. *Figure 48* shows completed deck framing in place with plywood decking and dome pans being installed.

Figure 46 ♦ Drop panel framing.

309F46.EPS

309F48.EPS

Figure 48 ♦ Completed deck framing with plywood decking and dome pan installation in progress.

309F47.EPS

Figure 47 ♦ Typical two-man installation in progress.

5.3.0 Handset Panelized Decks

Many of these types of deck systems use only two components: shoring and proprietary deck panels (*Figure 49*). The deck panels are manufactured in various sizes and shapes, with the supporting framing and decking material supplied as a complete unit. The replaceable decking material is normally plywood. One Asian manufacturer supplies deck panels made entirely of plastic. These deck panels can be interlocked with other panels for ganged placement.

All of the manufacturers of panelized deck systems require proprietary drop-heads for shoring and stripping purposes. These types of decks are initially expensive, but they are the fastest decking to handset and strip that is available. Contractors for large projects use panelized deck systems to shorten construction time and reduce labor. *Figure 50* shows typical erection of a panelized

309F49.EPS

Figure 49 ♦ Panelized decking under construction.

deck. The 6 × 6 panels in this installation weigh about 100 pounds so that two workers can lift and hook them onto proprietary drop-heads. Then, the panel is raised and propped into position with an erection pole. Finally the shoring, set to a predetermined length, is placed at the unsupported corners of the panel. This process is repeated for each panel.

When each panel is being stripped and the slab reshored, the process is reversed. The drop-heads are released, the panel is propped, and the shoring is removed from one end. Then, the panel is swung down and removed. After the panel is

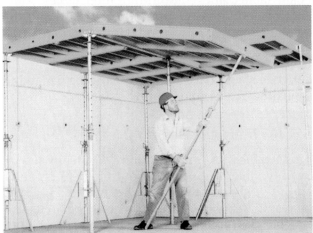

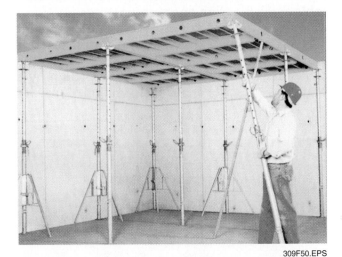

309F50.EPS

Figure 50 ◆ Typical erection of panelized decking.

removed, the drop-heads are removed from the shoring, and the same shoring can be reset against the slab. For fill-in around columns, curves, and other objects, specially shaped panels, adjustable panels, and smaller panels are available that are used with nailer strips as shown in *Figure 51*.

309F51.EPS

Figure 51 ◆ Small panels with nailer strips used for fill-in around a column.

INSIDE TRACK

Site-Built Panelized Decks

Some contractors fabricate their own deck panels using standard engineered wood I-joists and HDO plywood as shown in the figure. Like proprietary panelized decks, they are faster to erect, but require mechanical lifting to set or strip because of their weight. For post-tensioned 6" slabs, the contractor claims that longer spans were possible with the I-joists than with aluminum joists. The panels shown averaged 24 reuses before the plywood surface had to be replaced.

309SA04.EPS

5.4.0 Outriggers

When stripping and reshoring slabs constructed with handset decks, many contractors use one or more outriggers, sometimes called poke-outs (*Figure 52*), as material staging platforms. The outriggers allow the stripped formwork to be placed outside the slab for transfer to the next slab being constructed or to the ground. In the figure, note the side guardrails and the netting at the end of the outrigger. These prevent material and workers from falling to the ground below. The side guardrails also extend into the building. Outriggers like the one shown have two horizontal beams that extend into the building.

When a slab is going to be stripped, some of the shoring and formwork is removed at the edge of the slab and the outrigger is placed by crane so that the beams are inside the building as shown in *Figure 53*. The beams are braced against the slab

below and the slab being stripped by post shoring set into cups on the beam. Once braced, the crane lifting slings are removed. The beams function as cantilever supports for the outrigger. Note the bottom portion of a guardrail fastened to the post shoring inside the building.

5.5.0 Flying Decks

Flying decks are, essentially, complete slab-forming units with their own framing members, deck, and shoring. They are tables that are moved (flown) by crane from one floor slab to the next slab location to be constructed at a project. There are three basic types in general use: truss tables, beam tables, and column-mounted tables. They are normally used for forming flat slabs and the decking is usually plywood. However, pan forms and cast-in-place beam forms can be mounted on truss or beam tables depending on the height between slabs. Truss tables can also be ganged to save time in stripping and resetting.

5.5.1 Truss and Beam Tables

These tables use an aluminum or steel truss or beam system to support aluminum deck framing and the plywood deck (*Figures 54* and *55*). Truss tables up to 30' wide and exceeding 35' in length can be assembled and flown as a single unit. *Figure 56* shows the components of a typical truss table available from one manufacturer.

Various manufacturers recommend different methods for the extraction and flying of their truss tables. One method involves tilting the table outside the building to allow pickup by a crane as described in this section. Another

309F52.EPS

Figure 52 ◆ A typical outrigger.

309F53.EPS

Figure 53 ◆ Outrigger beam bracing.

ONE OF FOUR KNOCKOUT DECK PANELS REMOVED FOR SLING CONNECTION TO TRUSSES

309F54.EPS

Figure 54 ◆ Truss table system.

309F55.EPS

Figure 55 ◆ Beam table system.

method involves the use of an auxiliary electric hoist attached to a crane hook (*Figure 57*) so that the table does not have to be tilted. The auxiliary hoist method is described in the next section for column-mounted tables.

For a typical truss table, all filler panel shoring is removed and the jacks supporting the trusses are lowered until the table is placed on anchored tilt rollers at the outer edge of the slab and rollers or positioning dollies under other portions of the trusses. All filler panels around columns and across adjacent tables are removed as required. The table is then tethered to an anchor point or points (columns) with 1" diameter rope(s) that are only long enough to allow all the knockout panel openings on the table to be outside the building when the table is pushed out to the end of the

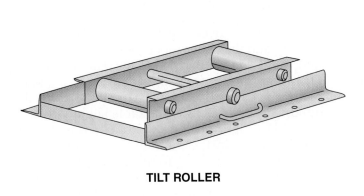

TILT ROLLER

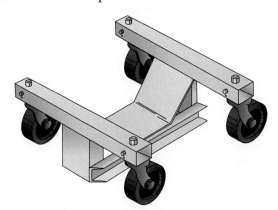

POSITIONING DOLLY

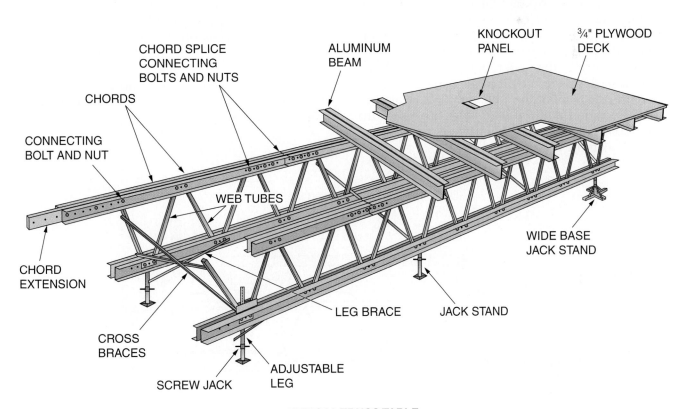

TYPICAL TRUSS TABLE

309F56.EPS

Figure 56 ◆ Typical truss table components.

Figure 57 ◆ Truss table being lifted by a crane equipped with an auxiliary electric hoist.

Figure 58 ◆ Truss tables partially rolled out of floor bays.

tether. With the table pushed by two to four workers a short distance out of the building (*Figure 58*), relatively long equal length slings from a crane hook located outside the building are connected through the knockout panel openings to the trusses (*Figure 59*).

The table is then pushed farther out of the building until the center of gravity (C.G.) is beyond the tilt rollers at the edge of the slab. This causes the table to tilt up gently until the rear of the table rests against the upper slab (*Figure 60*). After the table tilts, the crane hook, positioned over the outer knockout panels, lifts the table slightly and moves slowly away from the building, while lowering the hook to maintain the tilt, until table movement is limited by the tether rope(s). During this operation, the rear slings remain slack due to the tilt of the table. The crane then lifts the front of the table until it is rotated to a level position and the rear slings are also taut. The table is then lifted slightly so most of its weight is off the rollers.

The crane moves the table into the building slightly, and the tether rope(s) are disconnected. A long guide rope is then tied to the rear of the table. The guide rope is from the area where the table will be positioned after it is removed from the building. The crane lifts the table slightly to take the table weight off the rollers. Then, with help from workers in the building, the crane moves away from the building to remove the table.

When the table is clear of the building, workers use the guide rope to eliminate horizontal rotation. The crane lifts the table to the next floor location to be constructed (or to the ground) while workers guide it into position (*Figure 61*). Once the table is in position on jacks (*Figure 62*), it is raised to the correct level for the slab and graded (leveled). Then the filler panels, previously removed, are placed across the adjacent tables and around any columns. They are supported by additional shoring (*Figure 63*).

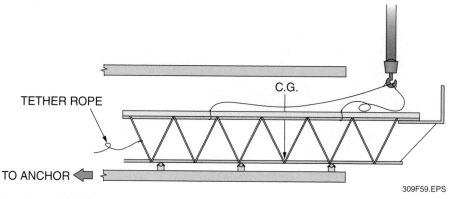

Figure 59 ◆ Preparing a truss table for removal.

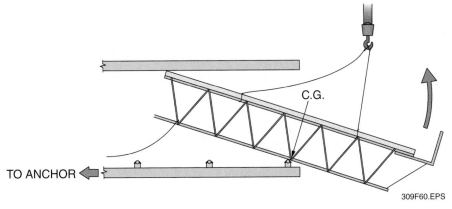

C.G.

TO ANCHOR ←

309F60.EPS

Figure 60 ◆ Tilting a truss table.

309F61.EPS

Figure 61 ◆ Truss table being guided into place on the next floor level.

309F63.EPS

Figure 63 ◆ Filler panels and shoring between tables.

309F62.EPS

Figure 62 ◆ Truss table on jacks.

INSIDE TRACK

Tunnel System

Another flying form system used is the room tunnel system. A room tunnel system is an all-steel forming system with wheels. It is advertised as a self-supporting room-a-day system where the deck and two or three walls are all placed around the form at the same time. The system is then collapsed slightly and is flown whole, or in halves, to the next level for formation of the next room.

5.5.2 Column-Mounted Tables

Column-mounted tables, called roller decks by one manufacturer, are supported by jacking attachments that are anchored by bolts to the columns or walls for the floor under construction (*Figure 64*). Each jack is rated to support a working load of 50,000 lbs. The tables are constructed of heavy-duty aluminum or steel side stringers, aluminum joists or wood I-joists, and a plywood deck that can support clear spans up 26' wide with an 8" slab. The advantage of these types of tables is that the area underneath the table allows free access to other trades, finishing operations, and space for material storage. Once the slab poured on the table as well as any columns/walls for next higher or adjacent floor level have sufficient strength and their vertical formwork has been removed, the table can be stripped and moved by crane to the floor location above or another location.

Table removal and transfer to another location or to the ground is similar to the method used for truss tables. If the transfer is to the next higher or an adjacent floor level, jack attachments are attached at the proper positions on the columns/walls for that location. Then, any shoring for filler panels around the table to be stripped is removed. Each jack attachment for the table is lowered, one at a time, to allow a roller assembly to be inserted between the jack head and the stringer (refer to *Figure 64*). Then all the jacks are incrementally lowered to strip the table from the slab. Any filler panels are removed as required. Then, a crane with an auxiliary electric hoist attached to the hook, along with a pair of slings from the hook and a pair of slings from the auxiliary hoist hook, are positioned outside the building. The slings are lowered so that there is enough slack to attach them to the stringers through knockout panels in the table decking. The slings from the crane hook are connected through the knockouts at the end of the table nearest to the slab edge. The slings from the auxiliary hoist are connected through the knockouts at the other end of the table. Tether rope(s) are tied to the table and to anchor(s) within the building. A long guide rope from the intended location is also tied to the back of the table. Then, workers with push poles or a forklift push the table part way out of the building to allow the crane to apply a light tension to the front slings at the outer edge of the table. The auxiliary hoist slings remain slack. As the table is moved further out of the building, the crane maintains the table in a horizontal position with the front slings (*Figure 65*). Once the rear slings are clear of the upper slab edge, the auxiliary hoist is operated to tighten them and center the crane hook over the middle of the table. As the rear slings are tightened, the crane hook is moved downward to maintain the table in a horizontal position. After the hook is centered,

309F64.EPS

Figure 64 ◆ A column-mounted table.

309F65.EPS

Figure 65 ◆ Column-mounted table being removed from floor bay.

the table is raised slightly to take some of the weight off the bottom rollers. The tether rope(s) are removed and the crane hook is moved away from the building as workers push the table the rest of the way out of the building. Workers use the guide rope to keep the table from rotating horizontally when it clears the building. The crane lifts the table to the next floor location to be constructed (or to the ground) while workers guide it into position over the retracted jack assemblies that were previously placed (*Figure 66*). Once the table is in position on the jacks, it is raised by the jacks to the correct slab level and graded. Then, filler panels with their shoring, removed from the previous table position, are placed across the adjacent tables and around any columns.

5.5.3 Flying Deck Safety

This section describes safety procedures related to the use of flying deck form equipment. To ensure your own safety as well as that of others, strictly adhere to the manufacturer's instructions, all applicable codes, and the following guidelines:

- Follow all state, local, and federal codes, ordinances, and regulations pertaining to shoring.
- Inspect all equipment before using it. Never use damaged equipment.
- Ensure that a shoring layout is on the job site at all times.
- Inspect erected shoring and forming:
    - Immediately prior to the pour
    - During the pour
    - After the pour until the concrete is set

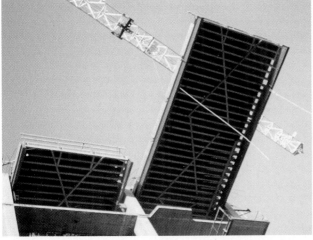

309F66.EPS

Figure 66 ◆ Column-mounted table being guided into position.

- Consult your shoring equipment supplier when in doubt. Shoring is their business. Never take chances.
- Do not exceed the manufacturer's recommended safe working load for the equipment being used.
- All flying deck forms must be assembled, moved, and maintained in accordance with the supplier's recommended procedures.
- If motorized concrete equipment is used, be sure that the shoring layout has been designed for use with this equipment and that this is noted on the layout.
- A method of adjustment should be provided on all flying deck form supporting members for form leveling, vertical positioning, ease of stripping, and adjusting to uneven grade conditions where applicable.
- Make certain that all supporting members are in firm contact with the flying form stringer/ledger and that supports are located in position as shown on the shoring layout.
- Use special precautions when shoring from or to sloped surfaces.
- The reshoring procedure, if applicable, must be approved by the engineer on record.
- Use deck form materials with properties as stated on the shoring layout drawing. Do not splice joists or ledgers between supports unless details are given on the shoring layout.
- Do not release forms until the proper authority has given approval to do so.
- All field operations must be under the direct authority of a supervisor who is qualified and familiar with the procedures for assembly, erection, flying, and horizontal movement of the flying deck form system being used.
- Make certain that a positively controlled method of tieback or braking is used when moving the deck form. The system must never be allowed to have free, uncontrolled horizontal movement.
- Ledgers/stringers and joists must be stabilized and laterally braced to ensure that the deck form system is stable against any foreseeable lateral loads.
- The crane used to fly the deck form must not be used to pull the deck form out of the building bay. A controlled and independent device or force must provide for horizontal movement of the deck form.
- Slings and rigging used in flying the deck form system must comply with all safe practices, applicable codes, and regulations governing their use.

- Do not make unauthorized changes or substitutions of equipment; always consult your supplier prior to making changes required by job site conditions.
- Safety measures must be taken for all personnel involved in the rigging of the flying deck form.
- During concrete placement and deck form rigging, the free end cantilever of a deck form may not exceed the amount recommended by the supplier. Follow the recommended flying procedure as given by the supplier.
- Any and all loose components of the deck form system (bulkheads, beam sides, filler strips, etc.), if flown with the form, must be securely fastened to the deck form prior to moving.
- Consult your supplier if a weatherproof covering or similar material is to be attached to the flying system.
- All personnel in the area must be advised and protected during all flying operations.
- All attached perimeter guardrails, midrails, and toe boards must conform to applicable codes and regulations.
- The weight of the flying deck form must not exceed the capacity of the crane over the full range of the working radius.

6.0.0 ◆ GRADING ELEVATED SLAB DECKS

Prior to placing concrete on a handset or flying deck, the deck must be graded (leveled). This is usually accomplished by checking the bottom of the deck at periodic points along stringers and long span joists across the entire deck and adjusting the shoring as required. It can be done using one person and a rotating beam laser level set up at various spots near the center of the deck as shown in *Figure 67*. Two workers using a builder's level can also be used. Immediately after concrete placement and before the concrete sets, the deck should be rechecked for grade to determine if any appreciable movement has occurred that may require height adjustment of some shoring or some spot addition of shoring.

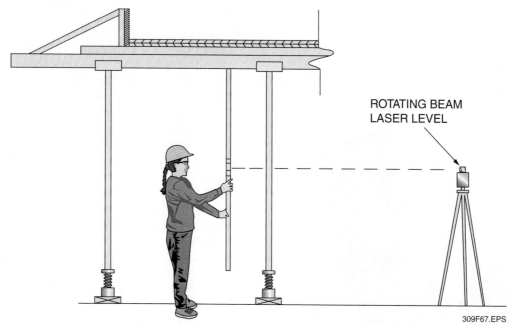

ROTATING BEAM
LASER LEVEL

309F67.EPS

Figure 67 ◆ Checking deck grading with a rotating beam laser level.

7.0.0 ◆ ELEVATED SLAB EDGE FORMS, BLOCKOUTS, EMBEDMENTS, AND JOINTING

Before concrete can be placed on a graded slab deck, edge forms, blockouts, embedments and any construction joints must be installed along with the required slab reinforcement.

- *Edge forms* – Conventional site-built wood edge forms, with bottom-edge kickers and wood braces fastened to the decking, are used extensively to contain elevated slab concrete at the perimeter of a slab and within the slab to form blockouts for large openings such as stairwells. To save on wood, many larger contractors are using adjustable metal braces, sometimes called adjustable kickers, to replace the wood braces and kickers normally used. These devices, which can be used many times over, are shown in *Figure 68*. They can be fastened to a wood deck or concrete surface, or staked in the ground for slab-on-grade applications. The vertical stiffener is hinged so that it can be adjusted to any angle. For repetitive use on flying decks, the kicker can be fastened to the deck using a bracket that allows the entire device, including the form, to be moved back a distance for form stripping as shown in the figure. When the deck is repositioned for a new slab, the forms can be returned to the same position and secured for placement of the next slab. Brackets are also available for the vertical stiffener to allow the attachment of metal edge forms instead of wood edge forms.

309F68.EPS

Figure 68 ◆ Typical adjustable kicker installation.

- *Blockouts* – If possible, blockouts for any required elevated slab penetrations, including piping, conduit, or ducts, should be placed prior to placing concrete. Preplacement prevents having to drill through the slab and possibly damage reinforcement after the slab has cured.
- *Embedments* – Before concrete placement, the elevation of the bottom of the slab decking, the elevation of the reinforcement used, and any embedments such as piping, electrical conduits, and outlet boxes must be checked. Deck forms that are too high can result in slab reinforcement and embedments being above the desired elevation of the slab. Screed rails or guides should be set to compensate for any initial downward movement of cambered deck forms during concreting. They also may be set to compensate for downward deflection of the structure after concrete placement and stripping of the forms.
- *Jointing* – Construction joints, if required for elevated slabs, should be specified by the designers of the building. Because joints can introduce weak vertical planes in a monolithic concrete member, they are located where shear stresses are low. Under most conditions, shear stresses are low in the middle of a span. As a guideline for slabs on removable forms, construction joints in floors are normally located within the middle third of spans of slabs, beams, and primary beams. Joints in girders should be offset a minimum distance of two times the width of any intersecting beams.

For composite slabs, construction joint location can affect the deflection of the floor framing near the joint. Construction joints that parallel secondary structural steel beams should normally be placed near the midpoint of the slab between the beams. Construction joints that parallel primary structural steel beams and cross secondary steel beams should be placed near the primary beam. The primary beam should not be included in the initial concrete placement. Placing the joint a distance of 4' from the primary beam allows nearly the full dead load from concrete placement to deflect the secondary beams included in the initial placement. This action also partially loads and deflects the primary beam. The second placement at the construction joint should include the primary beam. This will fully load the primary beam and allow complete deflection of the primary beam before the concrete at the primary beam hardens. Construction joints that cross a primary steel beam should be placed near a support at one end of the primary beam. This allows the beam to deflect completely before the concrete hardens. The placement of construction joints in noncomposite slabs on a metal deck follow the same guidelines as for removable forms.

8.0.0 ◆ BRIDGE DECK FORMS

Bridge decking is the riding surface of a bridge. Forms for bridge decks support the concrete between adjacent structural members until it hardens sufficiently to stand alone. Deck forms must be concrete tight and sufficiently rigid to support the concrete without distorting under load. Deck forms are either removable or permanent. Most removable forms are made of wood. Permanent forms are usually made of metal or pre-stressed concrete. Removable wooden forms used with conventional reinforced concrete decking are typically made of ¾" exterior-grade plywood sheets for the flooring (*Figure 69*). It is common for the decking to be supported by wooden or metal joists and stringers hung from adjustable metal joist hangers.

Preformed metal bridge decking panels made of corrugated steel are commonly used as permanent forms over which concrete is placed. They are similar to the metal forms described earlier for composite floor decking. Like composite floor decking, they serve several purposes. They act as a working platform, stabilize the frame, and serve as concrete forms for the bridge deck slab. They also reinforce the concrete slab to carry the design loads specified for the bridge deck. Typically these panels are supported by metal angles that are welded or strapped to the top flanges of the supporting steel beams or girders. However, it is important that no

support angles are welded onto flanges of steel beams or girders that are in tension. Metal deck panels are overlapped and installed in the opposite direction of the concrete placement to prevent loss of concrete through the joints. The panels should be welded in place as soon as they are placed and aligned to prevent them from being misaligned or blown off by wind.

Today, a decking method widely used for bridges involves the use of modular Exodermic™ bridge deck panels. Each of these modular deck panels consist of a reinforced concrete slab placed on top of an unfilled steel grid. By this method of construction, the strength of the steel grid takes the place of the bottom half of a conventional reinforced concrete slab. The result is that an Exodermic™ deck panel normally weighs about 35 to 50 percent less than a conventional reinforced concrete deck of the same size and span, without sacrificing strength or stiffness. By reducing the deck weight, the deck dead load is reduced, thus a higher live load rating for the bridge can be achieved. The concrete portion of Exodermic™ deck panels can be precast by a licensed manufacturer before the panels are placed on the bridge, or they can be cast in place at the bridge site. Because of their modular construction, use of both precast and cast-in-place panels reduces construction time when compared to the construction of conventional reinforced concrete decks.

Before placing either precast or cast-in-place deck panels on the bridge, **haunches** are usually formed using self-adhesive foam clamps, galvanized sheet steel, or structural angles connected with straps or welded to the supporting beam or timber. Precast deck panel construction provides for blockouts in the panels so that there is no concrete over the grid in the areas that are located

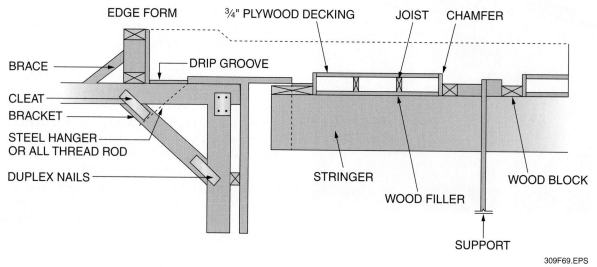

Figure 69 ◆ Typical wooden bridge deck formwork.

directly over the top flanges of stringers, girders, or floor beams in the bridge superstructure. Installing precast panels involves positioning the panels in place on the bridge superstructure and setting them to the correct elevation using built-in leveling bolts. The panels are attached to the bridge superstructure via welding of headed shear studs onto the stringers, girders, or floor beams below that are accessible through the blockout areas in the panel. Following this, the blockout areas are filled to full depth with rapid-setting concrete to make the deck composite with the superstructure.

When the concrete is cast in place, precut, preformed, steel Exodermic™ grid panels are placed on the bridge support structure to serve as a permanent form. The panels are placed and set to the required elevation using built-in leveling clamps and fastened to the steel superstructure of the bridge by welding headed shear studs through the grid to stringers, floor beams, and main girders below. Rebar is then placed on the grid. Following this, the headed studs in the haunch areas are embedded in concrete at the same time as the concrete is placed for the deck. This procedure makes the deck composite with the superstructure.

Bridge decking panels made of fiber-reinforced polymer (FRP) material are also available. Use of FRP deck panels increases the ability of bridge decks to resist the corrosive effects of weather and road deicing salts over that of decks made with concrete and steel materials. This helps increase the deck longevity and reduces deck maintenance. FRP panels are normally prefabricated into large, lightweight modules that can be installed easily and with light-duty equipment. FRP decks are increasingly being used as replacement solid-surface decks for existing deteriorated concrete decks of older bridges and drawbridges. This is because their use reduces the deck dead load, thus increasing the bridge's live load capacity. For these reasons, their use can sometimes enable the bridge deck to be widened. FRP deck panel construction is somewhat similar to that of precast concrete deck panels. This allows the deck-to-

beam connections to be made using shear studs encased in concrete in the same manner as done in conventional precast concrete deck construction.

9.0.0 ◆ EFCO CULVERT-FORMING SYSTEMS

Culvert forms (*Figure 70*) are used for a variety of jobs, including storm drainage, utility tunnels, sanitary sewers, main tunnels, irrigation canals, and mass-transit tunnels.

These patented forms are easily moved from one concrete placement to the next because the entire inside traveler form is set on wheels and can be moved without disassembly. The headers and legs of the traveler frame are adjustable so that more than one box size can be formed with a single traveler frame.

In a typical setup, a ratchet is attached to several headers (*Figure 71*). The ratchet will retract the headers approximately 2" to pull the form

309F70.EPS

Figure 70 ◆ Example of a culvert-forming system.

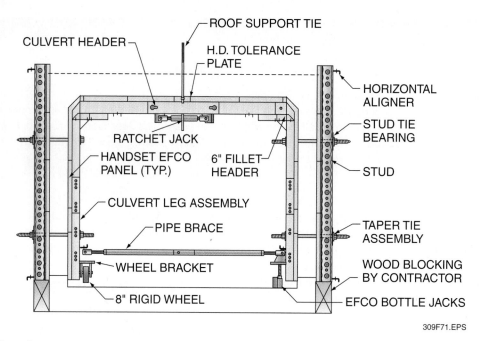

Figure 71 ◆ Culvert form setup.

away from the wall. A pipe brace between the leg assemblies on the bottom pulls the form away from the wall at the bottom of the setup. Secondary vertical adjustment is made with hydraulic hand jacks on both ends of the setup. Base jacks are used under each frame section to maintain position when the setup is raised off the wheels.

10.0.0 ◆ GENERAL FORMING AND SHORING SAFETY

WARNING!

Serious injury can result if safe practices are not followed when erecting, dismantling, or using forming and/or shoring equipment. Only persons familiar with current safety practices and the laws and regulations concerning shores should engage in the erection, dismantling, or use of shoring equipment. OSHA regulations require the use of guardrail systems and/or personal fall protection devices at all working levels, open sides, and all other openings on platforms and work areas above certain heights. In all cases, where a worker is exposed to a fall hazard, guardrail systems or other personal fall protective devices must be used.

OSHA regulation *Subpart Q, 1926.703* of *29 CFR Part 1926* requires the following with regard to shoring and reshoring:

- All shoring equipment, including equipment used in reshoring operations, shall be inspected prior to erection to determine that the equipment meets the requirements specified in the formwork drawings.
- Shoring equipment found to be damaged such that its strength is reduced to less than that required by *1926.703(a)(1)* shall not be used for shoring.
- Erected shoring equipment shall be inspected immediately prior to, during, and immediately after concrete placement.
- Shoring equipment that is found to be damaged or weakened after erection, such that its strength is reduced to less than that required by *1926.703(a)(1)*, shall be immediately reinforced.
- The sills for shoring shall be sound, rigid, and capable of carrying the maximum intended load.
- All base plates, shore heads, extension devices, and adjustment screws shall be in firm contact, and secured when necessary, with the foundation and the form.

- Forms and shores, except those used for slabs on grade and slip forms, shall not be removed until the employer determines that the concrete has gained sufficient strength to support its weight and superimposed loads. Such determination shall be based on compliance with one of the following: the plans and specifications stipulate conditions for removal of forms and shores, and such conditions have been followed, or the concrete has been properly tested with an appropriate ASTM standard test method designed to indicate the concrete compressive strength, and the test results indicate that the concrete has gained sufficient strength to support its weight and superimposed loads.
- Reshoring shall not be removed until the concrete being supported has attained adequate strength to support its weight and all loads in place upon it.

Other safety considerations specific to forming, shoring, and reshoring are:

- Use lumber rated for the stress, species, grade, and size specified on the layout drawing. Use only lumber that is in good condition. Do not splice timber members between their supports.
- Provide a proper foundation below the base plates for the distribution of leg loads to concrete slabs or ground. If installed on ground, mudsills must be used. The foundation must be level and thoroughly compacted prior to erection of shoring to prevent settlement. The area must be cleared of all obstructions and debris. Consideration must be given to potential adverse weather conditions such as washouts, freezing, and thawing of ground. Consult a qualified soils engineer to determine the proper size foundation required for existing ground conditions.
- Do not make unauthorized changes or substitutions of equipment.
- Provide guardrail systems on all open sides and openings in formwork and slabs.

- Access must be provided to all forming deck levels. If it is not available from the structure, access ladders or stair towers must be provided. Access ladders must extend at least three (3) feet above formwork.
- If motorized concrete placement equipment is to be used, be sure that lateral loads, vibration, and other forces have been considered and adequate precautions taken to assure stability.
- Plan concrete placement methods and sequences to make sure that unbalanced loading of the shoring equipment does not occur.
- Fasten all braces securely.
- Check to see that all clamps, screws, pins, and all other components are in a closed or engaged position.
- Make certain that all base plates and shore heads are in firm contact with the foundation and forming material.
- Avoid eccentric loads on U-heads and top plates by centering stringers on these members.
- Avoid shock or impact loads for which the shoring was not designed.
- Do not place additional temporary loads on erected formwork or poured slabs without checking the capacity of the shoring and/or structure to safely support such additional loads.
- Make sure that the completed shoring setup has the specified bracing to give it lateral stability.
- Make sure the erection of shoring is under the supervision of an experienced and competent person.
- When constructing frame shoring, follow the shoring layout drawing and do not omit required components. Do not exceed the shore frame spacings or tower heights as shown on the shoring layout. The shoring load must be carried on all legs, and all shoring frames must be made plumb and level as the erection proceeds. Also make sure to recheck the plumb and level of shoring towers just prior to concrete placement.

Summary

This module has provided an overview of horizontal concrete forms used in commercial construction. It also focused on the shoring and reshoring methods and equipment used to support the various types of horizontal forms. Construction for floor-forming typically involves use of pan forms, composite deck forms, or flying deck forms. Slab-and-beam forms are constructed for slab interior beams, cantilever beams, inverted or T-beams, and spandrel beams. Bridge decks can be constructed using conventional wood or metal formwork. Newer methods for forming bridge decks involve the use of patented modular precast deck panels or metal cast-in-place deck panels. Patented modular bridge decking panels made of fiber-reinforced polymer (FRP) material are also coming into increased use, especially for replacement decking on older bridges. Patented movable culvert forms are used when constructing storm drainage systems, sanitary sewers, and similar structures. Horizontal forms can be constructed either of wood or by assembling appropriate patented manufactured metal forms and equipment. Patented forms are more widely used today because they are easy to assemble and disassemble and can be reused many times. In order to safely assemble and use patented forms, the carpenter must be thoroughly familiar with the particular forms being used, especially the limitations of those forms. The instructions supplied with the forms must be followed.

Shoring is required to support elevated concrete decks while the concrete is hardening. In multi-story construction, reshoring is used on the deck below the shored deck.

Notes

1. One-way solid slabs are generally used for spans of *less than* _____ feet.
   a. 10
   b. 20
   c. 50
   d. 100

2. Two-way flat slabs are normally used for _____.
   a. high-rise apartment buildings
   b. industrial floors
   c. office buildings
   d. parking garages

3. Slabs comprised of reinforced concrete ribs that run at 90 degrees to each other are called _____ slabs.
   a. post-tensioned concrete
   b. two-way flat plate
   c. waffle
   d. composite

4. Slabs that use concrete bonded to steel decking are called _____ slabs.
   a. composite
   b. reinforced
   c. waffle
   d. post-tensioned

5. The component designated C in *Figure 1* is a(n) _____ beam.
   a. spandrel
   b. inverted
   c. cantilever
   d. interior

6. The component designated B in *Figure 1* is a(n) _____ beam.
   a. spandrel
   b. inverted
   c. cantilever
   d. interior

7. The component designated A in *Figure 2* is a _____.
   a. stringer
   b. scab
   c. kicker
   d. ledger

8. The component designated B in *Figure 2* is a _____.
   a. stringer
   b. scab
   c. kicker
   d. ledger

9. The component designated A in *Figure 3* is a _____.
   a. joist
   b. kicker
   c. stringer
   d. ledger

10. The component designated B in *Figure 3* is a _____.
    a. shore
    b. kicker
    c. stringer
    d. ledger

11. The form shown in *Figure 4* is a typical form for a _____.
    a. small beam
    b. large beam
    c. spandrel beam
    d. beam and column intersection

12. When using composite steel deck panels to form a floor slab, the deepest and strongest floor slab will be produced when the profile of the raised portion of the deck panel is _____ high.
    a. 1"
    b. 1½"
    c. 2"
    d. 3"

13. When a floor slab is made from composite steel deck panels, the phosphatized/painted surface is the one that comes into contact with the concrete.
    a. True
    b. False

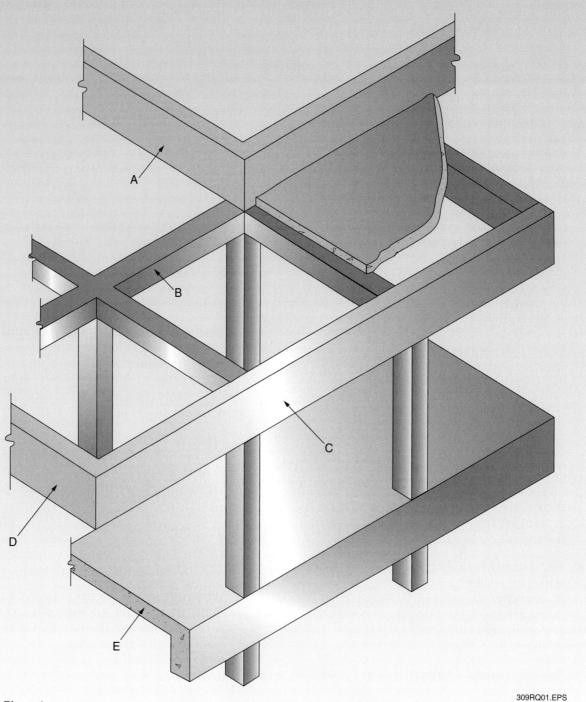

Figure 1

309RQ01.EPS

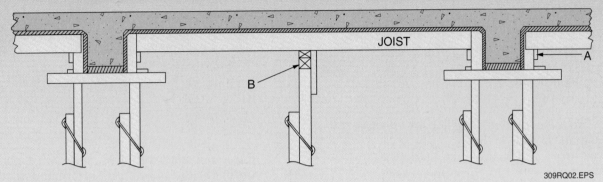

JOIST

A

B

Figure 2

309RQ02.EPS

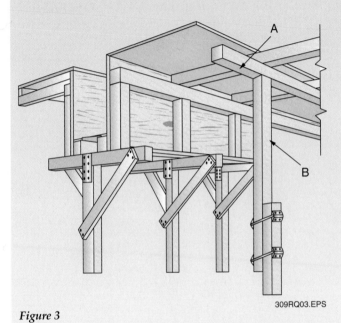

A

B

Figure 3

309RQ03.EPS

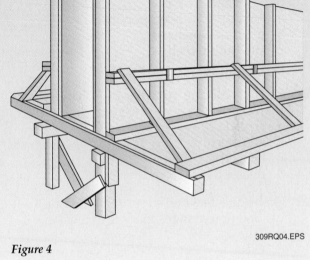

Figure 4

309RQ04.EPS

14. The temporary structure used to support the weight of fresh concrete and other loads while the concrete hardens is known as the _____.
   a. footings
   b. foundation
   c. vertical stiffeners
   d. shoring

15. When constructing wooden adjustable shores using Ellis™ shore clamps, the clamps should be placed on the lower shore post _____ apart on center.
   a. 6"
   b. 10"
   c. 12"
   d. 16"

16. Typical frame shoring has a load capacity of _____ pounds per frame.
   a. 1,000 to 5,000
   b. 2,000 to 5,000
   c. 20,000 to 50,000
   d. 100,000

17. Standard steel post shores can support loads of _____ pounds.
   a. 1,000 to 3,000
   b. 4,000 to 7,000
   c. 8,000 to 11,000
   d. 12,000 to 15,000

18. The least labor-intensive type of deck is the _____ deck.
    a. multi-component
    b. panelized
    c. composite
    d. flying

19. The type of deck most cost effective for small projects is the _____.
    a. truss and beam table
    b. handset multi-component deck
    c. column-mounted table
    d. flying deck

20. The type of decking that is the fastest to handset and strip is a _____ deck.
    a. handset multi-component
    b. handset panelized
    c. site-built panelized
    d. flying

21. Prior to placing concrete on a handset or flying deck, the deck must be _____.
    a. rigged
    b. adjusted
    c. leveled
    d. released

22. On bridge decking, support angles must be welded onto flanges that are in tension.
    a. True
    b. False

23. Compared to a conventional reinforced concrete deck slab, a bridge deck constructed of Exodermic™ panels typically weighs about _____ percent less.
    a. 10 to 20
    b. 20 to 25
    c. 25 to 30
    d. 35 to 50

24. Removal of forms or shores *cannot* occur until: (1) the conditions stipulated in the project plans and specifications have been followed or (2) the concrete has been tested using an appropriate ASTM standard test to indicate the concrete's compressive strength.
    a. True
    b. False

25. Just prior to concrete placement, recheck the plumb and level of _____.
    a. extension devices
    b. equipment devices
    c. foundation material
    d. shoring towers

Trade Terms
Introduced in This Module

Capital: A flared section at the top of a concrete column.

Corrugated: Material formed with parallel ridges or grooves.

Dead load: In a bridge, the actual weight of the deck itself.

Haunch: A structure provided on all bridges with steel girders or prestressed concrete I-beams. They provide a means of final adjustment of the deck slab elevation to match the design roadway profile and cross slope. The haunch allows this adjustment without having the top flange of the girder project into the structural deck.

Live load: In a bridge, the carrying capacity of the deck including the deck dead load weight.

Phosphatized: The treatment of metal with a phosphoric acid to prepare it for a finish coat. In composite floor decking, this unpainted surface will contact the concrete.

Profile: The appearance of a floor deck viewed cross-sectionally.

This module is intended to be a thorough resource for task training. The following reference works are suggested for further study. These are optional materials for continued education rather than for task training.

American Concrete Institute (ACI). www.concrete.org.

Cement Association of Canada. www.cement.ca.

Portland Cement Association. www.cement.org.

NCCER makes every effort to keep these textbooks up-to-date and free of technical errors. We appreciate your help in this process. If you have an idea for improving this textbook, or if you find an error, a typographical mistake, or an inaccuracy in NCCER's Contren® textbooks, please write us, using this form or a photocopy. Be sure to include the exact module number, page number, a detailed description, and the correction, if applicable. Your input will be brought to the attention of the Technical Review Committee. Thank you for your assistance.

Instructors – If you found that additional materials were necessary in order to teach this module effectively, please let us know so that we may include them in the Equipment/Materials list in the Annotated Instructor's Guide.

Write: Product Development and Revision
National Center for Construction Education and Research
3600 NW 43rd St., Bldg. G, Gainesville, FL 32606

Fax: 352-334-0932

E-mail: curriculum@nccer.org

Craft _____ Module Name _____

Copyright Date _____ Module Number _____ Page Number(s) _____

Description _____

_____

_____

_____

(Optional) Correction _____

_____

_____

(Optional) Your Name and Address _____

_____

_____

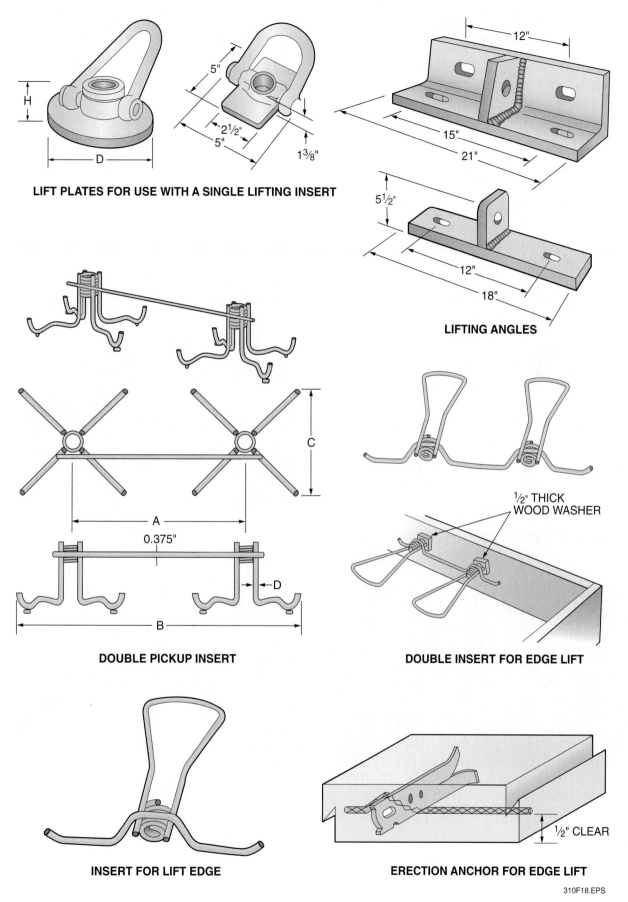

LIFT PLATES FOR USE WITH A SINGLE LIFTING INSERT

LIFTING ANGLES

DOUBLE PICKUP INSERT

DOUBLE INSERT FOR EDGE LIFT

½" THICK
WOOD WASHER

INSERT FOR LIFT EDGE

ERECTION ANCHOR FOR EDGE LIFT

½" CLEAR

310F18.EPS

Figure 18 ◆ Applications of form inserts.

3.0.0 ◆ ARCHITECTURAL TREATMENTS

A large variety of finish looks can be obtained with the use of exposed aggregates, sandblasting, reveal strips, color admixtures, and form liners. In some cases, the aggregate is incorporated into the concrete mix. This is typical with smaller aggregates between ¾" and 1½". Once the panel is raised, the aggregate is exposed by pressure washing or sandblasting, which should be performed as soon as possible after the panel is raised. Larger aggregates are placed by hand in a light bed of masonry sand that is spread over the casting bed. The sand bed is sprayed with a cement **slurry** to ensure that the aggregate is not dislodged during the lift. The concrete is then placed over the aggregate. Once the panel has been erected, the sand is washed away with a pressure hose. *Figure 19* shows an example of a pebble finish achieved using aggregates. In addition to these common methods of controlling the appearance of tilt-up buildings, artistic finishes can be obtained by the use of cutouts inserted in the form (*Figure 20*).

One method that has become popular is the use of face brick to create a brick or block appearance (*Figure 21*).

Some very attractive looks can be obtained by adding reveals (indents) to the finish. This is accomplished by inserting reveal strips, also called rustication strips, into the form. The strips are usually made of fiber board or 1" nominal lumber, and are nailed to the casting surface. *Figure 22* shows the effect that can be obtained with the use of reveal strips.

A wide variety of effects can be obtained with the use of form liners. The principle is the same as placing a form liner in a wall form, except the form is horizontal in this case. *Figure 23* shows panels that were formed using form liners. Form liners are usually made of plastic or galvanized metal.

310F20.EPS

Figure 20 ◆ Artistic finish.

310F19.EPS

Figure 19 ◆ Aggregate finish.

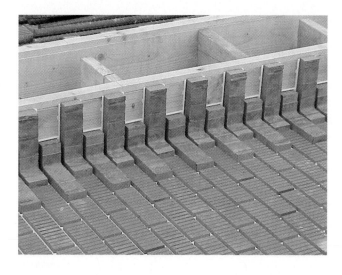

310F21.EPS

Figure 21 ◆ Achieving a brick finish.

INSIDE TRACK

Design Flexibility

At one time, tilt-up construction was used largely to make featureless, solid panels used in warehouse and similar construction. Today, there is almost no limit to the architectural design capabilities available with tilt-up construction.

310SA03.EPS

310SA02.EPS

Figure 22 ◆ Panels formed with reveal strips.

Figure 23 ◆ Panels formed using a form liner.

INSIDE TRACK

Arches

In today's world, it is not uncommon to find arches integrated into the designs of a tilt-up building. Within the practical constraints of tilt-up construction, architects and form designers today are limited only by their imaginations.

4.0.0 ◆ PLACING AND FINISHING THE CONCRETE

In general, the procedure for placing and finishing tilt-up panels is the same as that for slab-on-grade. It is good idea on a hot day to spray the reinforcing material with water before the concrete is poured. This will help reduce cracking. When it is very hot, it may be necessary to spray water on the concrete surface to keep the concrete from drying too fast.

In very cold weather, where the air temperature is consistently below 40°F, use heating equipment to protect the concrete. Use insulation blankets if the concrete is to cure overnight in freezing temperatures. Some contractors use tents and other structures to protect the panels in cold weather. However, if gasoline heaters are operated inside these enclosures, they must be vented to the outside. This precaution is not only for the obvious safety reasons associated with gasoline and gasoline engines. Carbon monoxide blends with the calcium hydroxide on the surface of the concrete to produce calcium carbonate, which can cause the surface of the panel to deteriorate. Water should not be allowed to pond on the surface of the panel. Freezing of the water can cause the surface to flake.

A low-slump concrete—4" to 5" maximum—is generally used in tilt-up panels. The low-slump concrete may not flow readily into corners and around reinforcement and inserts, so it should be vibrated. The drier concrete is generally used because the concrete casting slab will not readily absorb water.

CAUTION

Do not let the vibrator touch the casting bed, as this could cause the bond breaker to separate from the bed. Also, do not use the vibrator to move concrete, as this could result in segregation.

When the flow of concrete is started from the chute or pumper, a piece of plywood or a shovel should be used to disperse the concrete so that it does not affect the bond breaker. After that, the flow should be controlled so that wet concrete falls on wet concrete.

The concrete is typically screeded and finished with a wooden bullfloat (*Figure 24*). During the finishing process, the inserts and embedments are located and exposed.

310F24.EPS

Figure 24 ◆ Finishing a tilt-up panel.

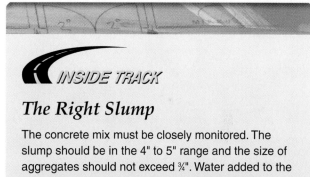

INSIDE TRACK

The Right Slump

The concrete mix must be closely monitored. The slump should be in the 4" to 5" range and the size of aggregates should not exceed ¾". Water added to the mix at the job site must be carefully monitored. As a rule of thumb, the slump will increase by 1" for every gallon of water added to a cubic yard of concrete.

310SA06.EPS

5.0.0 ◆ ERECTING AND BRACING THE PANELS

Once the concrete has cured sufficiently, the form is stripped, and lifting eyes and braces are attached to the inserts (*Figure 25*). This work is typically done by a professional rigging crew supported by carpenters and laborers. The braces are placed on the panel in preparation for the lift (*Figure 26*). Because they are angled, the braces will extend past the bottom of the panel. To prevent damage, lifting crew personnel support the braces as the panels are being lifted (*Figure 27*).

Before the panel is lifted, there are several additional tasks that should be performed:

- Lifting inserts should be tested and the correct locations of lifting inserts and braces should be verified.
- Standing water should be removed from around the panel and openings, as it will prevent air from getting under the panel, creating an added lifting load.

- Shelf angles and beam seats should be installed at this time, because it is easier to do so while the panel is on the ground.

Before the panels can be erected, a footing must be prepared to receive them. The panels are supported by either spread or continuous footings. Spread footings are placed under the joints between panels. It is more common these days to use continuous footings with dowels placed to help control the panels while they are being placed (*Figure 28*). Grout setting pads are placed on the footing to hold the panel up until it can be grouted in place (*Figure 29*). The grout setting pads are a few inches wider than the panels and must be long enough to support the panels until the space under the panels is grouted. All the setting pads must be placed at the correct elevation; otherwise, the panels will not be level. This will

310F26.EPS

Figure 26 ◆ Braces in place.

310F25.EPS

Figure 25 ◆ Preparing for lift.

310F27.EPS

Figure 27 ◆ Supporting the braces.

310F28.EPS

Figure 28 ◆ Continuous footing.

310F29.EPS

Figure 29 ◆ Grout setting pads.

require shimming, which is a time-consuming, and therefore expensive, process.

The rigging crew connects the lifting slings from the crane to the pickup shackles on the panel (*Figure 30*). Note the fine chains attached to the lifting lugs. These chains are attached to quick disconnects that are used to disconnect the lifting hardware once the panel is in place and braced. The use of these devices eliminates the need for workers to climb the panel in order to release the rigging gear.

NOTE

It may be necessary to use wedges or pry bars to break the bond between the panel and the casting bed.

310F30.EPS

Figure 30 ◆ Hooking up.

As the panel is moved into position, workers will jockey it into position on the footing, using the dowels inserted in the footing as a guide (*Figure 31*).

While the crane is still holding the panel erect, workers attach the braces to brackets that were previously placed in the casting slab (*Figure 32*). The braces are adjusted using their built-in screw adjustment until the panel is plumb (*Figure 33*). After the panels are installed, the joints between the panels are filled with polyethylene backer rod and sealant.

Some buildings may not have a concrete slab for attaching the braces. In other cases, it will be necessary to brace the panels on the outside. If the braces cannot be attached to the casting slab, a temporary footing called a deadman must be constructed. This footing is an auger-drilled hole filled with reinforced concrete (*Figure 34*). Concrete blocks are used for temporary footings in some instances (*Figure 35*). The braces remain in place until the roof structure is installed. This bracing must be designed by an engineer.

Panels containing lintels usually require additional support during the lift to overcome bending stresses. This support is obtained by attaching strongbacks to the panel before it is raised (*Figure 36*). The strongbacks are essentially the same as those used on wall forms, and may be made of wood or steel. Inserts can be embedded in the panel to provide attachment for the strongbacks (*Figure 37*).

310F31.EPS

Figure 31 ◆ Positioning the panel.

310F32.EPS

Figure 32 ◆ Attaching the braces.

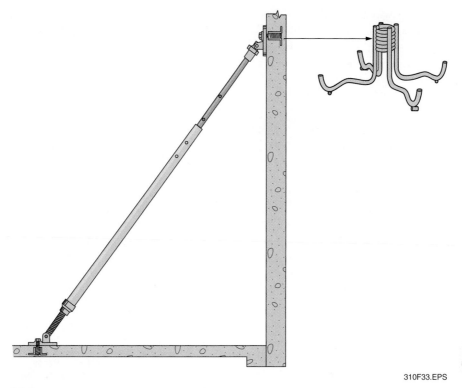

310F33.EPS

Figure 33 ◆ Adjustable brace.

310F34.EPS

Figure 34 ◆ Deadman footing.

310F35.EPS

Figure 35 ◆ Concrete block deadman.

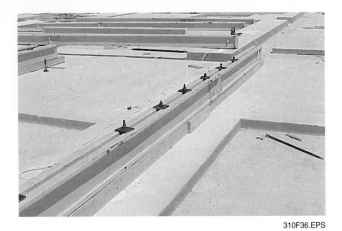

Figure 36 ◆ Strongback attached to panels.

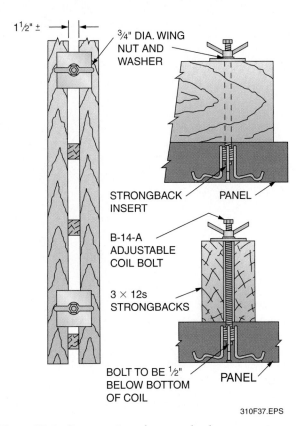

Figure 37 ◆ Cross-section of a strongback.

Summary

In tilt-up construction, concrete wall panels are generally formed on the finished floor slab of the building and then lifted into position by a crane. In some instances, the panels are formed on a separate casting bed near the building. The rigging used to raise the panels is attached to inserts that are anchored into the form before the concrete is poured. Inserts used to secure temporary braces to the panels are also tied into the form.

Tilt-up panels are generally 5" to 8" thick, so the edge forms used to form the panels are typically made from nominal 6" or 8" dimension lumber. A wide variety of finishes can be obtained using exposed aggregates, form liners, reveal strips, and other materials such as face brick.

When the panels are erected, they are set onto prepared footings, then leveled and braced. Continuous footings are the most common. The braces remain in place until the roof structure is installed.

Notes

1. Tilt-up construction was first used _____.
   a. in the late 1800s
   b. around 1950
   c. in 1995
   d. before the Civil War

2. Tilt-up construction is *not* considered cost-effective for buildings below _____ square feet.
   a. 5,000
   b. 10,000
   c. 15,000
   d. 20,000

3. Any openings in a casting bed must be completely filled with concrete and smoothed over.
   a. True
   b. False

4. Which of the following is a correct statement about tilt-up panel forms?
   a. Plywood sheets are the most common form material
   b. Openings for windows and doors are cut out of the panel shortly after the concrete is poured.
   c. The joint between the bottom edge of the form and the casting bed should be sealed.
   d. Engineered lumber is not suitable for building forms.

5. Reinforcing material is placed in the form before anything else.
   a. True
   b. False

6. Which of the following is a correct statement about lifting and bracing inserts?
   a. Inserts and related hardware are interchangeable among manufacturers because they are all made to the same industry standard.
   b. Inserts are placed so that they extend above the concrete.
   c. Only metal inserts can be used in tilt-up panels.
   d. The type and location of inserts are generally determined by the hardware supplier.

7. Rustication strips are used to _____.
   a. keep the panels from rusting
   b. brace blockouts for openings
   c. form reveals in the tilt-up panels
   d. fill the openings between panels

8. Carbon monoxide should not be allowed to come into contact with the surface of curing concrete because it will _____.
   a. slow down the curing process
   b. accelerate the curing process
   c. cause the concrete surface to deteriorate
   d. cause the concrete surface to become discolored

9. Grout setting pads are added to footings in order to _____.
   a. level the panels
   b. hold the panel up until it can be grouted in place
   c. make it easier to connect adjoining panels
   d. make it easier for the crane operator to find the panel locations

10. A deadman is a _____.
    a. temporary footing for panel braces
    b. type of building footing
    c. panel that cracked during a lift
    d. type of form liner

Trade Terms
Introduced in This Module

Beam seat: A tilt-up panel embedment used to support wood or steel beams after the panel is erected.

Edge lift: A lift performed using lifting inserts that are embedded in the top edge of the tilt-up panel. Used for lighter panels.

Grout: A pourable mixture of portland cement, lime, and water, with or without a fine aggregate.

Shelf angle: A metal plate embedded in a tilt-up panel as a support for joists.

Slurry: A thin liquid mixture of a substance such as cement.

Instructions for Installing and Removing Tilt-Up Inserts

How to Use Coil Face Inserts

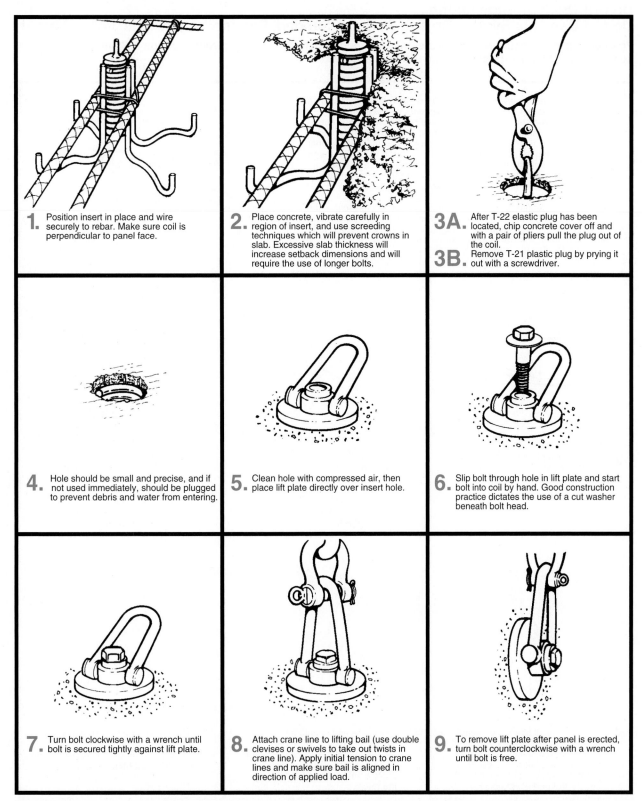

1. Position insert in place and wire securely to rebar. Make sure coil is perpendicular to panel face.

2. Place concrete, vibrate carefully in region of insert, and use screeding techniques which will prevent crowns in slab. Excessive slab thickness will increase setback dimensions and will require the use of longer bolts.

3A. After T-22 elastic plug has been located, chip concrete cover off and with a pair of pliers pull the plug out of the coil.

3B. Remove T-21 plastic plug by prying it out with a screwdriver.

4. Hole should be small and precise, and if not used immediately, should be plugged to prevent debris and water from entering.

5. Clean hole with compressed air, then place lift plate directly over insert hole.

6. Slip bolt through hole in lift plate and start bolt into coil by hand. Good construction practice dictates the use of a cut washer beneath bolt head.

7. Turn bolt clockwise with a wrench until bolt is secured tightly against lift plate.

8. Attach crane line to lifting bail (use double clevises or swivels to take out twists in crane line). Apply initial tension to crane lines and make sure bail is aligned in direction of applied load.

9. To remove lift plate after panel is erected, turn bolt counterclockwise with a wrench until bolt is free.

Warning! Crane line loads and bail of double-swivel lift plate must be turned in direction of crane forces before lifting operation begins. Crane line loads must not be allowed to apply sidewards loads to bail; this condition is dangerous and could lead to premature failure of hardware.

310A01.EPS

How to use the Ground Release II System

Do Not Use For Edge Lifting
Do Not Use This System On Top Surface, Seeded, Exposed Aggregate 3/4" or Larger

Precheck all insert holes with hardware prior to erection date, following instruction steps 2, 3 and 4, so that during tilting, proper hardware action is assured.

1. Install the insert so the directional arrow on the plastic recess plug points to the top or bottom of the panel. Wire tie the insert into position using a short length of additional reinforcing steel (rebar) placed tight against each side of the insert. Next, near each end of the plastic void former, secure a tie wire to one of the additional rebars, running the wire over the top of the plastic void former and back down, securing it to the additional rebar on the other side of the insert. Be sure to run the tie wire between the metal ring and the plastic void former as shown in the sketch to the right.

Note: The short length of rebar recommended is an aid to prevent the insert from moving during concrete placement. When this rebar is added for insert stability, it should be placed against the vertical portion of the insert and at least 1" away from the insert's foot. This extra rebar is not required to develop the inserts safe working load.

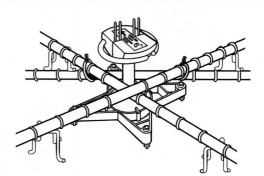

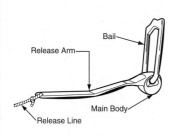

2. The various parts of the T-43-R Ground Release II Lifting Hardware are shown above.

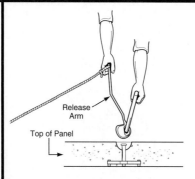

3. To install the lifting hardware onto the insert, hold the hardware by the bail and release arm, and lower it onto the head of the insert. Check to make certain that the release arm points to the top of the panel.

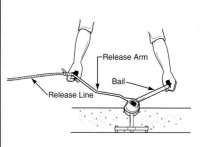

4. Lower the release arm until the arm comes in contact with the panel. Lay the release line along side of the lifting hardware so that the line goes to the bottom of the panel. With the crane lines attached, the panel is now ready for lifting.

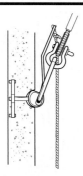

5. As the panel is lifted, the release arm is trapped between the panel and the crane line, which insures that the lifting hardware cannot be prematurely released. Brace and secure the panel into position.

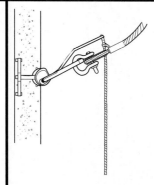

6. The crane line should be slackened slightly to permit the release of the lifting hardware. To release the lifting hardware, apply a single downward force to the release line.

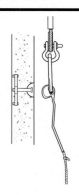

7. The lifting hardware remains in the open position, ready to be lowered to the ground and attached to the next panel.

Warning! The crane line and bail of the lifting hardware must be turned in the direction of the cable forces before the lifting operation begins. The crane line must not be allowed to apply a sideward force on the bail, as this condition is dangerous and could lead to premature failure of the hardware or insert.

310A02.EPS

How to Remove the Ground Release ^{II} Plastic Recess Plug

1. The Ground Release^{II} Insert's location in the panel is easily found by locating the antennae which will project through the surface of the concrete.

2. Using an ordinary claw hammer, tap lightly around the antennae, breaking through the thin skin of concrete to expose the insert. Avoid striking the concrete too hard so as not to break through the plastic recess plug.

3. Drive the claws of the hammer down about 3/8" between the end of the recess plug and the concrete.

4. Pry up on the end of the recess plug until one half of it "pops up" to a point where it is about one third of the way out of the concrete. For the time being, leave it as it is and proceed with step #5.

5. Repeat steps #3 and #4 to loosen the opposite half of the recess plug.

6. Grasp both halves of the recess plug between the thumb and finger and squeeze.

7. Both halves of the recess plug should now be easily removed, exposing the insert.

8. If one half of the recess plug should be hard to remove, drive the claws of the hammer as deeply as possible between the recess plug and the top of the insert, as shown above. Push forward on the hammer with one quick motion. This will remove the recess plug.

9. Use a blower to remove all debris from around the insert and the recess plug. The insert is now ready to receive the lifting hardware.
Note: For proper hardware release do not "round" out void holes.

Proper Hardware Usage

Prior to lifting any tilt-up panel, apply an initial load to the crane lines, making certain that the hardware is properly attached to the head of the T-41 Ground Release^{II} Insert and that the bail of the lifting hardware is aligned with the crane line.

Warning! Do not apply a sideward load to the bail

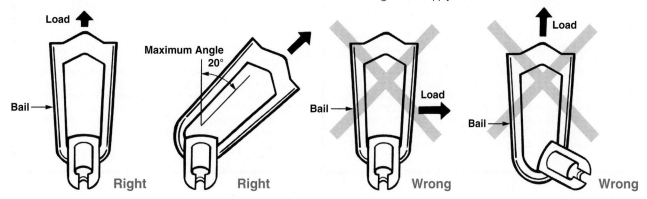

Warning! Do not modify, weld or alter in any way Ground Release^{II} Hardware units. Such actions could lead to premature failure of the hardware.

310A03.EPS

How To Install the Swift Lift Anchor

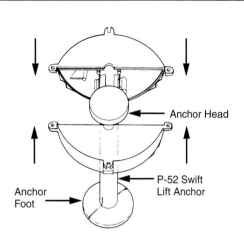

1. Assemble the P-54 Recess Plug by placing the head of the P-52 Swift-Lift Anchor inside any two halves of the recess plug. Then snap the two halves together. It is very difficult to assemble the unit with the foot of the anchor inside the P-54 Recess Plug and still get the two halves to close together correctly. If the two halves of the P-54 Recess Plug do not fit closely together, it could be because the anchor is in upside down. In such a case, reverse the anchor and try again.

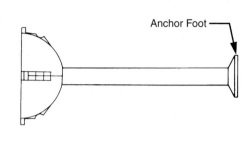

2. A correctly assembled P-54 Recess Plug and anchor.

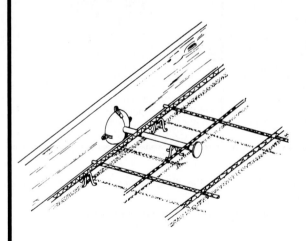

3. Attach the assembled P-54 Recess Plug and anchor to the formwork in its predetermined location with the recess plug seam in the vertical position. Use common (not double headed) nails in the upper three tabs of the recess plug. The plug and anchor assembly can also be attached to the formwork by using a 2 ton stud and wingnut if desired. Provide bar supports around the anchor as shown to prevent displacement during the casting process.

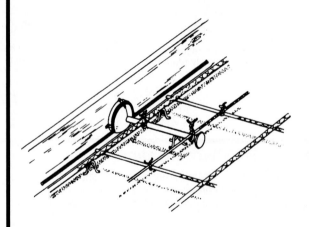

4. Slip the preformed shear bar onto the P-54 Recess Plug as shown. The receiving tabs of the P-54 Recess Plug will correctly position the shear bar. Usually, additional support wiring is not needed to hold the shear bar in place. However, prudent users will provide an additional wire tie or two to make certain the shear bar will not dislodge during concrete placement. Wire tie the P-52 Swift-Lift Anchor to reinforcing steel as shown.

310A04.EPS

This module is intended to be a thorough resource for task training. The following reference works are suggested for further study. These are optional materials for continued education rather than for task training.

The Tilt-Up Construction and Engineering Manual, Sixth Edition. Tilt-Up Concrete Association, Mount Vernon, IA.

Tilt-Up Concrete Construction Guide, 2005. American Concrete Institute, Farmington Hills, MI.

Tilt-Up Concrete Association, www.tilt-up.org.

Simple beam: A beam that is supported at each end (two points) and not continuous.

Single-curtain wall: A concrete wall that contains a single layer of vertical or horizontal reinforcing bars in the center of the wall.

Skeleton: A condition that occurs when individual timber uprights or individual hydraulic shores are not placed in contact with the adjacent member.

Slab-on-grade (slab-at-grade): A term used for a reinforced concrete slab, 3½" or thicker, that is placed over foundation footings or walls and on prepared soil. The slab usually has construction joints to allow expansion and contraction. The soil is the base material for its strength.

Slag: A product of a blast furnace or other metal smelting process that consists mostly of waste silicates and other compounds that are lighter than the metal and are removed from the surface of the molten metal.

Sleeve: A tube that encloses a bar, dowel, anchor bolt, or similar item.

Sling angle: The angle formed by the legs of a sling with respect to the horizontal when tension is put on the load.

Slipform: A form that moves continuously while the concrete is being placed.

Slump: The distance a standard-sized cone made of freshly mixed concrete will sag. This is known as a slump test.

Slurry: A thin liquid mixture of a substance such as cement.

Spalling: The condition of concrete breakup, chipping, splitting, or crumbling.

Span: The horizontal distance between supports of a member such as a beam, girder, slab, or joist; also, the distance between the piers or abutments of a bridge.

Special bending: All bending to special tolerances; all radius bending in more than one plane; all multiple-plane bending containing one or more radius bends; and all bending for precast units.

Spreader: A wood or metal device used to hold the sides of a form apart.

Staggered splices: Splices in bars that are not made at the same point.

Stirrups: Reinforcing bars used in beams for shear reinforcement; typically bent into a U shape or box shape and placed perpendicular to the longitudinal steel.

Strips: Bands of reinforcing bars in flat-slab or flat-plate construction. The column strip is a quarter-panel wide on each side of the column center line and runs from column to column. The middle strip is half a panel in width, filling in between column strips, and runs parallel to the column strips.

Strongback: An upright supporting member attached to the back of a form to stiffen or reinforce it, especially around door and window openings.

Studs: Vertical members of a form panel used to support sheathing.

Subsidence: A depression in the earth that is caused by unbalanced stresses in the soil surrounding an excavation.

Sulfate-resistant cement: A cement that is generally used only in concrete exposed to severe sulfate action caused by high-alkali water and/or soil.

Support bars: Bars that rest upon individual high chairs or bar chairs to support top bars in slabs or joists, respectively. They are usually #4 bars and may replace a like number of temperature bars in slabs when properly lap spliced; also used longitudinally in beams to provide support for the tops of stirrups. Also called raiser bars.

Temperature bars: Bars distributed throughout the concrete to minimize cracks due to temperature changes and concrete shrinkage.

Template: A device used to locate and hold dowels, to lay out bolt holes and inserts, etc.

Tie: A reinforcing bar bent into a box shape and used to hold longitudinal bars together in columns and beams. Also known as stirrup ties.

Tie wire: Wire (generally #16, #15, or #14 gauge) used to secure rebar intersections for the purpose of holding them in place until concreting is completed.

Uprights: The vertical members of a trench shoring system placed in contact with the earth and usually positioned so that individual members do not contact each other. Uprights placed so that individual members are closely spaced, in contact with, or interconnected to each other are often called sheeting.

Voids: Open space between soil or aggregate particles. A reference to voids usually means that there are air pockets or open spaces between particles.

Wales: Horizontal members of a shoring system placed parallel to the excavation face whose sides bear against the vertical members of the shoring system or the earth.

Water-cement ratio: The ratio of water to cement, usually by weight (water weight divided by cement weight), in a concrete mix. The water-cement ratio includes all cementitious components of the concrete, including fly ash and pozzolans, as well as portland cement.

Water table: The depth below the ground's surface at which the soil is saturated with water.

Weep hole: A drainage opening in a wall.

Figure Credits

Module 27301-07

Alan W. Grogono, M.D., 301F21 (bowline, round turn, clove hitch, square knot)
Chester Hoist Company, 301F24
Cianbro Corporation, 301F20
Coffing Hoists, 301F25, 301F26 (come-along)
The Crosby Group, Inc., 301F04
Duff-Norton, 301F27, 301F29
Insulatus Inc., 301SA02
JET brand of WMH Tool Group, 301F26 (ratchet-lever hoist)
Lehman's Non-Electric Catalog, 301F23
Lift-All Company, Inc., 301F15
Lincoln Fire & Rescue, Lincoln, NE, 301F21 (half-hitch safety, overhand safety)
J.C. Renfroe & Sons, Inc., 301F12
Dave Root, 301F21 (running bowline, timber hitch)
Vernon Smith, 301F30
SPX Power Team, 301SA06
Topaz Publications, Inc., 301F01, 301F11, 301F14, 301F17

Module 27302-07

Aearo Company, 302F01
Cianbro Corporation, 302F22
Construction Safety Council, Appendix
The Crosby Group, Inc., 302F30 (photo), 302F31 (photo)
E + K Equipment, Inc., 302SA03
Link-Belt Construction Equipment Company, 302F21, 302F34, 302F35, 302F40, 302F41
Manitowoc Crane Group, 302F36, 302F39
Rigging Handbook, © 2003 by Jerry A. Klinke, ACRA Enterprises, Stevensville, MI, 302F28, 302F29
Tilt-Up Concrete Association, 302SA02
Topaz Publications, Inc., 302F19, 302F20, 302F23, 302SA01
Wire Rope Sling Users Manual, Second Edition, 1997, Wire Rope Technical Board, 302F30 (art), 302F31 (art)

Module 27303-07

Calculated Industries, 303F21
ELE International, 303SA02 (middle)
John Hoerlein, 303F05
NDT James Instruments, Inc., 303SA02 (top)
Portland Cement Association, 303F02, 303SA02 (bottom), 303F17
Rosamond Gifford Zoo, 303F12

Module 27304-07

Bar Splice Products, Inc., 304SA09
Benner-Nawman, Inc., 304SA08
Brice Building Company, 304SA03, 304SA12
Don De Cristo Concrete Accessories, Inc., 304SA07 (right)
Klein Tools, Inc., 304F29, 304F37
MAX USA Corp., 304SA10
Oklahoma Steel & Wire Co., Inc., 304SA02
Portland Cement Association, 304SA04, 304SA05
Ridge Tool Company / RIDGID®, 304F27
Topaz Publications, Inc., 304SA01, 304SA06 (left), 304SA11, 304F61, 304F62
www.rebar.net, 304F19, 304F20

Module 27305-07

Baker Concrete Construction, Inc., 305F10, 305F24, 305F25, 305F28, 305F30, 305F35, 305F36, 305F39
Bon Tool Company, 305SA02, 305SA03, 305F38
Chapin International, 305F44
Photo courtesy of **constructionphotographs.com**, 305F07, 305F16
CS Unitec, www.csunitec.com, 305F31, 305F45 (middle)
Granite City Tools, 305F17
Metal Forms Corporation, 305F19
MK Diamond, 305F32, 305F45 (left, right)
Multiquip Inc., 305F20 (roller screed)
Portland Cement Association, 305F05, 305F06, 305F14, 305F15

REED Concrete Pumps, 305SA01, 305F11
Soff-Cut International, 305F33
Somero Enterprises, 305F21
Superchute, 305F12 (photo)
Topaz Publications, Inc., 305F08, 305F26
Wacker Corporation, 305F20 (steel truss screed)

Module 27306-07

BOMAG Americas, Inc., 306F07 (smooth steel wheel roller)
Reprinted courtesy of Caterpillar Inc., 306T01, 306T02, 306F07 (sheepsfoot roller, rubber tire roller), 306F36
Contractor's Depot and Multiquip, Inc., 306T03
Fluor Corporation, 306F31
Griffin Dewatering, 306F35
John Hoerlein, 306F07 (jump rammer, vibrating plate)
Humboldt Mfg. Co., 306F08, 306F09, 306SA02
JCB Vibromax, 306F07 (vibrating roller)
Lampson International LLC, 306SA01
Trench Shoring Services, 306F16, 306F19, 306F21
Wacker Corporation, 306F29, 306F30, 306F32
www.TrenchSafety.com, 306F12

Module 27307-07

American Concrete Institute, ACI 302.1R-04, *Guide for Concrete Floor and Slab Construction*, 307T01
Amico, 307F70–307F72
Bon Tool Company, 307F73
Brasfield and Gorrie LLC, 307F25, 307F26, 307F27 (bottom), 307F28–307F30, 307F35, 307F36
Brick Industry Association, *Bricklaying: Brick and Block Masonry* © 1988. Used with permission of the Brick Industry Association, Reston, VA, www.gobrick.com, 307F46
Concrete Form Services, Inc., 307F63–307F67
Photo courtesy of constructionphotographs.com, 307F75
Photo courtesy of Fab-Form Industries Ltd., www.fab-form.com, 307F68, 307F69
Gomaco Corporation, 307SA03
John Hoerlein, 307F05, 307F32
Photos provided by Mashburn Construction Company, Inc., Columbia, SC, 307F20, 307F39–307F42, 307F49–307F56, 307F76
Metal Forms Corporation, 307F61, 307F74
National Concrete Masonry Association, 307F47
Portland Cement Association, 307F44
Rosamond Gifford Zoo, 307F43
Sokkia Corporation, 307F08
Somero Enterprises, 307SA02
The Stanley Works, 307F13

Topaz Publications, Inc., 307F22, 307F24, 307F27 (top), 307F37, 307F60
Portions © 2004 Trimble Navigation Limited, All Rights Reserved, 307F16, 307F17
David White, 307F04, 307F06

Module 27308-07

Award Metals, 308F05 (snap tie)
Brasfield and Gorie LLC, 308F24, 308F40
EFCO Corp., 308F08, 308F10, 308F12, 308F26
Ellis Manufacturing Co., Inc., www.ellisok.com, 308F33 (photos)
Gates & Sons, Inc., 308F14–308F16, 308F19
Greenstreak, Inc., 308F51, 308SA07
MFG Construction Products Company, 308F27, 308SA04
PERI GmbH, 308F01 (bottom), 308F07(C), 308F20, 308F34, 308F39
Portland Cement Association, 308SA03, 308SA05, 308SA06
Premere Forms, Inc., 308F52
Reward Wall Systems, Inc., 308F54
Scanada International, 308F35–308F37
Sonoco, 308F28
Symons, 308F01 (top), 308F06 (lumber brace), 308F09, 308F11, 308F13, 308F17, 308F18, 308SA02, 308F30, 308F38
Topaz Publications, Inc., 308SA01, 308F53
Wall-Ties & Forms, Inc., 308F02
Western Forms, 308F07(A), 308F50

Module 27309-07

APA – The Engineered Wood Association, 309SA04
Brasfield & Gorrie LLC, 309F02, 309SA01, 309F12–309F14, 309F27, 309F32, 309F53, 309F63
Ceco Concrete Construction, LLC, 309F01, 309F03, 309F07–309F10, 309F23–309F26
Dayton Superior, 309F68
EFCO Corp., 309F57, 309F65, 309F70
Ellis Manufacturing Co. Inc., www.ellisok.com, 309SA02
Metal Dek Group® a unit of CSi®, 309F28
MFG Construction Products Company, 309F11
Photo courtesy of MSW Suspended Floor Solutions, 309F29
PERI GmbH, 309F31, 309F35–309F37, 309F40–309F42, 309F44, 309F55,
Symons, 309F04, 309F33, 309F38, 309SA03, 309F43, 309F49–309F51, 309F54, 309F56, 309F58, 309F61, 309F62, 309F64, 309F66
Titan Formwork Systems, LLC, 309F30, 309F39, 309F45–309F48
Topaz Publications, Inc., 309F52

Module 27310-07

Photo courtesy of
constructionphotographs.com, 310F24
Dayton Superior, 310F18, 310F33, 310F37,
Appendix
Meadow Burke, a Division of MMI Products,
310F27

Tilt-Up Concrete Association, 310F01–310F16,
310F19–310F23, 310SA02-310SA06, 310F25,
310F26, 310F28–310F32, 310F34–310F36
Topaz Publications, Inc., 310F17

Index

Figures are indicated with *f* following the page number.

Risers, and stair forms, 8.36, 8.42*f*
Riser/tread combinations, 8.36, 8.42
Rock caissons, 7.23
Rock mitigation, and trenching and excavation, 6.30, 6.31*f*
Rod accessories, 7.6, 7.8, 7.8*f*
Rollerbug tampers, 5.22, 5.22*f*
Roller-compacted concrete (RCC), 3.12, 3.37
Roman concrete, 3.10
Room tunnel systems, 9.33
Rope selection, and tag lines, 1.16
Rotating beam laser levels, 7.12, 7.12*f*, 9.36
Rough opening measurements, and wooden bucks, 8.20
Round pin anchor shackles, 1.4, 1.4*f*
Round slings, conditions for discarding, 1.14
Round turn and two half-hitches, 1.18*f*
Rubber-tired rollers, 6.6, 6.7*f*
Rule of sixes, 3.11
Running bowline, 1.18*f*
Running lines, 2.31
Rust, and concrete to steel bond, 4.10, 4.12
Rustication lines
   architectural forms and, 8.43
   defined, 8.51

S

Saddle ties, 4.33, 4.34*f*
Safety
   chain slings and, 1.14
   come-alongs and, 1.22
   composite decking and, 9.18
   concrete and, 3.5, 3.15, 3.18, 5.9, 5.10, 5.32–5.33
   concrete dust and, 5.24, 5.33
   cranes and, 2.16–2.17, 2.16*f*, 2.17*f*
   deep foundation excavations and, 6.11–6.13, 6.14*f*, 6.15*f*
   entering caissons and, 7.23
   flying decks and, 9.35–9.36
   forming-system manufacturers and, 8.3
   handling and placing concrete and, 5.32–5.33
   horizontal formwork and, 9.40–9.41
   inserts and, 10.8
   laser levels and, 7.12
   lifting gang forms and, 8.9
   lifting overhead steel and, 1.8
   lightning and, 2.21, 2.22*f*
   load-handling safety, 2.16–2.17, 2.17*f*
   mobile boom-type concrete pumps and, 5.11
   nuclear equipment and, 6.10
   pavers and, 7.52
   placing and tying rebar and, 4.30–4.31
   placing reinforcing steel and, 4.18
   power lines and, 2.18–2.19, 2.18*f*, 2.20
   reinforcing steel fabrication and, 4.23
   reshoring and, 9.19–9.20, 9.40–9.41
   rigging practices and, 2.2, 2.14–2.17
   scaffolds and, 8.19
   shackles and, 1.5
   shoring and, 9.19–9.20, 9.40–9.41
   site safety, 2.20
   tag lines and, 2.15–2.16, 2.16*f*, 2.17
   trenching and, 6.14, 6.15*f*, 6.16–6.24
   tuggers and, 1.25
   tying reinforcing steel and, 4.34
   water and, 6.16, 6.19*f*, 6.20, 6.23, 6.25
   weight of finished forms and, 8.21
Safety anchor shackles, 1.4*f*
Safety latches, and rigging hooks, 1.2
Safety shoes, 2.14

Safe working loads
   rigging hooks and, 1.2, 1.3*f*
   rigging precautions and, 2.15
   turnbuckles and, 1.7
Sampling concrete, 3.13, 3.15
Sand cone test, 6.9, 6.10, 6.10*f*
San Francisco rods, 7.6, 7.6*f*
Saw cut joints, 5.24
Saw kerfs, and bending sheathing, 8.17, 8.19*f*
Scaffold safety, 8.19
Scarifiers, 5.31, 5.32*f*
Schedules, 4.36
   defined, 4.57
Screeding, and finishing concrete, 5.18–5.19, 5.19*f*, 5.20*f*, 5.21
Screeds
   foundations and, 7.47–7.48, 7.47*f*, 7.48*f*
   handheld vibrating screeds, 5.17, 5.20, 5.21, 7.47, 7.47*f*
   manual screeds, 5.18–5.19, 5.19*f*, 7.47, 7.47*f*
   self-propelled laser screeds, 5.19, 5.20*f*, 5.21
   vibrating truss screeds, 7.47–7.48, 7.47*f*
Screw jacks
   rigging equipment and, 1.23, 1.23*f*
   slipforms and, 8.34
Screw pin chain shackles, 1.4, 1.4*f*, 1.5*f*
Screw spreaders, 5.8
Screw type plate clamps, 1.8, 1.9
Secondary control points, 7.3, 7.3*f*
Sedimentation, 6.25
   defined, 6.35
Segmented pad rollers, and compaction, 6.6, 6.7*f*
Segregation
   concrete placement and, 5.6, 5.12, 5.15
   defined, 5.38
   discharging concrete from bucket and, 5.9
   internal vibrators and, 5.17
   tilt-up wall systems and, 10.13
   transporting concrete in wheelbarrows and, 5.13
Seizing, 1.17
   defined, 1.29
Self-consolidating concrete, 3.12
Self-propelled laser screeds, 5.19, 5.20*f*, 5.21
Serrated jaw plate clamps, 1.8–1.9, 1.9*f*
Set, 5.3
   defined, 5.38
Setting
   of cement, 3.3
   defined, 3.31
Setting forms, 8.22
Settlement
   defined, 6.35, 7.56
   of fill, 6.4
   foundations and, 7.17
Settling, and dewatering systems, 6.30
Shackles
   bridle slings and, 2.24, 2.25*f*
   eyebolts and, 2.37, 2.38*f*
   as rigging hardware, 1.3–1.5, 1.4*f*, 1.5*f*
Shaft forms, 8.35, 8.35*f*
Shallow foundation elements
   cast-in-place walls, 7.28, 7.28*f*
   continuous strip, step, and spread footings, 7.26, 7.26*f*, 7.27*f*
   foundations at grade as, 7.25–7.26
   grade beams, 7.17, 7.27, 7.27*f*
   masonry walls, 7.28–7.29, 7.29*f*, 7.30*f*
Shape, of aggregates, 3.7